DISCARDED

PENSIONS
and
PROFIT SHARING

Third Edition

BY

HERMAN C. BIEGEL	WILLIAM W. FELLERS
GEORGE B. BUCK	WILLIAM B. HARMAN, JR.
DONALD F. FARWELL	FRED RUDGE
ARTHUR S. FEFFERMAN	JOHN B. ST. JOHN
	E. S. WILLIS

BNA Incorporated ● Washington, D. C. 20037

Third Edition
Copyright 1953, 1956, 1964
BNA INCORPORATED
WASHINGTON, D. C.

PRINTED IN THE UNITED STATES OF AMERICA
Library of Congress Catalog Card Number: 63-17944

CONTRIBUTING EDITORS

Herman C. Biegel, *Attorney*. Partner in the law firm of Lee, Toomey & Kent, Washington, D. C., New York, N. Y., and San Francisco, California. Member of the Bar of New York and the District of Columbia. Member of the Tax Section of the American Bar Association. Technical Adviser to the Trustees of the Council of Profit Sharing Industries.

George B. Buck, *Consulting Actuary*, New York City. Member of the Conference of Actuaries in Public Practice and Member of the Board of Actuaries, U. S. Civil Service Retirement System.

Donald F. Farwell, *Managing Editor*, Collective Bargaining Negotiations and Contracts, published by The Bureau of National Affairs, Inc., Washington, D. C.

Arthur S. Fefferman, Director of Economic Analysis, American Life Convention. Formerly Chief of the Personal Taxation Staff, Office of Tax Analysis, U. S. Treasury Department.

William W. Fellers, *Actuary*. Member of the firm of the Wyatt Company, Washington, D. C. Fellow of the Society of Actuaries and Member of the Economic Security Committee of the U. S. Chamber of Commerce.

William B. Harman, Jr. Associate General Counsel, American Life Convention. Member of the Bar of Virginia and the District of Columbia. Member of the Tax Section of the American Bar Association. Formerly attorney, Office of Tax Legislative Counsel, U. S. Treasury Department.

Fred Rudge, *Consultant*. President, Fred Rudge Associates, Inc. (Industrial Administration and Management Relations within and outside the corporation); and life member, Purdue Industrial Communication Research Council.

John B. St. John, *Actuary*. Penllyn, Penna. Consulting Actuary specializing in development and review of pension plans. Fellow of the Society of Actuaries. Fellow of the Casualty Actuarial Society.

E. S. Willis, *Manager*, Employee Benefits and Practices Service, General Electric Company, Schenectady, N. Y.

CONTENTS

Chapter   *Page*

PREFACE 9

I. FEATURES OF PRESENT-DAY PENSION PLANS, *by George B. Buck*

    First Considerations 11
    Basic Structure 13
    Extraneous Factors 14
    Treatment of Existing Benefits 15
    Extent of Coverage 17
    Fitting a Plan to the Pocketbook 19
    Existing Patterns 20
        Normal Retirement on Account of Age 21
        Retirement on Account of Disability 29
        Death Benefits 31
        Early Retirement or Vesting Benefits 34
        Optional Benefits 36
    Employee Contributions 37
    Conclusion 38

II. TAX ASPECTS OF PENSION PLANS, *by Herman C. Biegel and William B. Harman, Jr.*

    Introduction 40
    Qualifying a Pension Plan 41
    Securing a Ruling 51
    Amending, Suspending or Terminating a Plan 53
    Tax Problems of Employer 59
    Tax Problems of Employee 65
    Tax Problems of the Trust 74
    Pension Plans Covering Self-Employed People 80
    Conclusion 85

III. FINANCING A PENSION PLAN,
by *John B. St. John*

Introduction	87
Group Deferred Annuities	89
Plan Characteristics	90
Discontinuance of Annuity Purchases	105
Modification of the Contract	106
Premiums and Rates	106
Financial Operations	111
Administration of the Plan	113
Group Deposit Administration	114
Plan Characteristics	115
How Costs are Figured	116
Group Permanent Life Insurance	117
Plan Characteristics	118
Premiums and Rates	125
Individual Contract Pension Trust	127
Plan Characteristics	128
Premiums and Rates	129
Administration of the Plan	131
Ordinary Life Insurance with Supplemental Fund	131
Plan Characteristics	132
Premiums and Rates	133
Administration	135
Self-Administered Trust	135
Plan Characteristics	136
Premiums and Rates	138
Administration of the Plan	139
Underwriting	140
Variable Annuities	140
Tabular Analysis of Financing Methods	144

IV. PENSION COSTS AND COST EXPERIENCE,
by *William W. Fellers*

Reducing Pension Costs	146
Funding Methods	148
Cost Examples	151
Factors Affecting Costs	165
Mortality	165
Interest	169

Chapter		*Page*
	Capital Appreciation and Depreciation	170
	Withdrawal	171
	Salary Scales	174
	Administrative Expenses	175
	Retirement Age	175
	Other Plan Provisions Affecting Costs	176
	Conclusion	179
V.	DEFERRED PROFIT-SHARING PLANS, *by Arthur S. Fefferman*	
	Background	181
	What is a Profit-Sharing Plan?	182
	Profit-Sharing Compared With Pension Plans	184
	Example of Successful Profit-Sharing	185
	Qualification Rules	186
	Tax Deductions for Employer Contributions	193
	Employee Contributions	196
	Incidental Life Insurance, Hospitalization, and Medical Insurance	198
	Administration	199
	Termination or Amendment	201
	Tax Treatment of Distributions	202
	Profit-Sharing Plans Covering Self-Employed Individuals	203
VI.	BARGAINING ON PENSIONS, *by Donald F. Farwell*	
	Introduction	205
	The Rise of Pension Bargaining	206
	Prevailing Pension Patterns	210
	Current Issues in Pension Bargaining	217
	Normal Retirement Benefits	217
	Relationship of Benefits to Earnings and Service	218
	Adjustments Based on Living Costs	218
	Lump-Sum Benefit Upon Retirement	219
	Early Retirement	219
	Disability Benefits	222
	Integration With Social Security	222
	Benefits for Persons Already Retired	224
	Survivor Benefits	225

Chapter		Page
	Vesting	226
	Contributory vs. Noncontributory Plans	227
	Compulsory vs. Voluntary Retirement	228
	Investment of Pension Funds	229
	Legal Considerations	231
	Enforcement of Pension Agreements	232
	Compulsory Retirement	234
VII.	ADMINISTRATION OF PENSION PLANS, *by E. S. Willis*	
	Basic Questions for the Administrator	235
	Enrollment in the Plan	237
	Contact With Employees	246
	Contacts With Unions	249
	Retirement and After	252
VIII.	HOW TO ACHIEVE MAXIMUM RETURN ON PENSION COSTS, *by Fred Rudge*	
	Maximizing Benefits to the Company	258
	Why Analyze?	259
	Communication Policy and Method	259
	Some Guidelines to Content and Style	263
	Some Guidelines to Method	265
	The Challenge to Management	269
	Illustrative Pension Brochures	270
INDEX		275

PREFACE TO THE THIRD EDITION

The most important thing most managers have learned about pension plans is that they don't stand still. Decisions made a few years ago, during the great rush to provide employee security after World War II, must be constantly reviewed and revised—usually, from the standpoint of costs and benefits, upward. The National Industrial Conference Board estimates that employer payments for private pension and welfare funds have increased almost a half-billion dollars each year, reaching nearly 10 billion dollars in 1963, with no end in sight.

Hence this new edition of *Pensions and Profit Sharing*. In the years since 1949, when this book was first published (under its original title *Handbook for Pension Planning*) it has become the standard reference work for those concerned with private pension plans in business and industry. But in the eight years since the Second Edition was published, there have been many new rulings, new approaches to appropriate plans, and new demands by collective bargaining agents. It is hoped that this edition will continue to shed light on this complex subject in an up-to-date manner.

The great majority of executives who make the final decisions on private pension plans are, and will always be, laymen in pension matters. There is no need for them to absorb the "jargon of the trade" or the complicated, technical details of funding, qualifying a plan, or overseeing its operation. There are experts who can be consulted for such details.

Nevertheless, decisions must be made, and the intelligent executive will want to have the broadest possible *general* background of information against which to weigh these decisions. This book has been designed for that purpose. Each of the contributing authors has approached his assignment as if he were sitting down with the reader and explaining, as to a client, the particular points about pensions and profit sharing covered by his chapter.

CHAPTER 1

FEATURES OF PRESENT-DAY PENSION PLANS

By GEORGE B. BUCK

If you have more than an academic interest in pension planning, you may be either a prospective beneficiary of a pension plan or an employer faced with the problem of providing for the retirement of your employees. If you are an officer of a corporation considering the installation or revision of a pension plan, you probably will be interested from both of these viewpoints. This chapter is written with both in mind although it may seem that the greater emphasis is on the latter. Actually the two viewpoints are much more compatible when the basic problems are understood than would first appear.

First Considerations

Pension planning is long range planning. The benefits ensuing from a pension plan to both the employer and employee, by their very remoteness, are more conducive to objective thinking on both sides than is generally possible in the case of more immediate benefits. Unlike increases in pay, vacations, holidays, etc., which are of immediate value and consequently are judged solely on this basis by employees, a pension benefit is valuable to an employee not only in proportion to the amount of pension but also in proportion to the likelihood of his receiving it. Thus while John, who is ready to retire, may favor a plan paying $200 a month pension he may find himself opposed not only by the boss but by Tom, Dick and Harry who see much more merit in a plan paying John $100 a month while setting aside $100 for pensions to be paid to them at their retirement some years hence.

Obviously the above example is an over-simplification. Assuming that an employer with four employees could afford to pay $200 a month toward the cost of pensions, cutting John from $200 to $100 a month and accumulating $100 at interest may or may not produce the desired amount of benefit for Tom, Dick, and Harry. However, the actuarial solution of just such an equation would provide a sound basis for the establishment of a good pension plan. The problem might be presented to the actuary as follows:

> We can afford to contribute approximately $2,400 per annum to a pension plan. We wish to retire each employee at age 65 on a pension equal to some percentage of his average salary received during his final ten years of service multiplied by the number of years of service with the company. There will be no employee contributions. Pensions will be exclusive of Social Security benefits. No benefits will be payable upon death or withdrawal from service for any reason prior to retirement. Our present employees, all male, are:
>
> | Name | Salary | Age | Years of Service |
> |------|--------|-----|------------------|
> | John | $15,000 | 65 | 30 |
> | Tom | 4,500 | 55 | 5 |
> | Dick | 13,000 | 45 | 20 |
> | Harry | 3,900 | 25 | 1 |
>
> What percentage of such average salary can be provided for the above contribution?

After securing certain information as to the type of occupation in which the employees are engaged and some background in regard to the company's past and probable future history on which to base his actuarial assumptions, and after discussing the type of funding which seemed most suitable, the actuary could compute the answer to the above question relatively simply. Except for the volume of required computations, the same would apply if there were 40,000 instead of 4 employees. The point is that a simple formula has been chosen and there is but one unknown quantity to be determined.

Unfortunately such a direct approach to the determination of pension plan benefits is seldom possible. There is often a long period of trial and error before a satisfactory balance between desired benefits and acceptable costs can be reached. Such a period can be both confusing and discouraging to the would-be formulators of a pension plan who may become hopelessly entangled in a myriad of alternative benefit combinations and their resultant costs. A pension plan can be designed for your company which fits both your needs and your company's pocketbook. A good consultant can assist you in designing such a plan but the basic decisions should be yours. No matter how familiar with pension problems your consultant may be, he can never be as familiar with your own particular problems as you are yourself. He will, however, be able to help you in clarifying these problems as well as in suggesting possible solutions.

If the initiation of a plan is under consideration, it may be well to lean toward both a simple benefit structure and a cost well within the company's means. No pension plan need be static. Plans may usually be amended easily. However, an amendment toward more liberal benefits is far less troublesome than an amendment diminishing benefits. It is usually easier to increase the complexity of a plan than to simplify it. You will probably be in a position to find a better solution to some of the minor problems after you have had some experience in the operation of a simple basic plan.

So much for the note of caution as regards the end result. Now let us take a look at the preliminary considerations and features which are incorporated in plans now in operation and which might be included in your plan.

Basic Structure

Creation of a pension plan might be said to be analogous to the creation of a new product which management intends to sell to the consumers, i.e., ownership and employees. The first consideration, then, might be an analysis of the market. That is, for what reason, when, and upon what basis would the company be willing to buy benefits and of what benefits are employees most in need? Let us leave the question of "How much?" until a later stage after the engineers (actuaries) have our preliminary specifications and can give us an idea of the cost of production. For the time being let us limit our analysis to the following:
1. For which of the following causes of termination of service is it desired to pay benefits?
    a. Normal retirement on account of age
    b. Total and permanent disability[1]

---

[1] The company may also wish to cover cases of temporary disability or sickness but these are usually not included among the benefits of a pension plan, whose primary purpose is to cover permanent or presumably permanent termination of service.

c. Death
   d. Termination of service prior to normal retirement with income deferred to retirement age
   e. Termination of service prior to normal retirement with reduced income commencing immediately
2. For each of the above reasons for which it has been decided to pay a benefit, what qualification shall we require? (For illustrative purposes, I am inserting specimen, but not necessarily recommended, qualifications which might be imposed for each of the above categories.)
   a. Permissive at 65, compulsory at 70
   b. Ten years of service
   c. Five years of service
   d. Attainment of age 50 with 15 years of service
   e. Attainment of age 55 with 20 years of service
3. For each of the above benefits which it has been decided to pay, what factors should be used in determining the amount of benefit to be paid? (Again, for clarity, specimen answers have been inserted for each of the categories.)
   a. Compensation and years of service
   b. Same as a.
   c. Compensation
   d. Same as a. Benefits payable at age 65
   e. Same as d. or reduced actuarially if commenced at an earlier age

Extraneous Factors

The preliminary analysis has been made solely on the basis of marketability to our consumers. There may be other considerations in light of which the preliminary decisions will need to be reviewed. A major consideration, of course, would be the existence of a bargaining unit represented by a labor union within the consumer group. If such is the case and the union represents a relatively large portion of the employees, it may be expected, of course, that the union will wish to have a voice in setting the specifications in any plan covering its membership. This might range from simple approval of a plan proposed by the company for its other employees to submission by the union of a complete set of specifications devised by the union itself or following an industry pattern already set. The subject of collective bargaining on pensions is covered in Chapter VI. For the purposes of this chapter let it be assumed either that we are confident that the union will accept the company proposal or that the bargaining unit has been excluded from the group which we propose to cover.

Another consideration would be competition which our product must meet, that is, the pension plan or plans of other companies competing in the same labor market. While this is, of course, an important consideration, it may sometimes be given more emphasis than it deserves under present conditions. Employees are much more pension conscious than they were a few years ago and will probably become more so. However, it is not a simple task for even an expert to accurately appraise the relative value of two different plans. There are an infinite number of combinations of eligibility requirements, factors used in determining the amount of benefit and constitution of the membership. It is advisable in designing a plan to avoid as far as possible any obviously unfavorable comparisons between your plan and that of your competitor. If you cannot afford to match certain features of a competitor's plan, steer clear of such features and stress others wherein his plan may be lacking. Your primary purpose is to meet the needs of your company and its employees at a cost which can reasonably be afforded.

Treatment of Existing Benefits

After tentatively deciding upon the basic structure of the plan, a correlative decision might be made at this point with regard to the treatment of Social Security benefits. There are two basic methods of treating this problem. First, benefits of the plan may be stated as inclusive of Social Security. For instance, we may wish to provide that an employee meeting the necessary requirements would be entitled to a benefit of $200 a month including Social Security. The benefit payable under the plan would be determined by subtracting the monthly amount of Social Security benefit to which each individual employee becomes entitled from $200. Thus, an employee entitled to a Social Security benefit of $120 a month would receive $80 a month from the plan.

Under the second method, allowance might be made for the average Social Security benefit to which employees will become entitled in setting the formula for the plan benefit. The plan benefit itself would be stated as being independent of Social Security. Thus, if we find that the average employee's Social Security benefit would be $120 a month, and it is desired to produce an average benefit of $200 a month, the plan benefit would be set at $80 a month. The average employee would still receive a total benefit of $200 a month as under method 1, but in this case the total benefit would vary as the employee's Social Security benefit varies, whereas under the previous method the total benefit remains the same and the amount payable under the plan varies as the individual Social Security benefit varies.

The first method was widely employed in early negotiated pension plans, possibly because the employer felt that he would be benefited by any increases in Social Security benefits, which seemed more likely than any decreases, while the labor unions may have felt that any advantage thus gained by the company could be capitalized upon in subsequent negotiations. However, the method has a distinct administrative disadvantage. The disadvantage lies in the fact that benefits under the company's pension plan cannot be finally established until a determination has been made by the Social Security Administration.

Most plans employ the second method.[2] Where the second method is employed, a saving clause is frequently included in the rules governing the operation of the plan permitting the Board of Directors to reduce the benefits payable under the plan by any increase in Social Security benefits subsequent to the establishment of the plan. In this way a plan may be designed to dovetail or "integrate" with Social Security benefits in effect at the time the plan is established, while reserving the right to reduce benefits if subsequent increases in Social Security benefits tend to throw plan benefits out of line. Under this method, no action need be taken in the case of minor changes in Social Security benefits if it is desired to maintain plan benefits at their existing level.

There are, of course, other types of benefits which might have to be taken into account in addition to Social Security in certain cases, such as a previous plan instituted by the company or its predecessor, public pensions payable to employees of foreign subsidiaries, etc. These may be handled by one of the two methods

---

[2] There has been a marked trend toward benefits independent of social security. In many plans where benefits were originally established to include social security benefits, the amount of social security benefit used to establish the plan benefit has been limited or "frozen" arbitrarily at a level commensurate with previous social security levels.

already mentioned or a special procedure may be designed to fit the particular case.

Extent of Coverage

One of the early decisions that has to be made concerns requirements for eligibility for membership in the plan as distinct from the eligibility requirements for benefits. The primary purpose of such requirements is of an administrative nature. Typical categories into which employees may be classified are shown below:

1. By mode of compensation, i. e., salaried, wage, commission.
2. By status, i. e., full-time, part-time, temporary, permanent.
3. By union affiliation or representation.
4. By geographic location, e. g., it may be desired to exclude employees of certain plants or offices.
5. By age, i. e., employees may be excluded until the attainment of a minimum age or excluded if employed after the attainment of a maximum age.
6. By period of service, i. e., employees may not be covered until the completion of a required period of service.
7. By rate of compensation, i. e., employees may not become eligible for membership unless their annual compensation exceeds a certain minimum amount.
8. By occupational group. This classification is rarely found except when such group may correspond to a division determined under one of the first four categories.
9. By employee option. This would usually apply in the case of a contributory plan when employees in service on the date of establishment are given the choice of entering the plan and making contributions or remaining out of the plan entirely.

In setting eligibility requirements, groups should not be excluded simply because they are not likely to qualify for benefits. The exceptional members of the group who may otherwise qualify may prove embarrassing later if they have been excluded. Admission of those who never qualify for benefits will do no harm.

Service and/or age requirements are generally found in plans funded through the purchase of insurance company annuities in order to avoid the surrender charges occasioned by the high turnover at early ages and short service durations. In self-administered plans these charges do not occur and such requirements are less frequently encountered.

In contributory plans there is a distinct advantage in entering an employee in the plan as soon after hiring as possible, since the deduction required for pension purposes is less painful if begun with the first pay check rather than after full pay has been received for some period. While it is probably true that there is not much resentment on the part of young employees because of their exclusion prior to the attainment of a certain age, these same employees may feel somewhat mistreated when they are approaching retirement age and find that their first five or ten or even more years of service with the company are not counted for benefits. If credit is ultimately to be given for the waiting period, it would seem preferable to include the employee in the plan immediately and commence the funding of the benefit payable from the date that service credit begins to accrue.

There would appear to be an advantage to the employer also from a taxation and general financial viewpoint in covering employees as soon after employment as practicable. Although the rule does not always hold, of course, generally speaking there is a close correlation between profit expansion and payroll expansion and vice versa. Let us suppose that an industrial corporation operating a pension plan covering employees from their date of employment should enter upon a period of abnormally high activity requiring rapid expansion of employment and producing relatively high profits before taxes. The greatly increased number of employees covered under the pension plan would, of course, increase the amount of contributions required to fund the pension plan. Such contributions would constitute a deduction from taxable income during the period when taxes would presumably be at a maximum.

Suppose at the end of four years a reverse cycle should settle upon the industry requiring reductions in employment and substantially reducing profits. There would then be a reduction in required pension contributions attendant upon the reduction in payroll. Furthermore, the gains in the fund which would presumably result from an abnormally high rate of termination of coverage would tend to afford even greater relief to the company by further reducing the amount of current contribution required to fund the pensions of the employees remaining. Had this same company required a five-year waiting period prior to pension coverage, there would have been no increase in pension fund contributions resulting from the additional employees hired during the high tax years and relatively less contraction in the group of covered employees in the reverse cycle. Approximately the same pension contribution would be needed during the lean years as was required during the years when profits and taxes were high.

Many companies have separate plans for wage and salaried employees while others have over-all plans under which both groups are covered. This decision will, of course, depend largely upon the particular employee relationship situation. If labor conditions are such as to permit an over-all plan, there is much to recommend it as opposed to separate plans, from a general employer-employee relationship viewpoint as well as from the avoidance of the complications which arise upon the transfer of employees from one category to another.

It will not be necessary to make the final decision as to the groups of employees to be included or excluded in the early stages of the plan's development. The matter should be given careful consideration, however, and where doubt exists as to a group's inclusion or exclusion, separate cost figures should be developed so that the group may be added or subtracted without complete cost recalculations when the final decision comes to be made.

Fitting a Plan to the Pocketbook

We now come to the last two major decisions to be made. These are (i) how much should the pension be and (ii) how much should the company spend. There can be a great deal of variation in the amount of annual contribution which may be made, depending upon the speed at which it is desired to fund the existing liabilities. For the purposes of this chapter, however, let us think of cost as the over-all long-term cost. With this understanding, we can then say that an answer to either one of the above questions will mathematically determine the answer to the other.

Since it is seldom possible to say what a company is willing to spend until it is first known what that amount will buy, the answers to the two questions in actual practice are usually obtained simultaneously. Thus, having first decided upon the basic eligibility requirements of the plan, and the factors which are to be used in determining the benefits, we can then make a test calculation of the cost of the draft plan and proceed from there to the final plan of benefits desired. Simply stated, if an actuarial evaluation of our employee group shows that with the eligibility requirements selected a benefit of $100 a month per retiring employee will require an annual contribution of $1,000, we know we can produce under the same eligibility requirements a pension of $75 for a contribution of $750 per annum or a pension of $125 a month for a contribution of $1,250.

The point I wish to stress is that we can save a lot of time and expense by making as many preliminary decisions regarding the structure of the plan as possible before trying to match benefits with costs.

In actual practice, of course, the solution will not be as simple as that stated above. Benefits may vary by amount of compensation. They may be set at one rate for compensation not in excess of compensation covered by Social Security benefits and at another rate for compensation in excess of compensation covered by Social Security benefits. Benefits may depend on the number of years of service of each employee, and the credit allowed for service performed prior to the establishment of the plan may be somewhat less than the credit allowed for service performed subsequent to the establishment of the plan. Part of the company's cost may be offset by employees' contributions. Before the plan is finally decided upon, it may be found necessary to omit benefits for certain types of terminations which had originally been included, in order to provide greater benefits for other types of cases within the cost limitations believed to be necessary.

If the proper ground work has been done, however, this process of tailoring down is not nearly so complicated as it may sound and it is here that the technical advisers can offer the greatest assistance. At this stage the plan should be strengthened where needed and trimmed where necessary and least painful. Your consultant will probably have some suggestions of his own if an indication is given of the direction and degree of adjustment. The main danger at this stage is that of traveling in a circle with emphasis first on one benefit and then another. The best insurance against this, of course, is to have properly crystallized your own thinking during the preliminary stages to the point of setting primary objectives which you wish to achieve, so that in the latter stages of development the plan can continue to advance in that direction.

Existing Patterns

Now let us take the various causes of termination of service for which benefits might be paid and see what is generally being done by companies with plans already in operation with respect to each category.

A. Normal Retirement on Account of Age

The normal retirement age of 65 for male employees is almost universally found in pension plans of private corporations. A retirement age of 60 is quite common, however, for employees of public, quasi-public, and charitable organizations, as well as for female employees of some private organizations. It is interesting to note in this respect that the average life expectancy of women after retirement is substantially greater than that of men (with a consequent greater cost per dollar of pension for women than for men). It is therefore somewhat surprising to find companies desirous of retiring female employees at an earlier age than their male employees. The reason for this may possibly lie in the fact that fewer positions exist which are considered suitable for older women than exist for older men. With the general increase in the number of women employed, and as this increasing number begins to approach retirement age, we have found that the economics of the situation have forced companies to close their present gap in retirement ages between the sexes.

Service After Retirement Age

While a large number of companies insist upon retirement of employees upon attainment of normal retirement age, it is more usual for the pension plan to provide that employees may continue in service after normal retirement age with the consent of the company. A few plans provide for voluntary retirement after attainment of normal retirement age while setting some later age for compulsory retirement, such as 68 or 70. Unions have generally opposed the principle of compulsory retirement, but their positions have not been inflexible in the light of existing economic conditions. When a large proportion of younger union members are finding jobs hard to get, it is not surprising to find unions reversing their position.

There has been some criticism of the principle of using an employee's age as the criterion for retirement. It is argued that, where some employees are mentally and physically ready for retirement prior to age 65, other employees are perfectly capable of continuing to render valuable service well beyond that age. While this is undoubtedly true, there does not appear to be any easy solution to the problem of separating the profitable from the unprofitable employees without an appearance of discrimination on the part of the employer. Some labor unions have been active in the field of developing a system of job reassignment as employees grow older. It has been suggested that employees approaching retirement age be subjected periodically to clinical examination from a sociological, psychological, and medical standpoint to determine their eligibility for retirement. Such practices are not widespread, however, and we may expect that the time-honored criterion of chronological age will continue to be used to determine eligibility for retirement for some time to come. A plan which contains provision for retirement on account of disability prior to normal retirement age, and which permits an employee to continue working after normal retirement age where such continuance appears desirable, would seem to go a long way toward meeting the problems involved in the individual employee's capabilities.

Service Requirement

Plans in which benefits are directly proportional to years of service rendered seldom require any period of service as a prerequisite for superannuation retirement. If a plan pays a flat benefit regardless of years of service, there is an obvious need for requiring the completion of a certain minimum number of years of service as a qualification for the benefit. Similarly, plans containing provisions for a minimum pension will generally require the completion of a certain number of years of service to qualify for the minimum.

Benefits Related to Earnings

With respect to factors used in determining the amount of pension benefits, we may first divide pension plans into two main categories, those relating benefits to compensation and those which do not. There is some overlapping in the categories as some plans provide a certain flat amount of pension plus a percentage of compensation, while many others provide a percentage of compensation with a minimum expressed as a flat amount. Since by far the greater number of plans relate benefits to compensation, we may discuss these first.

The amount of compensation actually used in determining benefits may be defined in a number of ways. One basis is to use (1) compensation in effect at the time of the plan's establishment in determining the amount of benefit payable on account of service rendered prior to such date and (2) average compensation earned from the date of establishment to the date of retirement in determining the amount of benefit payable on account of service rendered since the date of establishment. Frequently a higher rate of benefit is payable on account of compensation earned in excess of the amount covered by Social Security benefits. A few plans go a step further in making an additional change in the rate of benefit at a lower level in order to take into account the higher rate of Social Security benefit payable at the lowest level. Generally, however, it is felt that the higher rate of Social Security benefit payable on account of the lowest salary level forms a minimum subsistence benefit for low-paid employees and no additional deduction in company benefit on this account is desirable.

Prior to the advent of Social Security benefits, many pension plans based their benefits on the average compensation earned during the five or ten years immediately preceding retirement. With the introduction of the Social Security benefit based on the average compensation over the whole period of employee service, company pension plans generally tended to follow suit. However, in recent years there has been some tendency to revert to the old method, when it was found that the inflationary cycle had tended to bring pensions based upon compensation averaged over a long period in the past out of line with current compensation rates. The same situation has caused Congress to amend the Social Security Act from time to time to permit a new start in computing average compensation for Social Security benefit purposes.

While basing benefits upon average compensation during the final years of service does tend to keep benefits more in line with inflationary and deflationary cycles, as opposed to basing benefits on the average compensation over the entire period of service with the company, the same objective could be accomplished by updating the period over which compensation is to be averaged when and if this is felt to be desirable. Moreover, this could be done without creation of any advance obligation to do so.

There is, however, another argument in favor of basing pensions on final average compensation and for which updating would not seem to be a satisfactory answer. Employees whose services have been most valuable to the company are apt to experience a much steeper rate of salary increase during their careers of service than the average employee. Such an employee's pension, if computed on the basis of his average salary over his full term of service, will be a much smaller percentage of the income which he is accustomed to receiving immediately prior to retirement than would be the case for the average employee. This might be especially true in the case of a senior officer of the company who experienced a rapid increase in income during the years just prior to retirement. While a pension based upon his average compensation received during the five or ten years immediately preceding retirement would automatically correct this situation, any attempt to correct it through arbitrary supplements to his pension might possibly give rise to charges of discriminatory practices.

A number of plans set a limit on the amount of compensation which may be used for the purpose of computing pensions. However, the tendency is away from such maximums and many plans which had them have found it desirable to increase the amount or to eliminate the maximum altogether.

Benefits Based on Contributions

A few plans, while not computing pensions directly on the basis of compensation, base benefits upon the amount of contribution made by the employee. However, where the contribution is fixed as a percentage of compensation the result is to relate benefits to compensation received during the period over which the employee contributed. In plans of the so-called "money purchase" type, the amount of benefit is directly related to the employee's contribution accumulated with interest. Since interest will operate to perhaps double or even triple the amount of contribution made by the employee during his very early years of service, while adding comparatively little to contributions made toward the end of his career, this type of plan tends to give relatively greater weight to compensation earned many years prior to retirement as compared to recent compensation. It therefore tends to produce pensions more out of line with current inflated compensation than in the case of plans relating pensions directly to compensation received over the whole term of service. For this reason, and because it is difficult to state the pension formula in definite terms to employees, this type of plan has gone more and more out of favor, although it is perhaps the most conservative type of plan from the viewpoint of funding liabilities.

Flat Benefits

Flat benefit plans, i.e., those which do not base benefits upon compensation, are generally only those negotiated to cover a group of wage employees. They are of two general types: those providing definite benefits independent of Social Security and those providing a flat amount of benefit inclusive of the Social Security benefit. If contributory, the benefit may be based directly on the amount of the employees' contribution. In plans covering both wage and salaried employees a combination of the two types of benefits is often found, the pension being stated as a percentage of compensation with a minimum flat benefit included in order to meet specific union demands.

Effect of Service on Benefits

Whether benefits are based upon compensation or not, the period of service is almost universally a factor in the determination of the amount. This may be done directly, as in a benefit equal to a certain percentage of compensation multiplied by the years of service or to a flat dollar amount multiplied by the years of service. Alternatively, service may be introduced indirectly in the determination of the benefit such as stating the benefit to be a certain percentage of compensation or a certain flat amount after completion of a fixed period of service, with proportionally reduced amounts payable if the period of service is less than the stated normal. Plans basing benefits upon the amount of employee contributions are, of course, automatically relating benefits to the period of service.

The Variable Annuity

The variable annuity fund is a rather widely discussed, but so far little used, vehicle for providing retirement benefits, the most notable now in existence being the College Retirement Equity Fund (C.R.E.F.), the public retirement systems of the State of Wisconsin, and the Employees' Retirement of the Tennessee Valley Authority.

The Teachers' Insurance and Annuity Association (T.I.A.A.) had for years been offering money-purchase type annuity contracts principally to the faculties and administrative staffs of institutions of higher education. As mentioned before, this type of plan is most seriously disrupted by inflationary cycles. In order to overcome the difficulty a scheme was devised under which a proportion of the contributions made could be allocated to a fund investing in corporate equities. The individual's contributions are converted to shares in this fund similar to shares in an investment trust. Upon retirement, the individual receives part of his benefit in the form of a standard annuity corresponding to the amount of contributions not allocated to the equity fund. The remainder of his benefit is an annuity provided by his share in the equity fund, the amount of which continues to vary after retirement in relation to the market value of the equities held by the fund.

This was C.R.E.F. and those few which have followed are generally modeled along the same lines.

Integration With Social Security

Before proceeding to a discussion of the amounts of benefits currently being provided, a brief definition of a term which invariably comes up in any discussion of pension benefits may be needed. In order to qualify a pension plan under the Internal Revenue Code for the purpose of exempting its income and the contributions of the employer from income tax, it must be shown that the plan is non-discriminatory. This means, among other things, according to the Treasury Department, that the benefits payable under a plan, when taken in conjunction with the Social Security benefit payable, must not be a greater proportion of compensation at any given level of compensation than is payable at any lower level of compensation. For example, if an employee earning $5,000 per annum can receive a benefit under a plan which when added to his Social Security benefit is equal to 40 percent of $5,000, then the plan must provide that any employee, with the same period of service, etc., earning less than $5,000 will receive combined benefits of at least 40 percent of whatever such lower compensation might be, and no employee earning more than $5,000, with the same period of service, etc., can receive more than 40 percent of such higher compensation. If a plan meets these conditions, it is said to be "integrated," that is, the benefits of the plan integrate with those provided under the Social Security Act in such a manner as to prevent discrimination in favor of more highly compensated employees.

A plan which provides the same rate of benefit for all levels of compensation is, of course, "integrated" in accordance with the Treasury's definition of the term. Since no account is taken of the benefit payable under Social Security, this is merely discrimination in favor of less highly compensated employees. A plan which provides the same rate of benefit for all levels of compensation but which deducts therefrom the amount of Social Security benefit payable is also "integrated" per se; however, even here certain limitations exist, notably in connection with the amount of reduction permitted in disability benefits.

A more common type of integrated plan, however, is one which adjusts or partially adjusts for Social Security benefits within its own benefit formula; for instance, one which provides a rate of benefit payable on account of compensation included under Social Security and a somewhat higher rate payable on account of compensation in excess of Social Security "wages." Since it would be rather difficult to integrate exactly, an approximation is usually made which favors the less-highly compensated employees to some extent. From time to time the Treasury Department releases rather detailed and somewhat complicated tests for the purpose of establishing whether or not certain types of benefit formulae integrate. It would not be feasible to attempt to go into any lengthy discussion of such rules for the purposes of this chapter. We might bear in mind, however, that if the Treasury adheres to past practice, and, thus, if benefits are based on the whole term of service, and there are no provisions in the plan which tend to make plan benefits dollar for dollar more valuable than Social Security benefits, the rate of benefit provided by company contributions on account of compensation in excess of Social Security "wages" may exceed the rate payable on account of compensation not in excess of such "wages" by $1\frac{1}{4}$ percent per year of service. Thus, you might have a plan which provided a pension equal to $1\frac{1}{4}$ percent of average compensation received in excess of $4,800 per year with no benefit whatsoever payable on account of compensation not in excess of $4,800 per year, or the benefits might be 1 percent on the first $4,800 of compensation plus $2\frac{1}{4}$ percent on the excess per year of service and so on. In actual practice, however, either because of the existence of provisions which require the reduction, or simply because it is desired to stay well within the defined limits, we seldom find more than a 1 percent differential used. In a contributory plan the differential may be increased to allow for any additional benefits provided by the employee's own contributions.

Size of Benefits

The actual percentage rates employed in determining benefits based upon compensation vary widely. As mentioned before, somewhat lower benefit rates are sometimes allowed for service rendered prior to the establishment of a plan. With but few exceptions, the benefit formulae produce benefits, inclusive of Social Security benefits, of anywhere from 30 percent to 60 percent of average compensation after 30 years of service. An average plan might be one which paid a pension equal to $1\frac{1}{2}$ percent of average compensation for each year of service, inclusive of Social Security, or, more commonly, one which paid a benefit, exclusive of Social Security, equal to $\frac{3}{4}$ of 1 percent per year of service on account of average compensation not in excess of $4,800 a year and $1\frac{1}{2}$ percent per year of service on account of average compensation in excess thereof.

It may be noted here that the second formula is somewhat more liberal than the first, especially in the case of low-paid employees, since the $\frac{3}{4}$ of 1 percent differential is more than compensated for by the present scale of Social Security benefits. In flat-benefit type plans the formula is usually designed to produce a monthly benefit, after 30 years of service, inclusive of Social Security, of between $150 and $250 a month with the average plan producing a combined benefit of about $200. A typical plan combining the two types of benefits might provide for a pension, inclusive of Social Security, equal to $1\frac{1}{2}$ percent of average compensation for each year of service with a minimum pension, inclusive of Social Security benefits, equal to $175 a month after 25 years of service.

Although other benefits may be included in a pension plan, the normal retirement benefit is the *raison d'etre* and other benefits are generally related to it. There may be other contingencies for which it seems desirable to provide for payments to an employee or his dependents and there should be a reasonable balance between the various benefits payable. If tailoring down is required, however, it is important to avoid attenuating the funds available in an attempt to cover all contingencies to such an extent that the amount remaining does not provide adequate pensions to the employees who have spent the better part of their working lives in the service of the company.

B. *Retirement on Account of Disability*

A large number of employers have more or less elaborate plans for providing compensation to employees during temporary illnesses and for paying medical and hospital expenses, in some cases not only for the employee but also for his immediate family. Still more employers provide some form of life insurance benefits to the dependents of deceased employees either through their pension plans or through group insurance. It is, therefore, somewhat surprising to find that many do not have any formal plan for providing for the employee who becomes totally and permanently incapacitated for the further performance of his regular occupation. Such cases of disability are relatively few in number and doubtless many employers make provisions for such cases on an informal basis as they occur. As the underwriting of a satisfactory disability benefit is difficult if not entirely impracticable from an insurance company's standpoint, benefits designed specifically to cover cases of total and permanent disability are more frequently found in self-administered plans.

Why Have Disability Benefits?

The inclusion in a pension plan of a retirement benefit for an employee, who after a long period of service becomes permanently disabled, is apt to be much more important from the employer's standpoint than the inclusion of a death benefit. The employee who dies is immediately and completely eliminated from the service of the employer. There is very little difference whether a death benefit is included in the plan or not as far as the efficiency of the employer's organization is concerned. It is said that the value of a death benefit to an employer lies in the good will and sense of security which it may instill in the minds of employees. While these are real values, not to be discounted, there are advantages in addition to these in the case of disability benefits.

The employee who is disabled but who appears at work is not able to perform his duties efficiently. He only interferes with other employees and his misfortune tends to lower their morale. He cannot be dismissed with any grace on the part of the employer. His disability creates more of a financial problem for his family than would his death. Adequate insurance against permanent disability is not readily available to the individual. However, many comprehensive pension plans have afforded such protection for many decades. Next to the normal age retirement benefit the disability benefit may be ranked second in importance.

Some plans provide special benefits in cases of disability or death resulting from accident in the performance of duty. Thus a uniform coverage of those cases which qualify for Workmen's Compensation may be afforded in companies which have employees in a number of states or who desire to cover their own compensation benefits. The pension plan may be used as the vehicle to average out such claims and forms an economical means of doing so.

Administering Disability Benefits

Cases of disability may be classed with other causes of early retirement and provided for on the same basis. Where a benefit is provided specifically for cases of disability, a medical officer or medical board is appointed for the purpose of making the necessary examinations and reviewing the reports of the employee's physician. This board or medical officer, in turn, reports the result of the examination to the managing board of the pension plan together with such recommendations as the findings may indicate to be proper. The final decision as to the employee's eligibility rests with the managing board.

There is almost invariably a period of service required for eligibility for disability benefits in addition to total and presumably permanent disability. The service requirement may range anywhere from five to twenty years with ten years as about the average. As in the case of death benefits, there would appear to be no logic in a minimum age requirement in addition to a service requirement in the case of disability benefits. Some of the negotiated plans have introduced a minimum age requirement of 50 or 55 in addition to a service requirement for eligibility for disability benefits, but the trend is to reduce or eliminate such requirements.

Computing the Disability Benefit

Generally speaking, the same factors used in determining the amount of normal retirement benefit are applied in the case of the disability benefit. A minimum period of service credit is sometimes used in determining the amount of benefit, provided the employee could have completed such minimum period had he continued working until normal retirement age. For example, a plan might require that an employee complete ten years of service with the company before becoming eligible for disability retirement. However, should he become disabled after completing ten years of service but before completing twenty years of service, he may be granted a benefit on the basis of his completion of twenty years of service, provided he could have completed at least twenty years of service by the time he reached normal retirement age.

Plans which are integrated with Social Security benefits frequently provide a special supplemental benefit to be paid in cases of disability until the employee qualifies for Social Security disability benefits or reaches age 65, at which time the supplemental benefit is reduced on account of the Social Security benefit which then becomes payable. Often the entire disability benefit is discontinued at age 65 and a normal retirement benefit is paid thereafter.

Since the disability benefit is generally related to the normal retirement benefit, the amounts of such benefits will vary accordingly. Care should be taken that, if minimum or supplemental benefits are provided in cases of disability, the combined benefits do not under any circumstances exceed the amount which would have been payable, including Social Security benefits, had the employee remained in service until his normal retirement age.

C. Death Benefits[3]

Coverage for a death benefit is usually dependent upon either passing a medical examination or completing a specified period of service. Sometimes both of these qualifications are required and, less frequently, neither may be required. Where completion of 5

---

[3] The death benefits discussed here are those generally applying in the case of employees dying while in the employ of the company. Death benefits may also be paid upon the death of pensioners or employees eligible for retirement, but such benefits are usually of a somewhat different nature and will be discussed later under *Optional Benefits*.

or more years of service is required, it is generally felt to be unnecessary to require a medical examination.

Since payment of a death benefit is a hedge against payment of a pension benefit, a period of coverage under the plan is sometimes required in order that sufficient reserves for the payment of pension benefits may have been accumulated should death occur cancelling the pension liability and making the reserve available for the payment of a death benefit. Where a large number of employees are covered under the plan, however, and death benefits are modest, this last requirement may not be necessary and employees who have completed the required years of service on the date of establishment may be covered immediately.

Computation of Death Benefits

The most frequent factor used in determining death benefits is compensation. However, while average compensation or average final compensation is almost invariably used in determining pension benefits and is sometimes used in determining death benefits, death benefits are frequently based on the compensation in effect on the date of death. Also, as under pension benefits, the death benefit may be an arbitrary flat amount unrelated to compensation. However, the latter type of benefit is generally of a very modest amount designed for the purpose of covering last illness and funeral expenses. In contributory plans the employee's contributions, usually with interest, are paid to his beneficiary; this may be in addition to a death benefit provided from company contributions. In a few plans death benefits are based on the amount of retirement benefit accrued to the date of death. In plans funded through the use of individual retirement income policies, the death benefit is usually set at an amount equal to 100 or 120 times the monthly retirement benefit to which the employee would have become entitled at the normal retirement age.

The period of service is also to be found as a factor in determining the amount of death benefit but much less frequently than in the determination of pension benefits. If service is used at all in the determination of the amount of benefit, it is usually only to the extent of grading the benefit during the early years of service, with the maximum reached after five or ten years of service. An exception, of course, would be in the case of death benefits related to employee contributions or the normal retirement benefit, which themselves are directly related to the period of service.

Among plans providing death benefits based upon compensation the amount of benefit will usually fall within the range of from one-half year's salary to two and one-half year's salary with a benefit of one year's salary being about the average. As mentioned above, this may be graded in the early years of service. For example, a very liberal plan might provide a death benefit equal to six months' salary after two years of service, increasing by six months' salary for each year of service thereafter, with a maximum death benefit equal to two years' salary after five or more years of service. Since the amount of an employee's contributions or the amount of his accrued pension benefit is generally low during the early years when the need for insurance protection is perhaps the greatest, death benefits based on these factors are not generally found to be satisfactory. One plan, however, seems to have provided a reasonable solution by providing a death benefit equal to one year's salary plus the employee's contributions with a minimum total benefit equal to two years' salary. This type of solution seems to have a great deal of merit both from the point of view of the employee and of economy. While the need may be greatest at the younger ages, most deaths occur at the older ages when the employees' contributions will be sufficient to make up the second years' salary.

Flat death benefits are infrequently found in pension plans and seldom exceed $2,500. The most satisfactory type of benefit from the married male employee's point of view is the widow's benefit which is in the form of an annuity payable to the deceased employee's widow until her death or remarriage. The amount of the widow's benefit is generally related to the normal retirement benefit to which the deceased would have become entitled had he retired on the day on which he died. Frequently the widow's benefit is set at one half the normal retirement benefit accrued to the date of death, with perhaps a minimum such as 20 percent of the employee's average compensation. While this type of benefit is common in England and other European countries, and is found in some plans in this country covering governmental employees, it was until quite recently rather rare among industrial pension plans. It is, of course, a relatively expensive benefit and is not popular with single employees, female employees, or married men who feel that they have sufficient insurance protection for their families and would instead prefer to have larger pension benefits.

D. *Early Retirement or Vesting Benefits*

Early retirement benefits and vesting benefits are frequently treated as separate benefits. However, as they are almost always of equivalent value, many plans make no distinction between the two as far as qualifications are concerned. Vesting is generally considered to mean the right of an employee to leave the service of a company prior to his normal retirement age and receive a pension upon his attainment of the normal retirement age equal to all or part of the pension accrued to the date of his termination of service. Early retirement generally refers to the right of an employee to leave the service of a company prior to his normal retirement age with a pension commencing immediately upon his termination of service. The amount of pension payable in the latter case is usually reduced to an amount such that its value is actuarially equivalent to the value of the pension commencing at normal retirement age. Thus, there is no difference in cost between the two benefits.

Advantages and Disadvantages

Many plans establish one set of qualifications and permit employees to choose between a pension deferred until normal retirement age or a lesser pension commencing immediately. Some plans, however, have two distinct sets of qualifications for vesting and early retirement, the latter usually being more stringent. Since vesting is of obvious value from an employee's viewpoint, most employees will quite naturally tend to favor minimum qualifications. From the employer's viewpoint, however, vesting is of questionable value, except under certain circumstances, and may be a distinct disadvantage. In the first place, any payments to employees leaving the service of the company prior to normal retirement tend to reduce the amount of funds which may be used to provide other retirement benefits. Secondly, one of the advantages of a pension plan from an employer's point of view is its tendency to hold employees who have gained valuable experience and, concurrently, valuable pension credits in the service of the company. Vesting benefits, obviously, tend to negate this advantage.

Under certain circumstances, however, an early retirement benefit may be of value to the employer as well as to the employee. A case in point would be the employee who, prior to his normal retirement age and short of being physically disabled, becomes psychologically or physiologically incapable of assuming satisfactorily the responsibilities of the position attained upon the basis of his past experience and performance. Such cases are particularly apparent, of course, at times when it becomes necessary to pare payrolls to meet contracting industrial activity. Many companies found their early retirement provisions of value in this respect during the great depression and subsequent recessions.

Eligibility

In setting the qualifications, therefore, for vesting or early retirement benefits, there is usually a compromise between the interest of the employer and the wishes of the employee. A number of plans make a distinction between employees leaving service with approval of the company and those who leave without its approval. Thus, one set of qualifications may be required for eligibility for a benefit in the former case with somewhat more stringent qualifications set for the latter case, or perhaps more frequently the latter case will not be covered at all. In recent years, however, the Internal Revenue Service has objected to the requirement of company approval, except in union negotiated plans, on the grounds that such a provision could be discriminatory. The qualifications for vesting or early retirement benefits are sometimes based solely upon completion of a period of service. More frequently the attainment of a minimum age is required, and most frequently the attainment of a minimum age and the completion of a minimum period of service are both required. An average plan might provide for vesting or early retirement upon the attainment of age 55 and the completion of 15 years of service with the company's consent, with perhaps an additional five years of both service and age required for the payment of a benefit upon termination without the company's consent. Where company consent is a requirement, great care must be taken to avoid exercising it in a discriminatory manner lest the plan lose its tax exempt status.

Computation of Benefit

The vesting or early retirement benefit is almost invariably related to the normal retirement benefit. Some plans have a graded system depending upon years of service, which permits partial vesting after the completion of a minimum period of service with the proportion increasing for each year of service until full vesting is attained. For instance, a plan might provide for an employee's becoming entitled to half his accrued pension at his normal retirement age if terminating his service prior thereto and after the completion of ten years of service, with an additional five percent of accrued pension for each year of service in excess of ten until full vesting is reached after twenty years of service.

With few exceptions, the vesting or early retirement benefit is (1) a pension payable at normal retirement age equal to the normal retirement benefit accrued to the date of termination of service, or (2) a reduced pension commencing immediately which is of equivalent actuarial value to the pension commencing at normal retirement age. Where the normal retirement benefit is not directly proportional to the years of service, as would be the case in a plan containing a minimum or maximum benefit, a special formula may need to be devised in order to determine equitably the amount of accrued benefit at the date of termination of service. Since such formulae may be more or less complicated depending on the complexity of the normal retirement benefit itself, no purpose would be served by attempting to detail any of them here.

In contributory industrial pension plans the right of an employee to the return of his contributions upon his termination of service at any time for any reason is almost universally respected, unless some other benefit is payable instead. Usually a return of contributions will include the interest accumulated on them.

E. Optional Benefits

Pensions are usually payable in the form of a life annuity with all payments ceasing on the employee's death. If the plan is contributory, provision is usually made, although not always, to return the remainder of the employee's contributions with interest if he should die before receiving pension benefits totaling this amount.

A few plans guarantee the payment of the pension for a fixed number of years, such as five or ten, irrespective of the fact that the employee himself might die before the expiration of the guaranteed period, payment thereafter being continued only while the employee is alive.

Most plans which provide substantial benefits in addition to Social Security benefits permit an employee to elect to receive a reduced pension in lieu of his regular pension in order that it may be continued in full or in some proportion to a beneficiary designated at the time of his retirement, if such beneficiary survives him.

Optional benefits such as those described above do not increase the cost of the pension plan since the reduced pension together with the pension to be continued to the beneficiary is computed, on the basis of the employee's and beneficiary's age and sex at the time of retirement, to be of equivalent actuarial value to the benefit otherwise payable.

A few plans which permit employees to continue in service after their normal retirement age provide for an employee's election of an optional benefit upon the attainment of his normal retirement age. In this way the employee may provide a pension for his dependents in the event that he should die in service prior to his retirement. This latter type of election, however, unless carefully restricted may add some additional cost to the plan.

Still other plans provide for the election of such an option at some point prior to the normal retirement date. Frequently employees may protect their dependents from the time they become eligible for early retirement either through election or through a provision which automatically provides for the payment of the optional benefit in the event of the employee's death in service. Such options do increase the cost of the plan unless provision is made for reducing the employee's own benefit after retirement to cover the cost of the coverage. The latter type of provision is somewhat hard to explain to employees, however, for it is only those who survive to retirement, i.e., those whose dependents received no benefits, who must pay for the cost.

Employee Contributions

The popularity of contributory over non-contributory plans has waxed and waned quite materially in recent years. Prior to

World War II the great majority of industrial pension plans were contributory. During the war years high profits and high taxes tended to swing the pendulum greatly in favor of non-contributory plans, employer contributions being deductible from taxable corporate income. Since the war the pendulum has returned to about center. While there is added administrative detail in the operation of contributory plans, many employers feel that there is a distinct psychological, if not economic, advantage in requiring an employee to share in providing for his old age. Some labor unions have adamantly opposed employee contributions in negotiating for pensions while others have supported employee contributions and used this as an argument for union participation in the administration of the plan.

Although pre-war plans and especially pre-Social Security plans were frequently designed on the basis that employee contributions would provide half the normal retirement benefit on account of service rendered after the commencement of contributions, more recent plans have generally fixed employee contributions at a considerably lower scale. The necessity of this reduction was readily apparent with the advent of Social Security and withholding taxes. Generally, employee contributions are related to the benefit accrual rate. If different benefit accrual rates are used for compensation under and over the Social Security maximum wage level, different employee contribution rates will be set proportionally. Thus, a plan providing a benefit equal to $3/4$ of 1 percent of compensation not in excess of \$4,800 per year of service and $1\frac{1}{2}$ percent on the excess might require employee contributions of 2 percent of the first \$4,800 of compensation and 4 percent of the excess. Employee contribution rates are generally fixed at from two to three and one-half times the benefit accrual rate, with the average plan set at a ratio of about two and two-thirds. Flat benefit plans will, of course, fix employee contributions at a flat amount in most cases.

Conclusion

Of the hundreds of pension plans in existence there are very few which are identical. There are many which are very similar and there are groups which seem to fall into fairly standard patterns. The number of combinations is infinite. If a company is about to establish a pension plan, in all probability it will, at least in some detail, be unique; but unless some experience has been gained with a plan already in operation, it will probably be best to adopt one of the standard patterns at the start. Many of the departures from established patterns, which are thought to represent new ideas, have been tried before, many without success. There is plenty of room for new ideas, however, and a good many of them are coming not from the professional experts but from the men who are facing the problems every day in the operation of their own plans. The professional consultant, in a sense, is acting in the capacity of a clearing house for his clients' inventions, for it is the retirement plan administrator who is most closely in contact with Mother Necessity.

Chapter 2

TAX ASPECTS OF PENSION PLANS

By Herman C. Biegel and William B. Harman, Jr.

Introduction

Retirement plans have shown outstanding growth in recent years. By September, 1963 there were in existence about 90,000 plans with favorable rulings from the Internal Revenue Service, more than five times the 17,000 plans in existence at the close of 1952. In the same period coverage of these plans doubled so that by the fall of 1963 an estimated 24 million individuals were covered by the plans.[1]

This marked upsurge in retirement plans reflects the vital role that they play in helping to meet the retirement needs of employees. But it also reflects in large measure the very substantial tax advantages given by the Federal tax law to encourage the growth of pension plans. The basic framework of the present tax treatment of pension plans was established by the Revenue Act of 1942. This Act confined the favored tax treatment to plans which do not discriminate in favor of executives, stockholders, or highly paid employees, and spelled out the broad tests which pension plans must satisfy in order to be eligible for the favored tax treatment. This treatment was incorporated in the Internal Revenue Code of 1954 with certain other amendments which will be discussed further on.[2] In 1962, P. L. 87-792, known as the Keogh-Smathers Act, allowed self-employed persons, who previ-

---

[1] These figures cover stock-bonus and profit-sharing plans as well as pension plans. Stock-bonus and profit-sharing plans are frequently used to provide benefits for employees at retirement. Figures regarding the number of plans are taken from *Internal Revenue Service Press Releases, Determination Letters Issued on Employee Benefit Plans.*

[2] References to sections of the Internal Revenue Code (IRC) are to the Internal Revenue Code of 1954 unless otherwise stated. References to sections of the Income Tax Regulations are to regulations issued under the 1954 Code unless otherwise stated.

ously were not eligible, to enjoy to a limited extent the tax advantages associated with coverage in qualified pension plans.

Because the favored tax treatment is granted only to those pension plans which meet the specified tests, the tax laws have had a tremendous impact on the shaping and formulating of pension plans. It is not enough for the pension consultant to determine what kind of plan is best suited to the needs of the particular employer and his employees. His consideration must be colored by the applicable limitations of the tax laws and the Internal Revenue Service's construction of them.

Even the give and take of the employer and the union representative around the collective bargaining table is now circumscribed by what the tax laws permit. For what the union wants may be limited by what the employer can give without visiting adverse tax consequences on the employer, the employee and the pension fund itself.

In the immediate wake of the 1942 Act and the Internal Revenue Service's regulations dealing with pensions it might have been fashionable for the tax lawyer and the pension consultant to quarrel with the narrow area into which qualified pension plans must fall. Today it is more profitable to face the facts of life in this field and draft the plan accordingly.

Essentially, the tax problems are these:

(1) What are the rules for qualifying a pension plan?
(2) How is such qualification obtained?
(3) Once having qualified, how can the plan be amended, suspended or even terminated?
(4) What are the tax consequences of a qualified plan to the employer?
(5) What are the tax consequences of such a plan to the employee?
(6) What are the tax consequences to the fund itself?

I. Qualifying a Pension Plan

Before considering the criteria for qualifying a pension plan, one might ask, "Why bother qualifying?" The answer is an eminently practical one. The qualification of a pension plan carries with it three important tax consequences:

First, the earnings of a qualified trust are exempt from Federal taxes under section 501 (a). (See p. 74.) If the plan is an insured one providing annuities, earnings on the pension reserves held by the life insurance company are similarly exempt from tax under section 805(d).

Second, the employer contributing under a qualified plan may, subject to certain limitations, take a current deduction for such contributions. (See p. 59.)

Third, the employee-beneficiary is not taxed upon employer contributions as they are made, but only as such amounts are distributed or made available to him under the plan. Because benefits are generally received in retirement years when other income tends to decline and older people receive favored tax treatment, including double personal exemptions, the deferment of tax until the employee receives the pension benefit ordinarily permits him to shift income to lower tax brackets and frequently to eliminate all tax. Quite apart from such a reduction in tax liabilities, the postponement of the time when tax is payable provides substantial interest savings to covered individuals. Moreover, when the amounts are distributed or made available to him or his beneficiary, additional tax benefits are extended (e.g., in some instances the capital gain rates will apply, a death benefit up to $5,000 is excluded from income taxes, and the proceeds of the plan are generally exempt from estate taxes). (See p. 71.)

Section 401(a) of the Internal Revenue Code of 1954 (formerly section 165(a) of the Internal Revenue Code of 1939) sets forth the following major criteria of a qualified pension trust:

(1) The trust must be created or organized in the United States;
(2) The plan (of which the trust forms a part) must be for the exclusive benefit of the employees or their beneficiaries;
(3) It must be impossible for the employer to divert or recapture the funds prior to the satisfaction of all liabilities under the trust;
(4) The plan must be established on an actuarially sound basis;
(5) The plan must cover either a specified percentage of employees or a class of employees which is not discriminatory (plans covering self-employed people must satisfy more stringent coverage rules for employees, see p. 80); and
(6) The benefits and contributions under the plan must not be discriminatory.[3]

In addition to these requirements, section 501(a) has made ap-

---

[3] The Internal Revenue Service has released a comprehensive ruling setting forth the guides to be followed in considering the qualification under section 401(a) of the Internal Revenue Code of a pension plan. (Rev. Rul. 61-157, 1961-2 C. B. 67). This should be consulted in considering any aspect of the qualification of such a plan.

plicable to pension trusts certain standards of trust conduct which were applicable only to charities and similar organizations under the 1939 Code.[4] As indicated below, if an otherwise qualified pension trust violates these standards, it may either lose its exempt status (e.g., if it engages in so-called "prohibited transactions"), or, at the very least, may subject a certain portion of its income to tax (e.g., if it engages in unrelated business activities).

A. Creation Within the United States

The requirement that a qualified trust must be created or organized within the United States[5] was inserted in the law by the Internal Revenue Code of 1954 and has no statutory counterpart in earlier Revenue Acts. However, under prior law, the Internal Revenue Service had ruled administratively that a trust created abroad did not qualify unless it was created by a United States employer and it agreed to restrict the source of its income to sources without the United States.[6] This latter provision was designed to prevent United States income from escaping taxation completely—e.g., in a situation where the employee-beneficiary was a non-resident alien.

B. Exclusive Benefit of Employees

The second requirement[7] that the trust must be for the exclusive benefit of employees or their beneficiaries—was not new in the 1954 Act. As a matter of fact, it has been in the law in substantially the same form since the Revenue Act of 1921.[8] This provision was generally overlooked in the controversy that arose over the new provisions relating to pension plans and trusts adopted by the Revenue Act of 1942. This criterion, however, became perhaps the most important provision in the statute enacted in 1942 with respect to the qualification of plans and trusts.[9] This test has been applied even when the other criteria in the statute have been met literally. There are probably more rulings under

---

[4] Cf. §. §. 421, 422, 3813, and 3814 of the Internal Revenue Code of 1939.

[5] §. 401(a)(1) of the Internal Revenue Code of 1954; §. 1.401-1(a)(3) of the Income Tax Regulations issued under the 1954 Code; see §. 7701(a)(9) for the applicable definition of the term "United States."

[6] IR Mim. 71, 1952-2 C. B. 170.

[7] §. 401(a)(2); §. 1.401-1.

[8] §. 219(f), Rev. Act of 1921.

[9] That this result was not wholly unexpected, see "Tax Phases of Pension and Annuity Plans" (1943) by Herman C. Biegel, Controller's Institute of America "Pension Plans; Social Security," Pamphlet No. 8, p. 348.

this provision than under any other single provision of the statute.

One of the problems treated by the Internal Revenue Service under this provision is the tax consequence of the termination of a plan. This is discussed separately below. (See p. 56.)

A plan may also fail to be "for the exclusive benefit of employees" within the meaning of section 401(a)(1) if it serves a corporate purpose as a source of disposing of the corporation's own securities. What the Internal Revenue Service is concerned with in this respect is that the trust may be used by the employer indirectly to create a market for its securities, or, by dealing in such securities, to rig the market price.[10] Accordingly, the District Director must be notified if stock or securities of the employer are acquired by the trust in order that a determination may be made as to whether or not the trust serves any purpose other than constituting part of a plan for the exclusive benefit of employees. Such notification must include a statement setting forth the amount to be invested in the stock or securities of the employer, the nature of the investment, the present rate of return, collateral or type of security for the loan, if any, and the reasons for the investment.[11] While the regulation (section 1.401-1(b)(5)(ii)) merely requires disclosure, if there is any question advance approval should be obtained.

To some extent the application of the prohibited transaction and unrelated business rules to pension trusts (see pp. 75-80) was designed to reinforce the "exclusive benefit" requirement insofar as it requires fair dealing between the employer and the trust created by that employer.

C. *Irrevocability*

The third requirement for a bona fide pension trust is that it must be impossible, prior to the satisfaction of all liabilities under the trust, for the corpus or income to be diverted to purposes other than for the exclusive benefit of the employees or their beneficiaries.[12] This provision was inserted in the law in 1938[13] and became effective in 1940.[14]

Prior to 1940 a qualified pension trust could be revocable by

---

[10] §. 1.401-1(b)(5)(i) and (ii); §. 503.

[11] Rev. Rul. 61-157, 1961-2 C. B. 67, Part 2(r); Rev. Proc. 56-12, 1956-1 C. B. 1029, Exhibit B.

[12] §. 401(a)(2); §. 1.401-2.

[13] §. 165(a)(2), Rev. Act of 1938.

[14] §. 218, Rev. Act of 1939.

the employer. At present the employer cannot recapture the funds except upon termination and then only to the extent that excessive amounts have been paid in because of "erroneous actuarial computations."[15] In case a group annuity contract is used to fund the pension benefits (without a pension trust), it must be provided in the contract that any refunds of premiums will be applied in the current taxable year or the next succeeding taxable year towards the purchase of retirement annuities.[16]

D. *Actuarially Sound Basis*

Another requirement for a qualified pension plan or trust is that the plan must be established on an actuarially sound basis, i.e., either the benefits payable to the employee or the required contributions by the employer can be determined actuarially.[17] In most privately conceived pension plans, no difficulty will be encountered on this score; a scale of benefits is agreed upon and the employer then pays in whatever his actuary or the life insurance company advises him is necessary to fund these benefits on an actuarially sound basis.

When unions started negotiating with respect to pension plans, considerable concern was expressed as to whether such plans would qualify in regard to "actuarial soundness." Some negotiated plans require that the employer contribute to a pension fund either a flat amount per employee, or flat percentage of payroll, or a certain amount per ton, or a specified amount per unit of production. If these amounts were used merely to provide such benefits as could be purchased with them, the plan would have no difficulty qualifying actuarially since it would be regarded as a "money purchase" arrangement. But many union plans go on to provide for a pension in a fixed amount regardless of the adequacy of the employer's contributions to provide that amount of pension. It is evident that in this type of case there is no necessary correlation between the contributions on the one hand and the specified benefits on the other.

In view of the importance of the issue, the Internal Revenue Service has ruled that if the relationship between the fixed benefits and the stated rate of contributions is supported by an actuarial computation to which the employer can certify, it will be accepted

---

[15] §. 1.401-2(b)(1).
[16] §. 404(a)(2); §. 1.404(a)-8(a)(3).
[17] §. 1.401-1(b)(1)(i).

as reasonable and the definiteness of the plan will not be adversely affected merely because it provides for a fixed benefit and a stated rate of contribution.[18] (For the problems relating to the employer's deductibility of contributions to such a plan, see section 1.404(a)-1 and the discussion on pp. 59-65.)

Another problem in determining whether the benefits under a plan are actuarially determinable arises in connection with the so-called variable annuity plan which is gaining some popularity. This type of plan attempts to correlate the purchasing power of the pension payments with the cost-of-living index and thus soften the impact of inflation on the benefits at retirement.

To do this, a portion of the overall pension fund is invested in the purchase of a minimum conventional pension, and the balance is invested in equity securities which tend over a long period to fluctuate with the cost-of-living index. The realized and unrealized capital gains and investment gains of the equity fund pass to the benefit of the participating employees, thus increasing their pension benefits. On retirement, the employee gets the minimum pension of a fixed number of dollars per month plus a certain number of annuity shares per month. The latter shares vary in value from year to year in accordance with the investment experience of the trust.

The problem under section 1.401-1(b)(1) of the Regulations is whether the plan is one which provides definitely determinable benefits and, therefore, satisfies the "actuarially sound" test. The Internal Revenue Service has ruled that the variable annuity plan qualifies on that score.[19]

E. *Coverage*

The fifth requirement for a qualified pension plan and trust relates to "coverage."[20] The statute now provides two tests for pension plans generally: one is based on an arbitrary percentage of employees; the other sets forth a rather general principle of non-discrimination. (The statute prescribes stricter coverage rules for pension plans covering self-employed people than for plans in general. See p. 81.)

---
[18] Rev. Rul. 55-681, 1955-2 C. B. 585.
[19] Rev. Rul. 185, 1953-2 C. B. 202.
[20] For detailed description of coverage requirements, see Rev. Rul. 61-157, *supra*, Part 4.

Tax Aspects of Pension Plans

The arbitrary percentage test applying to plans which do not cover self-employed people is this: 70 percent or more of all the employees must be covered; or, if 70 percent are eligible, then 80 percent of that 70 percent must be covered.[21] For this purpose a preliminary waiting period, not in excess of five years, may be specified in the plan. In other words, all employees with service of less than five years may be excluded—if the plan so provides—in making the computation. In addition, for purposes of this 70 percent computation, employees working less than 20 hours a week or less than five months in one year may be excluded.

It should be noted that an age limitation is not one of the specified exclusions. For example, suppose all employees having less than five years of service and under 35 years of age are excluded by the plan. All employees having more than five years of service, irrespective of age, must nevertheless be taken into account in determining whether the plan meets the 70 percent rule.

The failure to meet the 70 percent test does not necessarily disqualify a plan.[22] There is still the second—and somewhat broader —test, namely: the classification selected by the employer must not discriminate in favor of officers, stockholders, highly compensated or supervisory employees.[23] Here the Commissioner of Internal Revenue has considerable latitude as to what he will regard as a valid classification. In actual practice the great bulk of the plans qualify under this broader test rather than under the percentage tests indicated above.

The statute and regulations[24] describe certain classifications which in themselves will not be discriminatory. For example, a classification will not be discriminatory merely because it excludes employees all of whose earnings are covered by Social Security (i.e., employees earning $4,800 or less per year under the present Social Security law); or merely because it covers only salaried employees or only clerical employees. It is also possible to have a plan which covers salaried employees earning over $4,800.

One of the more important problems at the time the regulations

---

[21] §. 401(a)(3); §. 1.401-3.
[22] Conversely, meeting the 70 percent rule automatically satisfies the coverage test and makes moot the question as to whether the plan discriminates as to coverage under the alternate test. §. 1.401-3(b).
[23] §. 401(a)(3)(B); §. 1.401-3(b) and (d).
[24] §. 401(a)(5); §. 1.401-3(d); and §. 1.401-3(e)(1).

under the 1942 Act were being drawn up was the status of a plan which covered only employees earning over $3,000 a year, the maximum earnings then covered by Social Security. The Service finally took the position that, in order for an "over-$3,000 plan" to qualify, the benefits must be integrated with those provided by Social Security.[25] What this meant was that if the plan covered only employees earning over $3,000 per annum, no benefits could be given on the first $3,000 of earnings and the benefits on earnings over that figure had to be comparable to what Social Security provided on the first $3,000. The same is now true of the "over-$4,800 plan."

True, the Internal Revenue Service's insistence on the integration principle in determining whether a plan meets the non-discrimination test as to coverage has reduced the flexibility of section 401(a)(3)(B). But there are accompanying advantages to taxpayers. For what might have developed into a case-by-case wrangle between the Revenue Agent and a taxpayer as to whether a particular plan was discriminatory in coverage is now resolved quickly by the application of the simple rule of thumb: does the plan integrate with Social Security?

There is also the question as to whether the integration principle under section 401(a)(5) applies to a plan covering *all* salaried employees. An all-salaried plan, naturally, takes into account employees earning less than $4,800. It should be possible, therefore, not only to give benefits on the first $4,800 of income, but also to provide, on the earnings over $4,800, benefits in excess of the Treasury's formula.

However, there is one caution that should be kept in mind. Obviously, if the number of salaried employees under $4,800 is relatively small, and the amount contributed on behalf of that group as a whole is small in comparison with what is expended for the people over $4,800, the Service may question the validity of the all-salaried classification. Such a plan may be regarded as too transparent a dodge for converting an "over-$4,800 plan" into a broader classification and thereby avoiding the integration requirement. On the other hand, where the group under $4,800 in an all-salaried classification is substantial in number, and the amount expended on behalf of that group is large in relation to

---

[25] §. 29.165-3, Regs. 111. This will be discussed under "discrimination in benefits" text. A comparable provision is contained in §. 1.401-3(e).

the total expenditure, there should be no question as to the qualification of that plan under §401(a)(3)(B), and integration would not seem mandatory.

F. Discrimination in Benefits

The final requirement in the law with respect to a qualified plan and trust is: Not only must the classification as to eligible employees be good, but the contributions and benefits made on behalf of those employees must not discriminate in favor of officers, stockholders, supervisory or highly compensated employees.[26]

The law specifically indicates that a plan shall not be considered discriminatory merely because the contributions or benefits for employees bear a uniform relationship to the total compensation or to the basic or regular compensation.[27] Consequently, a qualified pension plan can provide larger dollar benefits or larger dollar contributions for higher paid employees than for lower paid employees—provided such contributions or benefits are not larger as a percentage of compensation for higher paid employees than for lower paid employees.

Similarly, the statute states that a plan will not be considered discriminatory merely because contributions or benefits applicable to the earnings covered by Social Security differ from those on the earnings not covered by Social Security. It is in this connection that the integration procedure was developed. Under this procedure, in order to integrate the two types of benefits, Social Security benefits are taken into consideration in determining whether the benefits or contributions provided by the private pension plan meet the non-discrimination test. In effect, the integration rules permit the pension plan to take credit for that part of Social Security benefits which is considered to be financed by the employer. In general, the portion of Social Security benefits recognized for such integration purposes is considered equal to a benefit amounting to 37½ percent of the first $4,800 of pay. (Different integration rules apply to plans covering self-employed people. See p. 82.) The effect of this can be seen by taking the case of a pension plan which provides benefits amounting to 37½ percent of pay. Such a plan can provide private benefits equal to

---
[26] §. 401(a)(4); see also Rev. Rul. 61-157, *supra*, Part 5.
[27] §. 401(a)(5), §. 1.401-4(a)(1).

37½ percent of pay for that part of wages over $4,800 a year without providing any private benefit for wages under $4,800. This is because an equivalent benefit for wages under $4,800 is deemed to be furnished by Social Security benefits. If, for example, the plan provided benefits of 40 percent of pay for wages over $4,800, it could qualify by paying benefits equal to 2½ percent of pay on wages under $4,800. The remaining 37½ percent of pay on the latter wages are deemed to come from Social Security benefits.

In terms of contributions to a pension plan, which does not cover self-employed people, the Social Security "integration" credit is now equal to 9⅜ percent of the first $4,800 of pay.[28] In other words, a pension plan which specifies that contributions shall amount to 9⅜ percent of all earnings in excess of $4,800 can meet the nondiscrimination test, since an equivalent contribution for wages under $4,800 is deemed to come from the Social Security system. If the specified contribution were 10 percent, this percentage would be contributed on wages over $4,800 and only ⅝ of one percent on wages under $4,800, since together with the Social Security credit of 9⅜ percent, this is all that would be needed to make up the required 10 percent for wages under $4,800.

This allowance for Social Security assumes that the pension plan provides a straight life annuity at normal retirement age (i.e., 65 for men and 60 for women). If the pension plan provides extra features such as early retirement, death benefits and annuities guaranteed for certain periods, the allowance is reduced. The purpose of this reduction is to ensure that the lower-paid employees, most of whose wages are under $4,800 a year, will get equivalent extra benefits under the private plan.

It should be noted that a plan which met the requirements of one of the old integration formula need not be adjusted even if it does not meet the requirements of the new formula.[29]

While the adoption of a benefit formula in accordance with the integration principle was fairly adequate protection against dis-

---

[28] The 9⅜ percent contribution figure is based on the assumption that an employee at the $4,800 salary level works 30 years to qualify for a benefit equal to 37½ percent of pay—the figure used to integrate Social Security benefits and private pension benefits. This amounts to a unit benefit of 1¼ percent of pay each year of service for 30 years. In order to finance a life annuity benefit for males at age 65 equal to 1 percent of pay, it would cost 7½ percent of pay. Therefore, a benefit equal to 1¼ percent of pay would cost 9⅜ percent of pay.

[29] §. 1.401-3(e)(2)(VI).

crimination, the Service at one time attempted still a further gloss on the requirements of section 165(a)(4) of the 1939 Code (as amended by the 1942 Revenue Act) where stockholders were covered by the plan. It held that if a pension plan covered stockholders, then the contributions which could be made on behalf of all employees each of whom owned more than 10 percent of the voting stock, directly or indirectly, could not exceed 30 percent of the contributions for all participants under the plan.[30] This was the so-called "30 percent rule."

The Tax Court failed to find any statutory justification for the 30 percent rule in the only case brought before it.[31] The Service thereupon revoked the 30 percent rule.[32] However, this does not mean that there are no limitations on what can be set aside for the stockholder employees covered by a plan. Instead, it means that each plan covering stockholder employees will be subjected to minute scrutiny by the examining Revenue Agent.[33]

One final word should be noted with respect to discrimination in benefits: that involves the question of vesting. There is no requirement that benefits be vested in the employee in order to qualify a plan. But if a plan does not vest benefits, it may be possible that discrimination may exist in favor of the stockholders, officers and supervisory employees because forfeitures will generally apply principally to their benefit. Accordingly, each case must be examined on the facts to determine whether the lack of vesting will tend to produce the proscribed determination.[34]

II. Securing a Ruling

So much for the principles applicable to qualifying a pension plan and trust. There is also the practical problem of just how

---

[30] I. T. 3675, 1944, C. B. 315; I. T. 3675, 1944 C. B. 316; I. T. 3676, 1944 C. B. 317.

[31] *Volckening*, 13 T. C. 723 (1949); Acq. 1950-1 C. B. 5.

[32] I. T. 4020, 1950-2 C. B. 61. The House bill dealing with the 1954 Code revived the "30 percent stockholder rule" (§. 501(e)(3)(A), H. R. 8300) but the Senate again reverted to existing law on this point. In conference, the House accepted the Senate position.

[33] See also, *Betty C. Stockvis*, 10 T. C. M. 74 (1951), where the Service attempted to disqualify a pension plan in which over 58 percent of the annual contribution was paid in for three highly compensated employees. The Tax Court held that even though so substantial a proportion of the total annual contribution was made on behalf of three highly compensated and supervisory employees, the plan was not discriminatory in coverage since it covered all employees with one year of service; nor was it discriminatory as to contributions and benefits, since the latter were proportionate to salary. See also Rev. Rul. 61-157, *supra*, Part 5.

[34] PS No. 22 (9/2/44).

this is accomplished.[35] While there is no legal requirement for a plan to secure an advance ruling as to qualification from the Internal Revenue Service, as a practical matter, such rulings are almost invariably secured in order to avoid the severe tax consequences resulting from failure to qualify. Original approval of a plan is obtained by filing a request for a ruling in duplicate with the District Director of Internal Revenue in which the employer's principal place of business is located; in the case of a plan of a parent and subsidiary companies, the request is filed with the District Director where the principal place of business of the parent is located (whether or not consolidated returns are filed); and in the case of an industry-wide plan or multiple employers, the request may be filed in the Office of the District Director where the trustee's principal place of business is located.[36] In this Office the case is assigned to a pension trust reviewer. Section 1.404(a)-2 of the Income Tax Regulations and Revenue Procedure 62-31 specify the rather extensive information which should be submitted with the request. A plan will be approved where payments are conditioned upon Service approval.[37] If, on consideration of the case, the pension trust reviewer believes the plan qualifies, he prepares and submits a favorable determination letter to a special reviewer for his consideration. If the special reviewer agrees, the District Director issues the favorable determination letter, without referring the case to the National Office in Washington. If the pension trust reviewer or the special reviewer feel some modification in the plan is necessary, they will suggest it to the taxpayer—generally prior to the issuance of any formal determination letter. When the change is made, the District Director will then issue a favorable ruling.

On the other hand, if the taxpayer disagrees with the suggested change, he may request that his case be forwarded to the National Office of the Internal Revenue Service at Washington for technical advice. The District Director is not bound to do this, but on most questionable matters he complies with that request. The Pension Trust Branch in Washington then advises the District Director of its reaction to the matter. If it is favorable, the ruling will be

---

[35] Rev. Proc. 62-31, 1962-2 C. B. 517; Rev. Proc. 62-28, 1962-2 C. B. 496; Rev. Proc. 63-23, 1963-41 I.R.B. 84.
[36] Rev. Proc. 62-31, *supra*, §. 4.07.
[37] Rev. Rul. 60-276, 1960-2 C. B. 150.

issued. The taxpayer will be afforded an opportunity to discuss the case with the experts in Washington in the event an adverse decision is indicated.

If the District Director refuses to forward the case to Washington for technical advice, the taxpayer may notify the District Director that he intends to request National Office consideration. If the District Director makes an adverse determination, or should take no action within 30 days after the notice is filed with him, the taxpayer then requests the National Office to consider its case. The National Office review will be granted only upon a clear showing:

1. That the position of the District Office is contrary to the law or regulations on the points at issue;
2. That the position of the District Office is contrary to the position of the Service as set forth in a Revenue Ruling currently in effect;
3. That the position of the District Office is contrary to a court decision which is followed by the Service, i.e., acquiescence in an adverse Tax Court decision;
4. That the contemplated District Office action is in conflict with a determination made in a similar case in the same or another district; or
5. That the issues arise because of unique or novel facts which had not previously been passed upon, in any published Revenue Ruling or announcement.

III. Amending, Suspending or Terminating a Plan

Pension plans are hardly static. No matter how much care and study have gone into the formulation of the plan, conditions change: Social Security benefits may be raised justifying a change of benefits under the plan. Inflation may render previously funded benefits inadequate. A contributory plan may prove burdensome on employees. The Service's attitude on a provision in the plan previously approved may change. The employer may be "strapped" temporarily for cash, requiring a suspension of the plan. Or business conditions may change so drastically as to require the termination of a plan in whole or in part.

Accordingly, pension plans should contain rather broad provisions permitting the employer to amend, suspend or terminate the plan. But while this reserved right may be exercised freely by the employer as a matter of trust law, there are tax problems involved when he attempts to do so. And this is true even if the initial approval of the plan recognized the right of the employer to make such changes.

A. Amendment

Changes in administrative or procedural aspects of the plan which have no substantive effect generally need not be submitted to the Service for approval. However, such amendments should be submitted with the annual filing of information by the Trustee[38] or by the employer.[39] Amendments which are substantive in character should be submitted to the Service for specific approval—precisely in the same manner and with the same degree of formality as the original submission of the plan. Moreover, in determining the validity of such amendments, the same elements require consideration as in the initial submission—namely, as to whether the amendment has the effect of causing the plan to violate any of the six criteria for qualifying a plan which were discussed above. (See pp. 43-51.)

There is still another class of amendments: those made involuntarily by the employer. A plan may be approved by the District Director. On post-review (perhaps several years later) by the Pension Trust Branch of the National Office in Washington, some aspect of the plan is discovered which may have been overlooked on initial processing or which is contrary to some recently adopted policy of the Service. In that event, the Pension Trust Branch refers the case back to the District Director for a revised ruling. The taxpayer is advised of the change in the Service's position and is requested to make an appropriate change in order to have the plan qualify from that point on.

Moreover, a plan may be approved in accordance with certain published rulings of the Internal Revenue Service. Thereafter these published rulings may be revised. In such event the rulings published subsequent to the issuance of approval letters are not usually applied retroactively; nor do they usually nullify approvals which had been previously made.[40] However, the new published rulings will be applied prospectively. A ruling in effect at the beginning of the year may be complied with at any time during the year, provided the amendment is made effective for all pur-

---
[38] §. 6033.
[39] §. 1.404(a)-2.
[40] Rev. Proc. 62-28, 1962-2 C. B. 496, Secs. 13 and 14.

poses as of the first day of the year. Where, however, it becomes necessary to amend the plan during the first taxable year the plan has been in effect in order to satisfy the requirements of sections 401(a)(3),(4),(5) or (6), the amendment may be made at any time up to the fifteenth day of the third month following the close of such year, provided the amendment operates retroactively to the date the plan was put in effect.[41]

Rulings may be obtained with respect to amendments on application to the District Director of Internal Revenue who would have jurisdiction if the plan were being submitted for initial approval. (See p. 52.) In such cases it is not necessary to submit the detailed information required with the initial submission; it is sufficient to furnish a copy of the amendment involved.[42]

B. Suspension

Suspension of a plan in this context means only a *temporary* halt in the employer's contribution with the intention that the contributions will be resumed. This may occur where the employer is temporarily short of funds or perhaps where a change in business is taking place which may require a change in the plan and thus makes it advisable to suspend the plan in the interim. What starts as a suspension may grow into a complete discontinuance or a termination (either partial or complete). The tax aspects of these situations are discussed below. (See p. 56.)

Assuming, then, a clear case of suspension with no immediate overtones of partial or complete curtailment, what is the effect of such action on the continued qualification of a pension plan? The prior ruling as to the qualification of the plan under section 401(a) will not be affected by a suspension of an employer contribution if (1) the benefits to be paid or made available under the plan are not affected at any time by the suspension, and (2) the unfunded past service cost at any time (which includes the unfunded prior normal cost and unfunded interest on any unfunded cost) does not exceed the unfunded past service cost as of the date of the establishment of the plan, plus any additional past service or supplemental costs added by amendment.[43] However, if both of these conditions are not met, the prior approval letter will

---

[41] §. 401(b); §. 1.401-5.
[42] Rev. Proc. 62-31, 1962-2, C. B. 517, §. 4.03.
[43] §. 1.401-6(c)(2).

no longer be applicable and the suspension may be treated as a discontinuance of the plan with the serious tax consequence that entails. In any event, the employer and the Trustee should notify the District Director—preferably before the suspension is made—so as to secure a ruling that the suspension will not affect adversely the prior approval letter.

C. Termination

There are two basic problems incident to a termination of a qualified pension plan: First, is the termination being effected at such a time and under such circumstances as to give rise to the inference that there never was a plan; and second, assuming the termination does not reflect adversely on the bona fides of the plan, is it being carried out in such a manner as to produce the discrimination in benefits prohibited by section 401(a)(4) of the Code?

With respect to the first problem, the Service's position is that the term "plan" implies a permanent, as distinguished from a temporary program.[44] This is especially significant where the plan contains a number of old, high salaried employees, and where the cost of the pensions for these employees will be funded within a few years. If such a plan is discontinued immediately after a substantial portion of the benefits for the top salaried people has been provided for, the Service may conclude that there never was a "plan" within the meaning of section 401.

Regulations under the 1954 Code (section 1.401-4(c)(1)) provide that a qualified plan may provide for termination at will by the employer or discontinuance of contributions and that this will not of itself prevent a trust from being a qualified trust. As a matter of practice, the discontinuance of a plan within a few years of its inception will be permitted by the Internal Revenue Service without adverse tax consequences only if it is abandoned because of business necessity.[45] What constitutes "business necessity" will vary from case to case.[46] However, certain situations have been held to qualify in that respect. For example, the business may be sold or transferred to a successor, which may terminate

---
[44] §. 1.401-1(b)(2); Rev. Rul. 61-157, *supra*, Part 2(p).
[45] §. 1.401-1(b)(2).
[46] Ingram & Co. v. Riddell (D. C. Cal., Nov. 29, 1955), 51 AFTR 1184; Kane Chevrolet, Inc., 32 T. C. 596 (1959).

the plan because it has no plan of its own or because it has an entirely different plan. Or the employer may be confronted with insolvency or bankruptcy, or with adverse business conditions (short of insolvency and bankruptcy) which are beyond his control and which make it quite burdensome to continue the required payments under the plan.[47]

It should be noted that if the Commissioner of Internal Revenue finds the termination was not required by business necessity, and so no bona fide "plan" existed, the plan will be disqualified with retroactive effect, even though a prior ruling approving the plan had been obtained. To the extent permitted by the statute of limitations, the employer's deductions in the prior years will be disallowed if the employees' benefits were forfeitable,[48] or the employees may incur tax liability with respect to the payments previously made on their behalf if their rights were nonforfeitable,[49] and, in either event, the trust will be taxable on the income earned by it in all open years.

It is extremely important, therefore, for the employer to notify the District Director of the proposed abandonment of a plan, to submit in advance all the facts which require such abandonment, and to request a ruling that the termination of the plan will not result in its disqualification for tax purposes.[50]

The procedure for securing approval of a termination is essentially similar to that for securing qualification. The District Director will render opinions both as to consummated or proposed amendments which involve curtailments or terminations, if the request for a ruling is accompanied by complete information as to the reason for the action taken and its effect on different groups of participants under the plan.[51] Requests for rulings should be sent in duplicate to the District Director of Internal Revenue which, as indicated above, would have jurisdiction if the plan were being submitted initially. (See p. 52.) The required information is extensive and the direction of the Service's scrutiny rather obvious.

---

[47] Discontinuance of a profit-sharing plan after one year's operation because of the adverse effect of complying with Salary Stabilization regulations was deemed to be within the "business necessity" rule. *Blume Knitwear, Inc.*, 9 T. C. 1179 (1947).
[48] §. 1.404(a)-12.
[49] §. 402(b) and §. 72, I.R.C.
[50] §. 1.401-1(b)(2).
[51] Rev. Proc. 62-31, 1962-2, C. B. 517, §. 4.04.

It should be noted that whether or not a plan is "terminated" is generally a question to be determined with regard to all the facts and circumstances of the particular case.[52] Thus, a plan is terminated when, in connection with the winding up of the employer's business, the employer begins to discharge his employees. A plan is not terminated, however, if the employer merely replaces a plan with a comparable plan.[53] The term "termination" includes both a partial termination and a complete termination.[54] A complete discontinuance of contributions (as contrasted to a suspension of contributions) is in effect a termination of the plan, except that the formal steps to accomplish such result have not been taken.[55]

The second problem relating to termination is that even if it is undertaken for "business necessity," the effect of curtailment must not produce discrimination in benefits with respect to employees covered. Accordingly, the law expressly provides that, upon termination of the plan or upon complete discontinuance of contributions under the plan, the rights of each employee to benefits accrued to the date of such termination or discontinuance, to the extent then funded, or the rights of each employee to the amounts credited to his account at such time, must be nonforfeitable.[56] Moreover, the regulations require that the plan must expressly incorporate provisions which will prevent the early termination from resulting in the prohibited discrimination, unless it is reasonably certain at the inception of the plan that the prohibited discrimination will not occur.[57]

In general, a plan will be considered acceptable if during the first ten years the employer's contributions which may be made for the benefit of any of the top 25 employees whose expected pension exceeds $1,500 per annum are limited in accordance with a specified formula and if the full current costs of the plan are being met.[58] The Service has been quite concerned with the possibility of discrimination in this connection and has described

---

[52] §. 1.401-6(b)(1).
[53] §. 1.401-6(b)(1).
[54] §. 1.401-6(b)(2).
[55] Rev. Rul. 61-157, *supra*, Part 5(f); §. 1.401-6(c)(1) and (2).
[56] §. 401(a)(7); §. 1.401-6(a)(1).
[57] §. 1.401-4(c)(1).
[58] §. 1.401-4(c)(2); Mim. 5717, 1944 C. B. 321. The formula is rather complicated and, accordingly, is not set out in detail.

fully the types of cases in which termination has produced the proscribed discrimination.[59]

While section 1.401-4(c)(2) and Mimeograph 5717 set forth general requirements as to the restrictions to be imposed on the distributions to the top 25 employees in the event of termination, no particular form is prescribed and any provision which effects the necessary limitations will be acceptable,[60] including one expressed in terms of a limitation on the amount of employee benefits rather than on employer contributions.[61] Conversely, no single provision for limiting contributions or benefits is appropriate for all plans.[62] Moreover, the limitations in regard to early termination of a plan are not intended to prohibit the payment of full current benefits to any employee upon retirement so long as the plan is in force and the employer continues his contributions.[63] Nor do such limitations prevent the payment of benefits to an employee who dies while the pension plan is in effect and prior to the commencement of his retirement income.[64]

IV. Tax Problems of Employer

Assuming the criteria for a qualified pension trust or annuity plan have been met, the problem naturally arises: What are the limits on the employer's deductions for his contributions to that plan? These limits are described below for the bulk of the plans which do not cover self-employed people. The stricter deduction limits applying to plans which cover self-employed people will be described later (see p. 80).

Prior to 1942 in the case of a pension trust there was deductible annually the future service cost[65] and 1/10 of the amount paid on account of past service.[66] In the case of an annuity plan, however, the Service held that section 23(p) of the 1939 Code (prior to the amendments made by the 1942 Act) requiring a ten-year spread of the past service contribution, was inapplicable; thus,

---

[59] Mim. 6131, 1947-1 C. B. 21.
[60] PS No. 8 (8/4/44).
[61] PS No. 38 (10/7/44).
[62] PS No. 42 (11/11/44).
[63] PS No. 25 (9/2/44) and §. 1.401-4(c)(4).
[64] PS No. 29 (9/16/44) and §. 1.401-4(c)(2)(vi)(a).
[65] §. 23(a), I.R.C. (1939).
[66] §. 23(p), I.R.C. (1939).

the entire past service cost purchased under such a plan could be taken as a deduction in the year of payment.[67]

The Revenue Act of 1942 changed that and the treatment provided therein has been carried over substantially intact by the Internal Revenue Code of 1954.[68] A single section now governs the deductibility of contributions to both pension trusts and annuity plans,[69] with respect to past service as well as future service costs. Some of the provisions of that section may now be considered.

The first requirement is that the employer's contribution on behalf of any employee must not, when added to the employee's other compensation, exceed reasonable compensation.[70] The test as to reasonableness here is that employed under section 162(a) with respect to all other compensation.[71]

In addition to this general requirement, section 404(a)(1) prescribes precise limitations as to the amount deductible annually under Clauses 404(a)(1)(A), (B), and (C) and the carry-over of excess contributions permitted by Clause (D).[72] Each of these will be discussed briefly.

Clause (A): This provides that the employer may deduct up to 5 percent of the compensation of the employees covered by the plan. No actuarial data will be required in the first year of the plan justifying an amount up to 5 percent. However, in the following year and every fifth year thereafter, or more frequently where preferable to the employer, actuarial data must be submitted to substantiate the amount contributed under the 5 percent test. The Commissioner will make periodic examinations of such data to determine whether the amount contributed under the 5 percent test exceeds the amount necessary to provide the remaining unfunded cost of past and future service for the employees under the plan.[73]

---

[67] I. T. 1810, II-2 C. B. 70 (1923); I. T. 2910, XIV-2 C. B. 152 (1935).
[68] §. 162, Rev. Act of 1942; §. 404.
[69] §. 404.
[70] §. 404.
[71] What constitutes reasonable compensation is a difficult question. It is apparent that if the Service makes a successful attack on the reasonableness of the employee's *direct* compensation, the amount paid into the plan on his behalf will constitute unreasonable compensation.
[72] §. 404(a)(1) applies to amounts deductible for contributions to a *pension trust*. §. 404(a)(2) adopts those limitations for amounts contributed to an *annuity plan* in which a trust is not used.
[73] §. 1.404(a)-4(b).

Clause (B): This provides that if the annual cost of the plan exceeds 5 percent of compensation it may be deducted as a level amount (or as a level percentage of compensation) over the remaining service of the employee.[74] For example, if a plan provides for retirement at age 65, the cost with respect to an employee age 45 would be funded over the remaining 20 years of his service; with respect to an employee age 55, it would be funded over the remaining 10 years; and in the case of an employee age 35, the cost would be funded over 30 years.

The only limitation in Clause (B) is that if the remaining unfunded cost of the plan for three individuals exceeds 50 percent of the total remaining unfunded cost then it must be spread over at least five years. This does not mean that the plan fails to qualify if the cost exceeds 50 percent for those three individuals. It merely means that the cost for those three people has to be spread over some reasonable period, not less than five years.

Clause (C): This provides that the employer can take a deduction for contributions in the current year equal to (1) the normal cost of the plan, and (2) not more than 10 percent of the past service or supplementary cost of the plan.

After the passage of the 1942 Act, the Internal Revenue Service was concerned with the possibility that some employers might be able to secure more rapid deduction of their pension costs by funding under the provision comparable to Clause (B) than under Clause (C). Accordingly, it provided in its regulations that any Clause (B) funding which paid off the cost of the plan faster than would be possible under Clause (C) would not be acceptable.[75] The courts, however, refused to approve the Commissioner's construction of the statute.[76] The existing regulations do not contain this restriction.[77] Accordingly, taxpayers have a choice of any one of the three methods of funding provided by the statute and may select the one which produces the most favorable tax results.

Clause (D): This provides that if the contribution of the employer in any given year is in excess of the limitations prescribed

---

[74] See §. 1.404(a)-5(c) and (d) for methods of determining the excess deductible under §. 404(a)(1)(B).

[75] §. 29.23(p)-6, Regs. 103 and 111.

[76] *Saalfield Publishing Co.*, II T. C. 756 (1948); Acq. 1952-2 C. B. 3; Non-acq. 1949-1 C. B. 6 withdrawn; *Philadelphia Suburban Transp. Co. v. Smith*, 105 F. Supp. 650 (D. C. Pa., 1952); see Rev. Rul. 57-89, 1957-1 C. B. 169 and §. 1.404(a)-5(d).

[77] §. 1.404(a)-6.

62 PENSIONS AND PROFIT SHARING

in Clauses (A), (B), or (C), then that excess is merely disallowed for the year in which made, but may be carried forward to the next succeeding year in which the amount actually contributed is less than that prescribed under those clauses.

The 1954 Code has provided, for the first time, statutory rules for the "survival" of the carryover credit when the employer corporation disappears in certain tax-free liquidations or reorganizations.[78] Previously, the Internal Revenue Service had ruled that the carryover credit survived only in the case of a statutory merger.[79] The new rules set forth in section 381 extend this to (1) the complete liquidation of subsidiaries under section 332 (except as to those liquidations where the distributee gets a "stepped-up" basis); (2) the acquisition of substantially all of a corporation's assets solely for voting stock of the acquiring corporation; (3) a transfer of substantially all the assets of a corporation to another corporation if immediately after the transfer the transferor or its shareholders is in control of the transferee; and (4) a mere change in identity, form or place of incorporation.

It should be noted that sections 404(a)(1) and (2) provide that the amount contributed by the employer is deductible only in the taxable year when *paid*, not when paid or accrued.[80] Thus, the distinction between taxpayers on the accrual and the cash method of accounting is disregarded. However, section 404(a)(6) provides that if a taxpayer on the accrual basis makes payment to a plan or trust not later than the time prescribed for filing the return for the taxable year or any extension thereof, that payment will be regarded as having been made on the last day of the taxable year provided that the liability to make the contribution is incurred during the taxable year (see section 1.404(a)-1(c)). In such a case, the requirement of sections 404(a)(1) and (2) that payment be made in the taxable year will be satisfied. Thus, the accrual basis taxpayer now has, in effect, 75 days plus six months following the close of the year (the due date for the return plus the maximum extension therefor) within which to make payment to a

---

[78] §. 381(c)(11) and (20); §. 1.381(c)(11)-1.
[79] PS No. 62 (5/5/50).
[80] Payment by demand note is payment where employer is solvent at delivery date. (*Time Oil Co.*, 294 F. 2d 667 (1961)). However, payment by the employer's note where the note has a maturity date after grace period permitted under section 404(a) is not considered as payment until the year when the note is satisfied. (*Logan Engineering Co.*, 12 T. C. 860 (1949); *Freer Motor Co.*, 8 T. C. M. 507 (1949)).

TAX ASPECTS OF PENSION PLANS 63

qualified plan or trust. This is in contrast to the 60-day period allowed under the 1939 Code[81] which was a wholly arbitrary period and had no relation to the time the books were closed or the tax returns were due or filed.

This does not mean that a taxpayer can postpone the adoption of a plan until the due date of the return for the taxable year, and then relate the tax benefits back to the prior year. In order to have a proper accrual within a taxable year, all the elements of an accrued liability of the employer to the pension trust or annuity plan must exist within the taxable year (although the plan may be amended retroactively after the end of the first year of the trust as described on p. 55).

In the case of a pension trust, this means that there must be in existence in the taxable year a plan and a trust recognized under local law; it is recommended that there be some corpus in the trust;[82] the trust instrument must be evidenced by an executed instrument; and the instrument must definitely and affirmatively preclude the diversion of funds prohibited by section 401(a)(2).[83] In the case of an annuity contract (where no pension trust is used), this means that within the taxable year the plan must be set forth in a resolution of the board of directors; the application accepted by the insurance company; the contracts prepared; the premium paid irrevocably; and the plan communicated to employees.[84]

While the Commissioner has been rather strict in his requirements that a valid pension trust[85] or annuity plan must be in effect within the taxable year in order to have a proper accrual under section 23(p)(1)(E) of the 1939 Code (comparable to section 404(a)(6) of the 1954 Code), he has not been uniformly successful in enforcing that requirement in the courts. In two cases an intention to create a trust, coupled with an irrevocable deposit in escrow, was deemed under local law (Arkansas) sufficient to create a trust as of the date of the escrow.[86] But the taxpayer

---

[81] §. 23(p)(1)(E), 1939 I.R.C.
[82] But see Rev. Rul. 57-419, 1957-2 C. B. 264 where a trust forming part of an accrual basis employer's qualified plan was complete in all respects under local law, except it had no corpus on the last day of the taxable year. There, the trust was deemed to have been in existence if the employer paid into the trust the required corpus within 60 days after the end of the taxable year. See Rev. Rul. 55-640, 1955-2 C. B. 231, where a mere enforceable promise was considered a sufficient trust res.
[83] §. 1.401-2(a)(2).
[84] Rev. Rul. 59-402, 1959-2 C. B. 122.
[85] Rev. Rul. 57-419, 1957-2, C. B. 264.
[86] *555, Inc.*, 15 T. C. 671 (1950); *Crow-Burlingame*, 15 T. C. 738 (1950).

should not count on either local law or a liberal construction by the courts to "bail him out" in all instances.[87]

Union-Negotiated Plans

One final word is in order with respect to the employer's tax problems—namely, the consequences under a union-negotiated plan. Unfortunately, the subject is too complicated to be treated summarily at this point. Suffice it to say that since most union contracts are for a stated period (e.g., three years), there are several basic questions:

>   (1) Is such a plan "permanent" within the meaning of the regulations?
>   (2) Does the fact that the plan provides for a fixed benefit (e.g., $100 a month) and a fixed rate of contribution (e.g., 5¢ an hour) violate the requirements that the benefits must be definitely determinable?
>   (3) What limits are applicable to the deductibility of amounts contributed by the employer?

The fact that the union contract may be renegotiated within the stated period, which may result in the amendment or termination of the plan, has not been deemed to make the plan a temporary, as distinguished from a permanent, arrangement. Moreover, if the relationship between the fixed benefit and the stated rate of contribution is supported by actuarial computations, the requirement of "definiteness" will be satisfied.[88] The applicable limits on the amount deductible by the employer under various approved methods of funding union-negotiated plans have also been spelled out by the Service.[89]

There is an even more serious problem incident to the deductibility of the employer's contribution arising out of the current pattern of union plans. The latter include not only pension benefits but benefits for disability, accident and health, unemployment, medical expenses, etc. The regulations state that section 404(a) of the 1954 Code does not apply to a plan which covers such "fringe benefits."[90] To alleviate this situation in one union plan, the 1954

---
[87] *Tavannes Watch Co. Inc., v. Comm'r.*, 175 F. 2d 211; See *Abingdon Potteries, Inc.*, 19 T. C. 23 (1952). *Dejay Stores, Inc. v. Ryan*, 229 F. 2d 867 (1956).
[88] Rev. Rul. 55-681, 1955-2 C. B. 585.
[89] PS No. 67 (4/26/51).
[90] §. 1.404(a)-1(a)(2); see §. 1.401-1(b)(1)(i).

Code provided that the employer's contributions in that one case could be deducted under section 162 of the 1954 Code, the provision dealing with trade or business expenses.[91] Another important liberalization was provided by P. L. 87-863 which specified that, for taxable years beginning after October 23, 1962, a qualified pension plan could pay benefits for sickness, accident, hospitalization and medical expenses of retired employees, their spouses and their dependents—provided, among other conditions, such benefits are subordinate to the retirement benefits, a separate account is established for them and the employer's contributions to the separate account are reasonable and ascertainable.[92]

Other problems in connection with union plans may arise as a result of an industry-wide plan (i.e., a single plan adopted by subscribing employers in a particular industry);[93] or an area-wide plan (i.e., a single plan adopted by subscribers in a particular locality); or, more recently, as a result of the guaranteed annual wage. A single plan and a single trust may be used by the group of employers involved even though there is no corporate affiliation among them; nevertheless, each employer must satisfy the requirements as to qualification under section 401(a) and deduction under section 404.[94]

V. Tax Problems of Employee

Assuming a pension plan or trust qualified under section 401(a) of the Code, the question naturally arises: What are the tax consequences to the employee?

A. Current Tax Aspects

As a general proposition, the employee is not taxed on the amount contributed to the qualified plan or trust by the employer in the year the contribution is made,[95] and this is true even though the employee's rights are fully vested (i.e., non-forfeitable) at the time the contribution is made. Nor is the employee taxable currently on the income which is accumulated in the plan or trust

---

[91] §. 404(c), cf. Letter Ruling to Ford Motor Co. dated December 2, 1955 with respect to "Guaranteed Annual Wage" trust contributions, P-H 1956 §. 76, 242.
[92] §. 401(h) as added by P.L. 87-863, October 23, 1962.
[93] See Plan of International Brotherhood of Electrical Workers (AFL) approved by Service 3/5/47.
[94] PS No. 14 (8/24/44). See also, PS No. 51, Part A (7/31/45).
[95] §. §. 402 and 403.

pending his retirement. Contributions to a non-exempt employee's trust, where the employee has non-forfeitable rights, are taxable to the employee in the year made.[96]

This postponement of tax on the employee only applies to the amount of the employer's contribution which is devoted to retirement purposes. If, for example, a qualified trust purchases a retirement income contract with life insurance protection which is payable on death to a designated beneficiary of the participant, then the portion of the premium applicable to such life insurance protection constitutes income to the employee in the year the contribution is made by the employer unless the premium is paid out of contributions made by the employee himself.[97] The cost of such insurance is considered as being the one year term premium for the amount of insurance in force in a given year (which is assumed to be the amount of the death benefit in excess of the cash value of the contract).[98] This also applies to amounts paid for insurance under a qualified combination insurance and annuity contract where no trust is used.[99]

Not all employer contributions to finance death benefits under qualified plans result in taxation to the employee currently. The foregoing tax consequences apply only where the death benefit is provided by means of an insurance contract. If a qualified plan or trust pays a death benefit from the trust funds or contract reserve (rather than from the proceeds of an insurance contract), no part of the amount paid into the trust or plan by the employer is currently taxable to the employee.[100]

B. *Taxation on Retirement*

Upon retirement or termination of employment, the payments made to the employee from the pension plan or trust will be taxable to him as an annuity—his contributions, if any, being regarded as his cost of the annuity, together with certain additional elements of cost to be discussed later.[101]

Since the tax treatment of annuities underwent a drastic revision in the Internal Revenue Code of 1954 (section 72), it is important

---
[96] §. 402(b), §. 403(b).
[97] §. 1.402(a)-1(a)(3); §. 1.72-16(b).
[98] Rev. Rul. 55-747, 1955-2 C. B. 228.
[99] §. 1.403(a)-1(d); §. 1.72-16(b).
[100] PS No. 65 (11/10/50); see also §. 1.402(a)-1(a)(4); §. 1.72-16(c).
[101] §. 72(f).

to review these provisions in some detail. The so-called 3 percent rule applicable to annuity payments prior to January 1, 1954 has been discarded.[102] In general the old 3 percent rule provided that the annuitant must report as gross income during the years he is receiving annuity payments 3 percent of the total premiums or consideration paid; the balance of each annuity payment was tax-free until the annuitant recovered his entire investment; thereafter each annuity payment was taxable in full.

The 1954 Code provides for the recovery of the annuitant's investment at a constant rate over the expected duration of the annuity payments (i.e., the annuitant's life expectancy). For example, if an employee having a life expectancy of 10 years is to receive a payment of a $4,000 annuity commencing January 1, 1955, and his cost or other consideration is $10,000 then each annual payment will be comprised of a $3,000 taxable element and a $1,000 nontaxable element.[103] Thus, the annuitant may be expected to recover his investment ratably over his life expectancy. If he survives his life expectancy, computed as of the annuity starting date, he may still continue to exclude $1,000 annually even though he has already recovered his investment tax-free. Where the annuity is not based on the life expectancy of one or more individuals but is payable, for example, in a fixed number of installments, the annuitant's cost is recovered tax free equally over each installment.[104]

Where payments under the annuity had already begun on January 1, 1954, the foregoing principles are equally applicable, using the *unrecovered* tax cost and expected duration of payments as of that date.[105]

The principal exception to this rule is in the case of an employee's annuity to which the employer has made a contribution where the aggregate amount receivable by the employee or his beneficiary during the three-year period following the first payment equals or exceeds the total investment in the annuity made

---

[102] See §. 22(b)(2)(B), 1939 I.R.C.
[103] Exclusion ratio =

$$\frac{\text{investment in contract}}{\text{expected return}} = \frac{\$10,000}{10 \text{ yrs.} \times \$4,000} = \frac{\$10,000}{\$40,000} = 25\%.$$

Therefore, 25% or $1,000 is excludable from income yearly; §. 1.72-4.
[104] §. 72(c)(3)(B); §. 1.72-5(c).
[105] §. 72(c)(4); §. 1.72-4(b).

by the employee.[106] In such a case, the employee is permitted to recover his entire cost tax-free and thereafter the annuity is wholly taxable.

The problem of computing the annuitant's cost or "investment in contract" is somewhat complex and can be only touched upon here. In general, it includes *all* premiums and other consideration paid by the employee for the contract *plus* any amounts paid by the employer which were previously includible in the employee's gross income, and *less* return of premiums or dividends.[107] Also, any amounts excludible by an employee's beneficiary under section 101 ($5,000 death benefit exclusion) must also be added to cost.[108]

Finally, one further adjustment must be made in determining an annuitant's investment. In the case of an annuity based on a life or lives where the contract provides for payments to a beneficiary in the nature of a refund of unrecovered premiums, then the actuarial value of such payments as of the annuity starting date must be deducted from the annuitant's cost.[109] The theory of this adjustment is that some portion of the consideration must obviously be attributed to the refund feature and that portion cannot be recovered tax-free over the life of the payments.

Where the total amount payable to the employee is distributed by a qualified pension trust or plan within one taxable year on account of either the employee's termination of service or his death, the distribution, to the extent it exceeds the employee's contributions, will be taxable to the recipient as a long-term capital gain and the annuity treatment is not applicable.[110] Since the capital gain treatment is so important, there are several factors worth noting in that regard:

(1) The capital gain treatment is available if the total distributions are made within one taxable year of the recipient from a qualified pension trust or plan. Prior to the 1954 Code, a disparity in treatment existed under the statute between total distributions from a qualified pension trust and from a qualified non-trusteed or insured plan.[111] To take advantage of the favored treatment accorded qualified pension trusts, some employers placed their

---
[106] §. 72(d); §. 1.72-13.
[107] §. 72(f); §. 1.72-6; §. 1.72-8.
[108] §. 101(b) and §. 101(b)(2)(D); §. 1.72-8(b).
[109] §. 72(c)(2); §. 1.72-7.
[110] §. §. 402(a)(2) and 403(a)(2); §. §. 1.402(a)-1(a)(6) and 1.403(a)-2.
[111] PS No. 61 (8/12/47); G.C.M. 25358, 1947-2 C.B. 901.

group annuity contracts in trust. However, section 403(a)(2) now renders this device unnecessary and provides for capital gain treatment for total distributions from a qualified plan.

(2) Capital gain treatment is still available for the total distributions payable with respect to a retiring employee even though the employee withdrew some portion of the amount paid to him while still employed and on termination of employment withdraws the balance to his credit in a single taxable year.[112] It will also be available where the employee retires, withdraws some of the money standing to his credit and then dies and the balance is paid to his beneficiary. Prior to the 1954 Code his latter case did not result in capital gain treatment since the Service concluded that the total amount payable with respect to the employee had not been paid on account of the employee's separation from service.[113]

(3) As indicated above, the capital gain treatment is available when the total distributions are made on account of the employee's separation from service. This is not satisfied where a qualified trust is terminated and distributions are made to the participants who continue working[114] (except in one very limited case where distributions were made in 1954 pursuant to a complete corporate liquidation prior to August 16, 1954).[115] However, the Tax Court has held in a case arising under the 1939 Code that capital gain treatment is available for a distribution under a terminated plan where the employee continued to work for a successor corporation.[116] The 1954 Code has not changed this result.[117] Similarly, the statutory requirement for the capital gain treatment is not satisfied if a distribution is made in a lump sum to an employee upon his formal retirement but he continues to be employed on a consulting or part-time basis for which he receives compensation.[118]

(4) In determining the amount of the capital gain, the fair market value of property distributed shall govern, except that if

---

[112] §. §. 402(a)(2) and 403(a)(2); §. 1.402(a)-1(a)(6)(ii); §. 1.403(a)-2(b)(1).
[113] S. Rep't. No. 1622, 83d Cong., 2d Sess., p. 289.
[114] *Edward Joseph Glinske*, 17, T. C. 562 (1951); *Estate of Frank B. Fry v. Comm'r.*, 19 T. C. 461 (1952), aff'd 205 F. 2d 517; Rev. Rul. 57-115, 1957-1 C. B. 160.
[115] §. 402(e); §. 1.402(e)-1.
[116] *Mary Miller*, 22 T. C. 293, aff'd 226 F. 2d 618.
[117] Rev. Rul. 58-94, 1958-1 C. B. 194; Rev. Rul. 58-85, 1958-1 C. B. 197; Rev. Rul. 58-96, 1958-1 C. B. 200; Rev. Rul. 58-97, 1958-1 C. B. 201; Rev. Rul. 58-98, 1958-1 C. B. 202; Rev. Rul. 58-99, 1958-1 C. B. 202.
[118] *Estate of Fry*, 19 T. C. 461 (1952), aff'd 205 F. 2d 517.

any portion of the distribution consists of securities of the employer corporation, any unrealized appreciation in such securities is not taxed to the employee until the sale or other taxable disposition of the securities by the employee.[119] These "securities" include stocks and bonds or debentures with interest coupons or in registered form issued by the employer or any parent or subsidiary corporation.[120] Parent and subsidiary are defined for this purpose to include a corporation standing in an unbroken chain of at least 50% stock ownership with the employer.[121]

Upon retirement or termination of employment, some qualified trusts, instead of distributing the amounts standing to the credit of the employee in a lump sum or over a period of years, may distribute an annuity contract previously acquired for that employee. Even though the contract contains a cash surrender value which is available to the employee merely by surrendering the contract, that value will not be taxable to him unless and until the contract is actually surrendered.[122] A similar rule of deferment is applicable where the contract purchased is an insurance contract that, within 60 days after the distribution of such contract, is irrevocably converted into an annuity contract.[123]

However, where a qualified trust distributes a contract to an employee which is not a straight annuity contract—as, e.g., an ordinary life insurance contract or a retirement income contract or a retirement endowment contract with insurance—a different rule applies. In those instances the employee must include in income in the year of distribution the entire cash value of the contract at the time of distribution.

It should also be noted that the 1954 Code included pension and annuity income within the definition of "retirement income" for purposes of the tax credit for retirement income. The recipient of pension and annuity income, if over 65 and otherwise qualified, can take this tax credit. As amended by the Revenue Act of 1964, the credit for single persons is computed by multiplying the first $1524 of retirement income by 17 percent for 1964 and by 15 percent for later years.[124] Under certain conditions where both

---

[119] §. 402(a)(2); §. 1.402(a)-1(b)(1) and (2).
[120] §. 402(a)(3); §. 1.402(a)-1(b)(1)(ii).
[121] §. 402(a)(3); §. 1.402(a)-1(b)(1)(ii); §. 421(d)(2) and (3).
[122] §. 1.402(a)-1(a)(2).
[123] §. 1.402(a)-1(a)(2).
[124] §. 37(a) and (d).

spouses have reached age 65 and file joint returns, a taxpayer may compute the credit on the basis of $2286 of retirement income. Retired government employees are entitled to take the retirement income credit with respect to their government pensions, regardless of their age.[125]

C. Taxation Upon Death

As a general rule, a death benefit paid by a qualified pension trust or plan is taxable to the recipient when received to the same extent that it would have been taxed to the employee if he had received it. Accordingly, if an employee dies either before or after retirement and a lump sum distribution is made by a qualified pension plan or trust, the beneficiary will be entitled to treat the distribution as a capital gain.[126] Or if payments are made on the installment basis, the recipient should treat those amounts as an annuity, using the employee's contributions as his cost. There are, however, certain qualifications to this rule which should be noted:

(1) If the employee elected a joint and survivor annuity (whereby a reduced annuity was paid for his life and continued after his death to a designated beneficiary) the contingent annuitant, with two exceptions, pays tax on each annuity payment exactly as the employee did, using the latter's contributions as the cost of the annuity for purposes of section 72. The first exception is that the beneficiary may add to his cost that portion of the $5,000 exclusion, hereinafter discussed, availed of with respect to the annuity. The second exception is that the contingent annuitant may take a deduction for Federal estate taxes paid on the annuity pursuant to the formula provided in section 691, as hereinafter more fully described.

(2) As indicated above, some qualified pension trusts and plans acquire annuity contracts with insurance to fund the benefits under the plan; and the current cost of the term insurance in force each year is taxable to the employee. In such cases if the employee dies prior to retirement and the face amount of the contract is paid to his beneficiary, then the portion of the proceeds representing the current insurance protection in force at the time of death is tax-free to the recipient and only the reserve accumulation de-

---

[125] §. 37(c)(2).
[126] §. 1.402(a)-1(a).

signed to provide the pension benefit is taxable.[127] This conforms to the rule excluding from income tax insurance proceeds payable by reason of the death of the insured.[128]

(3) Some pension plans or trusts do not contain any element of insurance but provide for the payment of a death benefit in the event the employee dies either before or after retirement. As indicated above, the general rule is that such payments are taxable to the particular beneficiary exactly as they would have been taxed to the respective employee. However, a provision, originally introduced in the Revenue Act of 1951 and substantially amended in the 1954 Code, allows the beneficiary a far more favorable treatment than the employee himself would have received if he had lived.[129]

Under section 101(b) of the 1954 Code, the beneficiary or the employee's estate, under prescribed conditions, is entitled to exclude up to $5,000 paid, by or on behalf of the employee's employers, "by reason of the death of the employee." It should be noted that the $5,000 maximum exclusion applies to the aggregate of all death benefits on the death of the employee from all employers. Prior to the 1954 Code, however, it was possible for an employee's beneficiaries to exclude $5,000 received from each of several employers.[130]

While the $5,000 exclusion is by no means limited to payments under qualified plans, such plans are particularly adaptable to qualifying for the exclusion. In general, payments as to which the employee had non-forfeitable rights immediately prior to his death do not qualify for the exclusion.[131] However, where the payments are made by a qualified plan or trust, constitute the "total distribution" of the employee's account, and are paid within a single taxable year of the distributee, the exclusion is available even though the employee's interest prior to death was nonforfeitable.[132]

If the beneficiary receives an annuity by reason of the death of the employee, the annuity is valued as of the employee's death and may be excluded up to the $5,000 maximum. The exclusion

---

[127] §. 1.402(a)-1(a)(4); §. 1.72-16(c).
[128] §. 101(a)(1).
[129] §. 302, Rev. Act of 1951; §. 101(b).
[130] §. 101(b).
[131] §. 1.101-2(a)(2).
[132] §. 101(b)(2)(B); §. 1.101-2(d)(3)(i).

is accomplished by adding the amount thereof to the beneficiary's investment in determining the taxable portion of each annuity payment under the method prescribed in section 72.[133] An exception to this rule exists, however, with respect to joint and survivor annuities. Amounts received under such annuities do not qualify for the exclusion if the employee had already received payments thereunder before his death, or, in any event after the date he would have begun to receive payments thereunder if he had lived.[134]

D. Estate Tax

The 1954 Code for the first time provides a specific statutory rule as to the includability, in the gross estate of a decedent-employee for estate tax purposes, of the value of payments to a surviving beneficiary under a joint and survivor annuity.[135] The 1939 Code was not clear as to whether an annuity to which the decedent's employer had contributed was so includable and to what extent.[136]

The 1954 Code specifically provides that such annuity contracts (entered into after March 3, 1931) are includable in the decedent's gross estate in an amount equal to the proportion of the total value of the annuity which the decedent's contributions to the annuity bear to the total cost. Employer's contributions to non-qualified plans and trusts made by reason of the employment relationship will be considered part of the employee's contributions. Employer's contributions to qualified plans and trusts are not so considered, in connection with estates of all decedents dying after December 31, 1953.[137] This exemption for qualified plans is available even though the plan is terminated prior to the decedent's separation from employment.

It should be noted that section 691 of the 1954 Code provides an income tax deduction to the surviving beneficiary for the estate tax payable on the net value of the annuity for estate tax

---

[133] §. 1.72-8(b); §. 1.101-2(e)(1)(iv).
[134] §. 101(b)(2)(C); §. 1.101-2(e)(1)(ii).
[135] §. 2039; for a definition of annuity contracts covered, see §. 2039(a) and §. 20.2039-1(b).
[136] S. Rep't. No. 1622, 83rd Cong. 2d Sess., p. 123; cf. *Comm'r v. Estate of Twogood*, 194 F. 2d 627 (2d Cir. 1952).
[137] §. 2039(c).

purposes.[138] The estate tax payable on such net value is an amount equal to the excess of the actual estate tax over the tax computed without including such net value in the gross estate.[139] In determining the net value of the annuity for estate tax purposes an adjustment is required for the amount of the annuity payments excludable under section 72 during the surviving beneficiary's life expectancy period.[140]

This deduction is spread ratably over the period during which the annuity is received but not beyond the life expectancy of the surviving beneficiary measured as of the first day of the period for which such beneficiary received a payment.

VI. Tax Problems of the Trust

Under the 1939 Code, section 165 prescribed the entire treatment of qualified trusts. The section contained a specific disclaimer that a qualified trust "shall not be taxable under this Supplement and no other provision of this Supplement shall apply with respect to such trust." If any legal restriction was to be placed on the activities of a qualified trust, it had to be predicated on the statutory limitation that the trust must be used for the exclusive benefit of the employees and their beneficiaries.

Under the 1939 Code, therefore, if a pension trust qualified, its entire income was tax-free; if it failed to qualify, then its entire income was taxable.

The House version of the 1954 Code attempted a major change in this respect: It placed the definition of qualified trusts in the chapter dealing with other types of exempt organizations. (Section 501(e), H. R. 8300). It spelled out certain transactions which were prohibited for qualified trusts. (Section 503(c), H. R. 8300). It provided that a qualified trust could not invest its income in a manner to jeopardize the functions of the trust. (Section 504, H. R. 8300). It described precisely the type of investments which a qualified trust could make. (Section 505). Finally, it made qualified trusts subject to the unrelated business income tests of other charities. (Sections 511–515).

The Senate retreated a good way in that respect and the pro-

---
[138] §. 691(d).
[139] §. 691(c)(2)(C).
[140] §. 691(d)(2)(A).

visions contained in the 1954 Code are in no wise as radical in their treatment of qualified trusts. Nevertheless, the 1954 statutory restrictions on the activities of a qualified trust are worthy of comment.

The 1954 Code subjects pension trusts to the standards of conduct previously applied only to organizations qualifying for tax exemption as charitable, educational, scientific or similar organizations. The 1954 rules may be discussed in three categories: (1) The "prohibited transactions"; (2) feeder organizations, and (3) unrelated business income. While the substantive context of the rules does not add very much to the "exclusive benefit" requirement of section 401(a), the language is more specific and provides a helpful guide for the operation and conduct of a pension trust.

A. *Prohibited Transactions*

Under the 1939 Code, if a qualified trust engaged in any particular activity, the Service could ask only:

(1) Does the transaction violate the trust instrument?
(2) Does the transaction violate the state law?
(3) Is the trust being used for the exclusive benefit of the employees and their beneficiaries?

Under this construction of the statute, the Service required a prior disclosure of any investment to be made in the employer's stock or securities.[141] No comparable disclosure was required for the acquisition of property from the employer although the Service could always question the propriety of any transaction between the employer and the trust on the "exclusive benefit" concept.

Under the 1954 Code, however, the "exclusive benefit" concept is implemented by specifically enumerating in the statute certain transactions which are expressly "prohibited transactions" as between the employer and the trust.[142] The penalties for engaging in a so-called "prohibited transaction" are essentially the same as are applicable to the violation of any other requirement—loss of exemption for the trust, possible loss of the deduction by the

---
[141] PS No. 49 (6/6/45).
[142] §. 503(c); §. 1.503(c)-1.

employer and possible loss to employees of the favorable tax treatment accorded the employer's contributions under qualified trusts and plans. With one exception, the exemption is withdrawn commencing with the taxable year following the taxable year in which the trust receives notice that it has engaged in a prohibited transaction.[143] The exemption may be restored if the trust satisfies the Commissioner that it will not "knowingly again" engage in a prohibited transaction.[144] If the trust was deliberately attempting to divert corpus or income and the transaction involved a substantial part of its corpus or income, the exemption may be revoked as of the date of the violation.[145]

The prohibited transactions are six in number and relate solely to transactions, taking place after March 1, 1954, between the trust and its creator or certain individuals or organizations related to or controlled by the creator. A trust may not:[146]

(1) Lend money without requiring adequate security and receiving a reasonable rate of interest. An amendment in 1958[147] permitted a pension trust, under certain conditions, to invest in unsecured bonds of the employer corporation. A second amendment to section 503 in 1958[148] modified the "adequate security" requirement in certain cases where the employer was prohibited by Federal law or regulation from pledging as security for a loan certain classes of property. Note that this requirement might prevent the purchase by the trust of bonds of the employer but not the employer's stock, even though the bonds are a safer investment.

(2) Pay compensation in excess of a reasonable allowance for salaries or other compensation for personal services rendered;

(3) Make any of its services available on a preferential basis;

(4) Make any substantial purchase of securities or other property for more than an adequate consideration in money or money's worth;

(5) Sell any substantial part of its securities or other property for less than an adequate consideration; or

---

[143] §. 503(a)(2); §. 1.503(a)-1(b).
[144] §. 503(d); §. 1.503(d)-1(a).
[145] §. 503(a)(2); §. 1.503(a)-1(b).
[146] §. 503(c).
[147] §. 503(h); P. L. 85-866.
[148] §. 503(i); P. L. 85-866.

(6) Engage in any other transaction which results in a substantial diversion of its income or corpus.

B. Feeder Organizations

Under the 1939 Code, prior to 1950 not only was a charitable organization tax-exempt on its income regardless of the form of its investments, but it could be argued that a "feeder organization" (i.e., any corporation or organization owned or controlled by a charitable organization, all the profits of which were payable to the charity) was also exempt on its income.[149] In the Revenue Act of 1950[150] a provision was added to section 101 of the 1939 Code that a feeder organization was not exempt and would be taxable on its income as a corporation or trust (depending on its form of organization) regardless of the fact that such income was payable to a tax-exempt charity.

However, this change in the 1950 Act was applicable only to feeder organizations related to charitable organizations. It did not affect feeder organizations related to qualified trusts. It was therefore possible for a qualified trust—even after the 1950 Revenue Act—to have a feeder organization and claim that the latter's income from the regular conduct of a trade or business was nevertheless exempt from tax because it was payable to, or would ultimately be payable to, a qualified trust.

The 1954 Code cured this.[151] It makes the feeder organization concept applicable to a qualified trust. This does not mean that an otherwise qualified trust will lose its exemption if it owns a feeder organization, or that the income actually paid in the form of dividends or interest by the feeder organization to the qualified trust will be taxable to it. It merely means that the feeder organization cannot claim exemption on its income because of the fact that it is owned by a qualified trust.

For these purposes, a feeder organization is defined as one operated for the primary purpose of carrying on a trade or business for profit. However, there is excluded from the term "trade or business" the rental by an organization of its real property (including personal property leased with real property).[152]

---

[149] *Mueller Co. v. Commissioner*, 190 F. 2d 120; *Roche's Beach, Inc. v. Commissioner*, 96 F. 2d 776.
[150] §. 301(b)(2).
[151] §. 502.
[152] §. 502.

C. Unrelated Business Income

As indicated above, under the 1939 Code a qualified trust could engage in any activity permitted by the trust instrument and state law and not in violation of the "exclusive benefit" test. Many trusts were thus able to acquire businesses and operate them within the tax-free shelter afforded the trust. Still other qualified trusts acquired property with borrowed funds and leased the property back to the seller (the "sale and leaseback" device), using the tax-free rent to pay off the loan.

Had Congress merely stopped with the "prohibited transaction" and "feeder organization" concepts in the 1954 Code, these activities would still be possible, for many activities were conducted with persons other than the employer—thus rendering inapplicable the prohibited transaction sanctions. And many other activities were conducted within the framework of the trust itself—thus avoiding the feeder organization proscriptions. Accordingly, it was necessary to adopt the "unrelated business income" concept to round out the "new look" in qualified trusts.[153]

This does not mean that if a qualified trust has unrelated business income it becomes disqualified. It merely means that if the trust has unrelated business income, it is subject to tax on *that* income—not on the balance. It should be noted that the tax rates involved are those applicable to individuals, not corporations.[154] For this reason, a qualified trust may prefer to place its business properties in a feeder organization that will be taxed as a corporation.

It should also be noted that there may be a fine dividing line between a trust which loses its entire exemption by reason of operating a trade or business and a trust which merely has unrelated business income and is taxable only on that income. This distinction would appear to depend on the quantum of the trade or business carried on—i.e., whether in view of the extent of the trust's activities it is being operated primarily for the purpose of carrying on a trade or business.[155]

What is unrelated business income? The definition of "unrelated business income" is extremely broad insofar as a qualified

---
[153] §. 511.
[154] §. 511(b); §. 1.511-1 and §. 1.511-2.
[155] §. 511-2(b).

TAX ASPECTS OF PENSION PLANS 79

trust is concerned. It means the income from any business regularly carried on by the trust or by the partnership of which it is a member.[156] However, there are a number of exclusions from the concept which limits it substantially. For example, dividends, interest, annuities, royalties and real property rentals (other than business lease income) are excluded.[157] Still caught is income from the disposition of stock in trade, property included in inventory, property held primarily for sale to customers in the ordinary course of trade or business[158] and—most important of all in the case of qualified trusts—business lease income.[159]

Since business lease income is so significant in the field of qualified trusts, a few words on this subject may be warranted. As defined here, a "business lease" is one for a term of more than five years, involving real property (including personal property leased in connection with real property) where borrowed funds were used to acquire the property.[160] In the case of rentals from a business lease, the qualified trust must include in income the same percentage of the rents that the amount of the business lease indebtedness at the end of the taxable years bears to the adjusted basis of the property at the end of the taxable year.[161] These rules as related to pension trusts apply only to years beginning after June 30, 1954,[162] and will not apply to indebtedness incurred before March 1, 1954 in connection with real property leased before March 1, 1954 or to indebtedness incurred after such date to carry out the terms of a lease made before March 1, 1954.[163]

It should be noted that the qualified trust may still invest its funds in real property and acquire rentals therefrom tax-free. The business lease rules apply only to such deals where borrowed funds are used to acquire the real property (including the case where property is acquired subject to a mortgage).[164]

Finally, a question might be raised as to why the tax on business lease income cannot be avoided by making the lease on a year-to-

---

[156] §. §. 512(a) and 513(b)(2); See §. 1.513-1 for definition of unrelated trade or business.
[157] §. 512(b); §. 1.512(b)-1.
[158] §. 512(b)(5)(A) and (B); §. 1.512(b)-1(d).
[159] §. 512(b)(4); §. 1.512(b)-1(c)(1).
[160] §. 514(b); §. 1.514(b)-1.
[161] §. 514(a); §. 1.514(a)-1; see §. 1.514(a)-1(b) for examples illustrating this rule.
[162] §. 511(c).
[163] §. 514(c)(5).
[164] §. 514(c)(2).

year basis. If the employer were the lessee, the trust could be sure of continuation on this basis. The practical answer is that mortgagees will not lend substantial sums on such a lease. The legal answer is that if the same tenant is in possession after the fifth year, the income from the sixth year on is taxable as business lease income.[165]

Pension Plans Covering Self-Employed People

The Self-Employed Individuals Tax Retirement Act of 1962 (P. L. 87-792—known as the Keogh-Smathers Act) allows self-employed persons to be covered by qualified pension plans for taxable years beginning after December 31, 1962. Previously, such individuals could not be covered by qualified plans because only employees were permitted to be covered. The result was that self-employed persons were treated less favorably than executives and owner-employees of corporations who were entitled to be covered by qualified plans in their capacities as employees.

The 1962 Keogh Act took a step toward equality of tax treatment for the self-employed under pension plans. It is important to note, however, that actual equality of treatment under pension plans for the self-employed has not yet been attained. Actually, the Keogh Act represents a compromise agreed upon after 15 years of legislative efforts to secure acceptance of the principle of coverage for self-employed persons under pension plans. As the price paid for the acceptance of this principle, the Keogh Act specifies that plans covering self-employed people are subject to special rules not applicable to pension plans in general. These special rules curtail the tax advantages of the self-employed under qualified plans. The rules applying to plans covering self-employed persons are described below.

Contributions and Benefits. In general, the contributions or benefits provided for self-employed persons must be non-discriminatory—that is, the percentage which they form to compensation must not be larger for the covered self-employed persons than for the covered employees.[166]

As noted above, there is no specific dollar ceiling on deductible employer contributions for employees generally. However, the

---
[165] §. 514(b)(2)(B).
[166] §. 1.401-12(f)(1) and (2).

1962 Keogh Act places a special limit on such contributions for self-employed people. The maximum annual contribution taken into consideration for deduction purposes is 10% of the self-employed person's earned income or $2,500, whichever is the less.[167] His income tax deduction is limited to one-half of these contributions up to a maximum of $1,250 a year.[168]

The term "earned income" includes professional fees and other amounts received as compensation for personal services actually rendered. Thus, the net earnings or net professional fees of a doctor or lawyer are treated as earned income.[169] If both capital and personal services are material income-producing factors, earned income is taken to mean not more than 30 percent of the net profits from the trade or business. The entire amount of the net profits, however, is considered earned income if the proprietors' or partners' profits are $2,500 or less.[170]

Coverage. Owner-employees (i.e., who own the entire interest in an unincorporated business or who own more than a 10 percent interest in a partnership)[171] who cover themselves under pension plans are required to provide comparable pensions under the plan for all of their full-time employees with more than three years of service. Seasonal, part-time and temporary employees, however, can be excluded.[172]

Owners of several businesses. Special rules also are provided which are designed to preclude the self-employed individual from increasing his tax advantages under the Act merely because he has several businesses. An owner-employee, for example, cannot make contributions under two or more retirement plans, which after being totaled, exceed the basic 10 percent-$2,500 limits.[173] In addition, if an owner-employee controls more than one business he must group together all of the controlled business activities for the purpose of determining whether all of his employees are covered by a qualified retirement plan.[174]

---
[167] §. 404(e)(1); §. 1.404(e)-1(a)(2).
[168] §. 404(a)(10); §. 1.404(e)-1(c).
[169] §. 401(c)(2)(A); §. 1.401-10(c)(3).
[170] §. 401(c)(2)(B); §. 1.401-10(c)(4).
[171] §. 401(c)(3); §. 1.401-10(d).
[172] §. 401(d)(3); §. 1.401-12(e)(1).
[173] §. 404(e)(2); §. 1.404(e)-1(d)(1).
[174] §. 401(d)(9); §. 1.401-12(1)(2).

Non-forfeitable contributions. If the plan covers owner-employees, employer contributions for their covered employees must be non-forfeitable at the time they are made.[175]

Integration with Social Security. Special rules are provided for integrating plans covering self-employed people with the Social Security system. Such plans may be integrated with the Social Security system only if contributions made for the owner-employees under the pension plan do not exceed one-third of the total contributions under the plan. In that event, the plan is given credit only for actual Social Security contributions made by the employer, which now amounts to $3 5/8\%$ of the first $4,800 of wages paid to an employee and $5 4/10\%$ of the first $4,800 of self-employment income of a self-employed individual.[176] The net result is to give plans covering self-employed people a smaller allowance for Social Security contributions under the integration procedures than is provided to plans which do not cover owner-employees. As noted above, the latter plans generally receive an allowance for Social Security under the integration procedures equal either to a contribution rate of $9 3/8\%$ of the first $4,800 of pay or a benefit rate of $37 1/2\%$ of the first $4,800 of pay (see p. 49).

Funding. A variety of funding methods is available to plans covering self-employed individuals. Such plans may be funded through contributions to a trust, by direct purchases of annuity or insurance contracts, or by direct investment in a new series of government bonds designed especially for retirement plans covering self-employed individuals. In general, a bank is required as trustee if the trusteed form is used for funding purposes.[177] A custodial account in a bank is permitted in lieu of a trust, however, if the investments are solely in regulated investment company stocks, or in annuity, endowment, or life insurance contracts.[178] Moreover, if the trust form is used for plans funded exclusively by life insurance, endowment or annuity contracts, there is no requirement to use a bank as trustee or custodian.[179]

Contributory plans. If the plan provides for employee contributions, a self-employed individual can supplement deductible con-

---

[175] §. 401(d)(2)(A); §. 1.401-12(g)(1).
[176] §. 401(d)(6); §. 1.401-12(h).
[177] §. 401(d)(1); §. 1.401-12(c)(1).
[178] §. 401(f); §. 1.401-8(a).
[179] §. 401(d)(1); §. 1.401-12(c)(4)(ii).

TAX ASPECTS OF PENSION PLANS 83

tributions by making non-deductible contributions on his own behalf.[180] However, an owner-employee's non-deductible contributions (1) cannot be at a higher rate in relation to compensation than the rate permitted for employees, and (2) cannot exceed 10% of his earned income or $2,500 a year, whichever is the lesser.[181]

Excess contributions. Special rules are provided to discourage owner-employees from investing in the tax-free retirement funds amounts exceeding the total of (1) allowable contributions on which deductions are based, and (2) the non-deductible voluntary contributions. If such excess contributions take place and were not willfully made, they must be returned to the owner-employee on whose behalf they were made, together with the interest earned on them.[182] However, to permit an individual whose earned income fluctuates from year to year to purchase level-premium annuity or life insurance or endowment contracts under the Act, an exception is provided from these excess contribution rules. This exception allows an owner-employee to make an annual level contribution toward the premiums on his policies, providing that the total contribution does not exceed the average of the contributions allowable for the three years preceding the tax year or the average amount which would have been allowed if the Act had been in effect during that period.[183] His deduction for the current year is determined, however, by applying the "10%-$2,500" limitation to his earned income for the current year.

Timing of Withdrawals. To qualify, a plan must specify that benefits are not payable to more than 10-percent owners before age 59½, except in the event of permanent disability or death.[184] This is intended to insure that plans established by the self-employed under the 1962 Act will actually be used for retirement purposes rather than for annual income averaging purposes.

The Act also seeks to prevent indefinite postponement of taxes on funds placed in the retirement plans on behalf of owner-employees by specifying that benefits must begin before age 70½.[185] At the death of an owner-employee any interest in the

---

[180] §. 1.401-13(a)(2).
[181] §. 401(e)(1); §. 1.401-13(b)(3)(ii) and (iii).
[182] §. 401(e)(2)(C); §. 1.401-13(d)(1) and (2).
[183] §. 401(e)(3); §. 1.401-13(c)(4).
[184] §. 401(d)(4)(B); §. 1.401-12(m)(1).
[185] §. 401(a)(9)(A); §. 1.401-11(e)(1).

retirement plan remaining to his account is required to be (1) paid out to the beneficiary within five years from the date of the owner-employee's death or, (2) used within such five-year period to buy an immediate annuity payable over the beneficiary's life or over a period not exceeding the beneficiary's life expectancy or (3) distributed, under a plan of distribution which has already commenced over a period not exceeding the employee's life expectancy or the joint life and survivor expectancy of the covered individual and his spouse.[186]

Tax on withdrawals. The benefits received by self-employed individuals from plans established under the 1962 Act are taxed as ordinary income in the year of receipt. In general, these benefits are taxed as annuities under the life expectancy method (see p. 67). For the purpose of finding his exclusion for the free return of capital, the self-employed individual's investment in the contract is considered to be the sum of the contributions he previously made to the plan for which he received no deduction. For example, if the self-employed individual contributed $2,500 in one year and deducted $1,250 in accordance with the limitations on the deduction, he is considered for that year to have made an investment of only $1,250 for the purpose of determining his exclusion for the tax-free return of capital.[187] This avoids granting an exclusion for amounts which have already been deducted for tax purposes.

Lump sum distributions received by a self-employed person from pension plans are not entitled to capital gains treatment but instead are eligible for a special averaging procedure. In general, the tax on such lump sum distributions is five times the tax attributable to including one-fifth of the lump sum in taxable income in the year of receipt.[188]

Moreover, any premature distributions which retirement funds may pay out before the owner-employee reaches age 59½ or becomes disabled are subject to a tax penalty. If such a premature distribution amounts to $2,500 or more, the tax on the distribution cannot be less than 110 percent of the additional tax that would have resulted if the payment had been received on a pro

---

[186] §. 401(d)(7); §. 1.401-12(m)(3).
[187] §. 1.72-17(b).
[188] §. 72(n); §. 1.72-18.

rata basis over the five years ending with the year of distribution.[189] Where the premature distribution amounts to less than $2,500, the tax amounts to 110 percent of the liability incurred by including the entire distribution in the taxpayer's gross income for the current year.[190]

In contrast to the treatment accorded to regular employees, self-employed individuals are not eligible for estate and gift tax exclusions on pension rights.[191] Moreover, self-employed persons cannot qualify for the $5,000 death benefit exclusion[192] or for the sick-pay exclusion with respect to distributions from qualified plans.[193]

Prohibited Transactions. If the plan covers an owner-employee who controls the business by means of an ownership interest of 50 percent or more, the plan is subject to stricter prohibited transaction rules than generally apply to pension plans. For example, while a trust which is part of a pension plan is generally prohibited from lending to the employer its income or corpus without the receipt of adequate security and a reasonable rate of interest, a trust forming part of a plan covering a self-employed individual who has a controlling interest is prohibited from lending any part of the corpus or income to him *even* if there is adequate security and a reasonable rate of interest. A trust forming part of a pension plan covering owner-employees who control the business is also prohibited from paying compensation for personal services to, from making services available on a preferential basis to, and from buying or selling property to the controlling self-employed individuals, a corporation controlled by any of them either directly or indirectly, or certain of their relatives.[194]

Conclusion

Time and space have not permitted the discussion of many other tax problems incident to the adoption of a qualified pension plan and trust. For instance, no treatment was accorded herein to the Federal gift tax consequences, Social Security withholding

---

[189] §. 72(m)(5)(B)(i); §. 1.72-17(e)(2)(i).
[190] §. 72(m)(5)(C); §. 1.72-17(e)(2)(ii).
[191] §. 2039(c) and 2517(b); §. 20.2039-2(c)(1) and 25.2517-1(c)(1).
[192] §. 101(b)(3).
[193] §. 105(g).
[194] §. 503(j).

tax problems, and the tax impact on United States citizens earning pensions while abroad. Moreover, the legal aspects other than Federal income taxes—e.g., wage and hour, S.E.C.—have not been mentioned, but should nevertheless be considered in connection with the adoption of a pension plan and trust.

This should not imply that the tax and other legal consequences present formidable or perhaps insuperable obstacles to the formulation of a pension plan and trust. It merely means that the applicability of these various laws should be explored before a plan or trust is adopted in any given instance. A comprehensive review of the various legal factors in advance will unquestionably remove many headaches that may be encountered by plunging headlong into a pension plan without adequate legal "know-how." But the advantages to both the employer and the employee in a proper case are so substantial that such a study is definitely worth while.

Chapter 3

FINANCING A PENSION PLAN

By John B. St. John

Introduction

There are essentially two different methods of financing a pension plan. Either may be used separately or the two may be combined in various ways for a particular program. The first method is to insure the benefits of the plan with an insurance company under one or more annuity or insurance contracts. The second is to accumulate the funds in a trust under the terms of which the accumulations in the fund will be used to provide the benefits of the plan.

The major kinds of plans in common use, which will be described in this chapter, are:
1. Group Deferred Annuities
2. Group Deposit Administration
3. Group Permanent Life Insurance
4. Individual Contract Pension Trust
5. Ordinary Life Insurance with a Supplemental Fund
6. Self-administered Pension Trust
7. Variable Annuities

While these are the main kinds of pension plans, there are other possible combinations or variations in operation, for example:

> The accumulations under a self-administered trust may be used at retirement to purchase annuities under individual or group annuity contracts. The pensioner would then receive his income from the insurance company as a guaranteed annuity.
> The group annuity contract may also be used to accumulate a part of the funds. Funds are then accumulated in both a group annuity contract and a trust. Annuities are purchased at retirement under the group annuity contract. This method may be called "Split Funding."
> Where there is an individual contract pension trust, the proceeds

of the insurance or the annuity contracts may be paid to the trust which will then pay the pensioner or the beneficiary. This procedure is appropriate if the insurance or annuity contracts provide somewhat more or different benefits from those of the plan. The contracts are, in effect, investments of the trust providing a reinsurance of the plan benefits.

Each of the seven kinds of pension plans listed above is discussed in this chapter with a brief description of the main characteristics and methods and with specific illustrations of these characteristics so far as is practical.

Each method of financing has its special advocates. Each may have particular advantages over any other method in particular circumstances. The order in which the kinds of plans are described in this chapter should not be taken as indicative of a preference for any particular method. The group deferred annuity method is described first because it has developed a certain degree of standardization which lends itself to a more detailed description.

If each of the seven methods accomplishing the same general results were to be described in detail, there would obviously be a considerable amount of repetition of features that are essentially similar. Such a repetition is avoided by describing the group annuity method in full and limiting the descriptions of other methods to those elements which are different, peculiar, or distinctive.

Following the description of principal methods, there is a chart analysis of the more important differences in the elements of each method.

The benefits of a plan including all the conditions for their payment constitute the disbursement phase of the plan. The disbursement phase may be quite independent of the method of accumulation of the necessary funds. Certain types of benefits, however, lend themselves to certain methods of accumulation because of the facility of administration or cost calculation. These natural or characteristic relations between benefits and methods of financing are brought out as far as possible in the description of each method.

The contributions to the fund and the accumulation of the fund with interest are sometimes referred to as the method of financing. The contributions to any plan are not the costs in any true sense. The real costs of the pension plan are the amounts of benefit to be paid out to future pensioners, plus expenses of administration of the plan. The contributions to the plan may be any arbitrary amount appropriated for the purpose, or they may be the estimated annual amounts required to meet the eventual costs, calculated in accordance with certain assumptions and distributed in accordance with a desired plan of advance payment. The contributions to the plan may properly provide for arbitrary margins of safety.

Because real costs are indeterminate and because the term "costs" is commonly used in referring to the amount of contribution made to the plan, no attempt is made in this chapter to distinguish these terms. In considering any comparison of costs, however, it must be remembered that unless there are differences in benefit amounts or administrative expenses, comparisons show only differences in the assumptions used to estimate the real costs or differences in the methods suggested for distributing these costs in the prepayment over a period of years.

Group Deferred Annuities

A group deferred annuity is a contract between an employer and the insurance company which provides for the purchase of annuities for the employees covered by the plan. In a multi-employer type of plan or a negotiated plan the group annuity contract may be made between the trustees of the plan and the insurance company. The employer purchases annuities under this contract in the amount of benefits earned by the employees for each year of service credited under the plan. The insurance company guarantees to pay the benefits of the plan to the extent that they have been so purchased. The insurance company also furnishes all necessary actuarial, investment, and administrative services ordinarily required by the plan.

The insurance company may specify a minimum number of lives or a minimum annual premium which will constitute an acceptable group. If the plan is contributory, there will be a requirement that at least 75 percent of the eligible employees must join the plan.

Although a group annuity contract may be issued without reference to a minimum number of persons covered, there is a practical point at which the cost of administration of a plan covering a small number of employees under the group-annuity form would be as expensive as the cost of the administration of an individual contract pension trust.

The annual premium will include a stipulated annual expense charge to cover the basic expenses that are related to all contracts. This policy charge is usually arranged to diminish with an increase in the annual contributions to the plan.

Securing a Group Annuity Contract

The procedure for securing a group annuity contract, usually carried out by an agent, broker, or consultant, requires the employer to make application to the insurance company. The application may be executed on an insurance company form or may be a simple letter signed by a responsible officer of the employer requesting the issuance of a contract and transmitting a deposit premium.

In practice, an insurance company representative, the agent, or consultant will usually assist the employer in developing specifications for the particular plan desired. The insurance company, on the basis of preliminary application and deposit premium, will then prepare a draft which, when finally in satisfactory form, will serve as a basis for a formal acceptance of the contract and the establishment of the plan on behalf of the employer. Such action may include acceptance by the Board of Directors and the stockholders and will usually be subject to approval by Internal Revenue Service.

Plan Characteristics

Retirement Income Formula

The characteristic group annuity plan, which may be referred to as the standard deferred annuity contract or a unit benefit type of plan, provides for the purchase each year of a small amount of paid-up deferred annuity for each member of the plan. The amount of annuity is expressed as an amount in dollars or as a percentage of the member's earnings for each plan year. The percentage may vary from $\frac{1}{2}$ percent to as much as 2 percent of the member's earnings. The benefit will usually provide a larger percentage of the employee's earnings with respect to earnings in excess of the amount covered by Social Security taxes and benefits.

The formula thus is integrated with Social Security. The objective of such integration is to provide a benefit percentage per year of service that is approximately the same, or a little less, on earnings in excess of Social Security earnings as the percentage based on Social Security earnings. The Social Security benefit on the lower earnings will supply a definite expected part of the total retirement benefit.

The amount of benefit per year of service may be determined by an earnings class schedule. For example, the earnings class schedule (Table 1) provides for benefits of 1 percent of earnings

TABLE 1

Schedule of Earnings Classes
Retirement Income and Employee Contributions

Earnings Class	Range of Monthly Earnings From	Range of Monthly Earnings To	Monthly Retirement Income for Each Year of Service	Employee's Monthly Contribution
1	Under	$175	$1.50	$ 3.00
2	$175.01	225	2.00	4.00
3	225.01	275	2.50	5.00
4	275.01	325	3.00	6.00
5	325.01	375	3.50	7.00
6	375.01	425	4.00	8.00
7	425.01	475	5.00	10.00
8	475.01	525	6.00	12.00
9	525.01	575	7.00	14.00

under $400 per month and 2 percent of earnings in excess of $400 per month. The amount of benefit is based on the amount of earnings at the midpoint of each earnings class. Employee contributions are illustrated at the rate of $2 monthly for each $1 of monthly income. This would be the equivalent of a contribution of 2 percent of the first $400 of monthly earnings and 4 percent of any excess earnings.

The schedule may be extended for additional earnings classes. The range of monthly earnings will increase in progressive steps of $50 a month. For each additional class the monthly retirement income will increase by $1 and the employee contributions will increase by $2. In accordance with this earnings class schedule, if an employee's earnings were $400 a month, he would fall in class 6 and he would receive for each year while in this earnings class an income benefit of $4 per month. At the end of 25 years of membership, if he remained in that earnings class, he would have accumulated 25 x $4.00 or $100 of monthly retirement income. During his membership he would have paid $8.00 a month, $96 a year, or a total of $2,400.

This typical group deferred annuity plan will provide for the purchase by the employer, or by the employer and the employee jointly, of the income shown in the schedule for each member in the course of each year of service. The schedule illustrates a contributory plan in which the employees share in the cost. If the plan were noncontributory, the column of employees' monthly contributions would be omitted. The same or lower schedule of benefits may be applicable to each of the years of service prior to the effective date of the plan.

The same benefit formula may be expressed in terms of exact earnings rather than earnings classes. For example, the above formula might be expressed in either of the following ways:

> (1) The retirement income for each year of service while a member of the plan shall be 1 percent of the first $400 of monthly salary plus 2 percent of all salary in excess of $400 monthly. Employees shall contribute 2 percent of the first $400 of monthly salary plus 4 percent of all salary in excess of $400, or
> (2) Employees shall contribute 2 percent of the first $4800 of earnings in any year and 4 percent of all earnings in excess of $4800. The employee's rate of annual retirement income for service while a member shall be one half of the total amount of his contribution during his total membership.

Money Purchase Plans

The money-purchase type of benefit was also at one time frequently used in group annuity plans. In this type of formula the contributions of both the employer and the employee are fixed as a percentage of the employee's salary. In the money-purchase plan the premium amounts are fixed and the benefits for the employee depend upon the sex and age when he and his employer start paying premiums and the continuity of such premium payments until his normal retirement date. Some plans provide benefits under a unit-benefit schedule from employer contributions and additional benefits under a money-purchase schedule from employee contributions.

Final Pay Plans

Some plans define the retirement benefit as a percentage of final average pay. The percentage may be either a flat percentage for all members eligible for normal retirement without reference to years of service, or it may be a smaller percentage multiplied by years of service. Because such benefits are not directly related to the salary earned during each year of membership, it is difficult to administer a final pay plan under a group deferred annuity contract. For this type of benefit the other types of financing discussed later are usually used.

The retirement incomes under the final pay type of plan or the contributions under a money purchase plan may, like the unit-benefit plan, be expressed by a formula or a salary class schedule. The illustrative schedule (Table 2) provides fixed benefits of 25 percent of the first $4800 and 50 percent of salary in excess of $4800, based on the average salary in the final five years of service.

TABLE 2

Schedule of Earnings Classes and Retirement Incomes

Earnings Class	Five Year Final Average Salary	Annual Retirement Income
1	Under $2,160	$ 480
2	$2,160-2,639	600
3	2,640-3,119	720
4	3,120-3,599	840
5	3,600-4,079	960
6	4,080-4,559	1,080
7	4,560-5,039	1,200
8	5,040-5,519	1,440
9	5,520-5,999	1,680

Past Service

Whether a unit-benefit or a money-purchase type of formula is used, there will usually be need for a past service benefit. Without this benefit the retirement income that can be provided for the employees who are near retirement when the plan is established will not be sufficient to offer a reasonable amount of retirement income.

The past service benefit will usually be a percentage of the current rate of pay at the effective date of the plan for each year of service prior to the effective date. Instead of the current pay, the average rate for 5 or 10 years prior to the effective date may be used. Instead of giving full credit for all the years prior to the effective date, service may be granted only for a limited number of years or with respect to service after a minimum attained age.

The percentage of benefit credit for each year of past service is sometimes somewhat smaller than that applicable to each year of future service. A smaller percentage applied against the current rate of earnings may be used to produce approximately the same total amount of benefit as the larger future service percentage applied against a smaller rate of actual past earnings. Past earnings generally will have been lower than the current rate of earnings. For example, assume that an employee has worked for a company for 10 years and during that time his earnings have averaged $3000 per year. At present, however, his rate of pay is $4000 per year. Then if the rate of benefit for future service is 1 percent, a past service benefit rate of .75 percent applied against $4000 of current earnings would produce the same benefits as 1 percent of average past earnings at the rate of $3000.

Another reason for having a smaller rate of past service benefit in a contributory plan is that the employer pays the entire cost of this benefit and consequently the benefit per year of service may reasonably be less than that for each year during which the employee contributes part of the cost.

Employee Contributions

Employee contributions under a standard group annuity plan will be related to the units of benefit being purchased. For example, employees may pay $3 a year or 25¢ a month for the purchase of $1 of annual benefit. The method of determining the group annuity rates requires this uniform relationship between the contributions and benefits for economical administration. A limited number of variations may be permitted, for example, one ratio for benefits on the first $4800 of earnings and a second ratio for earnings over $4800. Group deferred annuities do not lend themselves to a scale of employee contributions varying with the employee's age at entry into service or entry into the plan.

Employee contributions, if used, may not ordinarily exceed a ratio of 4 to 1 in relation to benefit units. At the younger ages a rate of contribution from the employee of 3 to 1 or larger will usually buy all of the benefits, leaving nothing for the employer to purchase. Carried to the extreme, this might result in the employees paying contributions which would purchase all of the benefits purchased under the plan for a major part of the employee's working lifetime. The rate of employee contributions should be no greater than the total cost of the retirement benefits except possibly at a few ages near the youngest probable age of employment. Where the employee contributions exceed the cost of benefits under the schedule, the whole employee contribution is used to purchase the larger amount of benefit it will produce. This larger benefit may be allowed to produce a larger total pension at retirement or the excess may be used to reduce the amount of retirement income purchased by the employer contributions when the employee reaches a higher age.

Employees will contribute exactly what the schedule requires and no more or no less. There is occasional demand for employees to contribute more or larger amounts voluntarily. Such additional contributions would tend to make use of the pension plan as a savings plan for a few individuals. Withdrawals and changes in amount to such additional contributions would complicate the administration. More essentially, however, if such additional purchases were allowed, they would have to be on a basis which would allow no substantial advantage as compared with employees using the same money to purchase an individual annuity contract from an insurance company.

On termination of employment, the employee may leave his contributions with the insurance company to provide a paid-up annuity with what he has already contributed. Generally, however, he will not be permitted to continue contributions to purchase any additional annuity since such additional contributions would again have no material advantage over the purchase of an individual annuity contract from the insurance company.

Normal Retirement Date

The normal retirement date is fixed primarily as a necessary device to determine a premium required in funding a group annuity contract. By common misconception it is frequently considered the date on which employees should retire. This is not necessarily the case because, practically speaking, employees do not suddenly cease to be useful in their employment; some employees should retire before they reach age 65, and others continue to function effectively after that age. A group annuity contract, therefore, may provide for optional retirements either before or after the normal retirement date. The normal retirement date is merely the date as of which the annuities under the contract will normally mature, or commence to be paid. If the retirement occurs before the normal retirement date, then either the retirement income must be smaller in amount or an additional premium will be required. If the retirement occurs after the normal retirement date, then either the income may be increased, or there will be an excess of funds over the amount actually needed.

Early Retirement

The usual procedure is to pay the employee a reduced income on early retirement in the amount that can be provided by the funds which have accumulated to the date of his early retirement. The contract will show a table for converting the amount of the employee's accumulated annuity credits into the amount of reduced income which has the same value as the regular credits. Table 3 illustrates the percentages of reduced annuity which would be payable.

It is not generally customary, but theoretically possible, to pay an additional premium so that there will be no reduction in the employee's income or a lesser reduction of an arbitrary amount according to a formula.

Thus, under many plans it is considered easier to explain to the employees the reduction of benefits on early retirement by using a specified discount per month between the date of early retirement and the date of normal retirement. A discount of $\frac{1}{2}$ percent for each month between the employee's early retirement date and normal retirement date is roughly equivalent, on the average, to

TABLE 3

Early Retirement Factors
Reduced Amount of Early Retirement Income As a Percentage of the Employee's Total Income Accumulated to his Date of Early Retirement

Age at Early Retirement	Normal Retirement Age 65	
	Male	Female
55	42.7%	48.3%
60	63.1	67.8
61	68.7	72.9
62	75.1	78.6
63	82.3	85.0
64	90.6	92.1

the actuarial reduction factor and is commonly used as an early retirement discount.

Social Security Adjustment

For normal retirement dates earlier than age 65 and for early retirements, the contract may also provide for an adjustment in the employee's annuity to take into account the employee's Social Security benefit which begins at age 65, or in a reduced amount of benefit at age 62. The employee's income from the group annuity plan will be larger from the early retirement date up to age 62 or 65, as the case may be, and smaller thereafter. The objective is to provide a total amount of combined income from the plan plus Social Security, which will be approximately the same amount before and after the Social Security benefits become payable.

This option provides for an earlier payment of a substantial amount of the annuities purchased. Hence, the insurance company may require evidence of the employee's insurability if the employee elects the option. If this adjustment is automatic for all early retirements, the evidence of insurability may be waived.

Deferred Retirement

If the employee continues to work after his normal retirement date, the usual practice is to pay him either commencing on his normal retirement date or at actual later retirement the amount of income he is entitled to on his normal retirement date.

If the income is commenced on his normal retirement date, the employer may arrange to reduce his salary by an equivalent amount so that his total income may remain unchanged or the employer and employee are free to arrange any other rate of compensation agreeable to both. Under such procedure, the income paid is exactly that purchased and no adjustment in cost is required.

The alternative procedure used, perhaps with a greater frequency, is to defer the commencement of the retirement income until the employee actually retires, and then pay the amount of income which would have been paid had he retired on his normal retirement date. In this case, the retirement income payments which would have been payable between the dates of normal retirement and actual retirement are returned to the employer in the form of credits to be used against further premiums due under the contract. The employee receives his full salary during the period of continued employment which will generally be far more attractive to him than his retirement income. Hence, he suffers no real loss in giving up the retirement benefits for his larger salary payments.

It is theoretically possible to accumulate the retirement income payments during the period of the employee's continued employment, and upon retirement purchase for the employee an additional piece of retirement income. The increase which may be obtained by this procedure for each year of continued employment is quite substantial. It may be roughly 8 to 10 percent of the retirement income previously accumulated for each additional year. This very substantial increase in income adds an important inducement for the employee to continue to work and to resist retirement. Since one of the primary purposes of the plan is to aid the employer to retire employees at the appropriate time, this treatment would tend to defeat the purpose.

Disability Benefits

If disability benefits are desired under the plan, they can be provided under a separate long-term disability insurance contract.

Death Benefits Prior to Retirement

At death of the employee before retirement, his total contributions accumulated with interest are payable to his beneficiary or estate. The practical problem of selling the employee on the contributory retirement plan requires that the employee be assured that his own contributions to the plan will always be available to him or his estate. A slightly higher benefit or lower cost to the employer may be had if the employee contributions are returnable without interest. Many employees have come to consider their retirement plan contributions as at least a savings fund which should earn interest. Consequently, interest is usually allowed on the contributions.

In calculating the interest credits for employee death benefits, the common practice is to allow interest for completed months from the end of the year in which any contributions were made to the first day of the month preceding the employee's death. Table 4 illustrates the accumulated amounts of contributions with interest at 2 percent and with interest at 3 percent, if death occurs at the end of a year of contributions. The same amounts are customarily used for the employee withdrawal values paid on termination of employment.

Prior to 1960, the rate of interest allowed on employee con-

TABLE 4

Employee Death or Withdrawal Benefits Including Interest

Number of Years Since Commencement of Contributions	Amount of Employee's Contributions	Employee Death or Withdrawal Benefit for each $1.00 of Monthly Contribution	
		2% Interest	3% Interest
1	$ 12.00	$ 12.00	$ 12.00
2	24.00	24.24	24.36
3	36.00	36.72	37.09
4	48.00	49.45	50.20
5	60.00	62.44	63.71
10	120.00	131.39	137.57
20	240.00	291.56	322.44
30	360.00	486.81	570.90

tributions was almost uniformly 2 percent under a group annuity contract. This may be compared with the assumed rate of interest returned in the insurance company's rate calculations of $2\frac{1}{4}$ or $2\frac{1}{2}$ percent. Since 1960, most insurance companies have changed the rate basis for group annuities and currently assume a rate of interest which is $3\frac{1}{4}$ or $3\frac{1}{2}$ percent. With these rates, it is a general practice to allow the terminated employee 3 percent interest on the return of his contributions at death or termination of employment.

Death benefits are seldom granted with respect to the employer contributions to the group annuity contract. These benefits are available, however, if desired. The inclusion of such benefits, depending on the exact benefits, might increase the employer's cost by substantial amounts.

Death Benefits After Retirement

After an employee's retirement, the annuity may be payable either with or without death benefit. If the plan is noncontributory, the usual form would be a life annuity without any death benefits. Some contributory plans allow the employee to elect an annuity without death benefit after retirement. In the latter plans, obviously, there could be a few deaths as a result of which the employee and his estate would not recover as much as the accumulated value of his contributions. This would only occur if the employee died shortly after his retirement, before he had received annuity payments equal to his contributions.

The standard normal form of annuity for a contributory plan is the "modified refund" annuity in which the beneficiary of the employee or his estate will receive at his death a sum equal to the difference between the accumulated value of his contributions including interest up to the date of his retirement and the aggregate amount of the retirement income payments which the employee has received before his death.

The following forms of annuity are also generally available. One of the first three forms will usually be the normal or automatic form, but any other form may be available as an option which the employee may elect under certain conditions.

(1) A life annuity without death benefit.
(2) A modified cash refund annuity.

Financing a Pension Plan 101

(3) An annuity payable for life with income guaranteed for a minimum period of 5 or 10 years.

(4) A contingent annuity, all or part of which will be continued to a second person designated by the employee for as long as that person survives the employee after his death. For example, an employee may elect to receive a reduced amount of income, one-half of which would be continued after his death to his wife, if she is living, for the remainder of her life.

The following example and tables illustrate the reduction in annuities which would be required to change from a life annuity normal form of benefit to any of the forms indicated.

Example: (*Modified Cash Refund Annuity*): The change to or from the modified cash refund annuity and the life annuity involves a very small death benefit value. In a plan providing employee contributions at the rate of $2.00 of contributions for each $1.00 of retirement benefit, the employee's contributions with interest after a lifetime in the plan would probably not exceed four times the annual rate of his benefit. Under the modified cash refund annuity he would receive a death benefit if he died within four years after his retirement. The value of this four-year possible death benefit at his retirement would be about 1 percent of the value of his annuity at that time. Therefore, if he changed from a life annuity to a modified cash refund, his income would be reduced by about 1 percent. If he changed from a modified cash refund to a life annuity, his income would be increased by about 1 percent.

The change from a life annuity normal form to a five-year guarantee or a ten-year guarantee would involve, respectively, higher values of death benefits and, correspondingly, larger reduction in the accumulated retirement income. Similarly, if the conversion were from annuities with five- or ten-years certain to a life income annuity, the proportionate increases would be similarly larger. The option factors for a five- or ten-year guarantee are contained in Table 5.

The contingent annuitant option election would result in more substantial reduction in benefits because this option provides for a lifetime income to the second beneficiary. The amount of reduction in the employee's annuity, in such an option, will depend on the age of the employee, the age of his wife or other beneficiary whom he selects as a contingent annuitant, and the amount of income which he elects to have continued to the contingent annuitant. Illustrative factors are shown in Table 6.

TABLE 5

Option to Change From a Life Annuity to an Annuity Payable for Life But Not Less Than 5 or 10 Years
Reduced Annuity Payable If an Annuity With a Minimum Guarantee Period of 5 or 10 Years is Elected to Replace a Life Annuity

| | Retirement Age 65 ||
	Male	Female
5-year guarantee	98.1%	98.9%
10-year guarantee	92.8%	95.7%

TABLE 6

Contingent Annuity Factors
Reduced amount of income payable during the life of the employee expressed as a percentage of the employee's normal income

| Age of Contingent Annuitant || Male Employee Age 65 | Female Employee Age 65 |
Male	Female		
		When the whole amount of the reduced income is to be continued to the contingent annuitant.	
50	55	64.4%	73.1%
55	60	69.3	77.8
60	65	74.9	82.6
65	70	80.7	87.2
70	75	86.2	91.3
		When one-half the amount of the reduced income is to be continued to the contingent annuitant.	
50	55	78.3%	84.4%
55	60	81.9	87.5
60	65	85.6	90.5
65	70	89.3	93.2
70	75	92.6	95.4

In general, no annuity form may be changed to another form with a larger amount potentially payable at death or with death benefits payable for a longer period of time, without evidence of good health at the time the employee elects the option. This is because the election of such an option involves the exchange of an annuity for its equivalent value in life insurance. The exchange may be allowed without evidence of good health if the election is made some time in advance of the effective date of the change. The exact length of time required may depend on the value of the insurance benefit involved but may be arbitrarily set by the insurance company at 1, 2, or 5 years prior to the option effective date.

Employee Benefits on Termination of Employment

On termination of employment under the plan, an employee will be entitled to a benefit based upon his own contributions and possibly further benefit provided by all or part of the employer's contributions.

In a contributory plan an employee is assured of a return of his contributions either with or without interest. On termination the employee may choose either:

> 1. To withdraw his contributions in cash, in which event the corresponding annuities which have been purchased for him will be cancelled, or
> 2. To leave his contributions with the insurance company and retain the amount of paid-up annuity they will purchase.

If he elects to leave his contributions with the insurance company, he nevertheless retains the right to withdraw their cash value at any time in the future prior to the commencement of his annuity.

If the plan provides for a return of the contributions with interest, the amount of cash withdrawal value is computed in the same manner as the amount payable at his death.

Modern plans usually provide for the vesting of all or a portion of the benefit purchased by the employer's contributions, if the employee has met certain minimum conditions as to age or length of service, or both. This vesting is usually, but not necessarily, conditioned on the employee's choosing to leave his own contributions, if any, in the plan. To the extent that the employee has met the requirements of the plan as to vesting, such annuities remain in force as paid-up deferred annuities and become payable to the employee upon his attainment of normal retirement age.

Employer Credits

The group annuity contract will customarily provide credits to the employer from several sources including:

1. Cancellation of annuities upon termination of employment.
2. Deferment of retirement of an employee to some date after his normal retirement date.
3. Dividends or retroactive rate credits.

In order to meet the requirements of the Internal Revenue Code, these credits may not be paid in cash but must be applied against future premiums due under the contract.

Upon termination of employment other than by death or retirement, the employer is entitled to a credit on account of any annuities cancelled. In the normal operation of a group deferred annuity, the employer purchases benefits each year for each employee in the plan. If the employee then resigns or is discharged and forfeits his accrued benefits, the annuities which have been purchased for him are cancelled and their value is credited to the employer account under the contract to be applied to future purchases of annuities. To the extent that annuities vest in the employee there will, of course, be no cancellation and no credits.

The employer's credit on termination of any employee's employment is payable only if the employee is in good health at the date of his termination. The employer premiums have been determined on the assumption that any premiums which have been paid for benefits for employees who subsequently die before retirement will be redistributed to help provide the benefits for those employees who live to retirement date. Thus, in any case in which the employee's termination might be due to ill health which would eventuate in his death, the value of his annuities would be required in the fund to help provide the benefits for the other employees. Furthermore, if there were no such condition, obviously the employer would theoretically have the opportunity to terminate the employment of each employee just prior to his death and secure a credit which would not be available if he died in service.

The evidence of good health required in most cases is of the simplest possible form. A statement of the employer's belief in the former employee's good health is usually acceptable. Where the amount of the value of the annuity is very large, the insurance company may reserve the right to require a medical examination of the employee. If this is not practical, the credit values may be placed in a suspense account pending future development. If at the end of five years the individual is still alive, then the credits may be released without further evidence of good health. Interest will, of course, be allowed on the amounts held in such an account.

The amount of credit allowed upon cancellation of any annuity may be the sum of the employer's payments plus accumulated interest at 3 percent, less a surrender charge of 4 percent of both employer and employee credits but not less than 100 percent of the past service premium.

The employer's credits in event of deferred retirement have already been described above. If there is a death benefit payable under the plan and the retirement is deferred, then the credits arising from deferred retirement may be retained temporarily by the insurance company in a suspense account to cover the amount of the death benefit required. Interest is allowed on the balance in this suspense account. The balance in this account for any employee, not required to pay the death benefit at his death, or after he has received annuity payments sufficient to exhaust this death benefit, will then be credited to the employer.

Dividends or rate adjustments will be covered more fully below. It is sufficient to note here that any credits arising from this source will be available along with the other credits to pay future premiums.

Discontinuance of Annuity Purchases

The employer is always in a position to terminate the further purchase of annuities under the contract (subject, of course, to the restrictions of the IRS and to any union contract the employer may have). The annuities that have already been purchased would in that case remain in force but no further premiums would be payable. Discontinuance can be effected by the employer giving notice to the insurance company.

The only conditions under which the insurance company can ordinarily discontinue the further sale of annuities to the employer are

(1) in event of the failure of the employer to pay premiums which are due within the grace period, and

(2) in event that the total number of employees covered in the contract falls below a specified number, such as 10, or the

number of contributing employees under the contributory plan falls below 75 percent of those eligible to join the plan.

However, the insurance company may agree to continue the sale of annuities in spite of the above conditions.

If the plan ceases to function by discontinuance of further purchases of annuities in accordance with any of the circumstances described above, the annuities which have already been purchased will automatically become vested in the employees in full.

The employer may have a continuing retirement plan to replace the contract under which the purchase of annuities is being discontinued. Such a replacing plan may be a group annuity contract or a trust fund. Under such circumstances, the contract may provide that the full vesting of annuities purchased will not occur. Upon termination of employment, the employer credits, which would otherwise be applied to pay premiums under the discontinued contract, may be paid by the insurance company to the new substitute plan whether it is an insurance company or trust.

Modification of the Contract

The plan and group deferred annuity contract may be modified at any time by mutual consent of the employer and the insurance company. No such modification or change in the contract will be allowed to alter adversely or affect the amount and terms of payment of any annuities which have already been purchased. In other words, the employees' rights to any annuities which have been purchased will be protected by the terms of the contract against adverse modification.

The insurance company also reserves the right to modify any terms of the contract at any time at which the rates may be changed. Such modification will normally be restricted to those provisions which would require appropriate change to correspond to the new rates.

Premiums and Rates

Both employee and employer premiums under a group deferred annuity contract may be paid either monthly or annually. In view of the general practice of deducting employee contributions from the employee's periodic pay, the monthly payment of premiums is generally used.

Premiums for the past service benefits are determined as a single premium on the effective date of the plan to purchase the entire amount of all past service credits under the plan. Considerable flexibility is available in the actual payment of this past service cost. The unpaid portion of the total single sum cost would be earning interest as if it had been paid on the effective date. Therefore, any delay in payment will increase the amount eventually required to be paid to complete the purchase of these annuities.

The past service benefits may be purchased by the payment of one lump sum covering the entire cost. The federal income tax law and regulations, however, provide that in no event shall more than 10 percent of the amount of the single sum cost be deductible in any year in computing the employer's income tax. Therefore, the amount usually paid in one year will not exceed the 10 percent of the single sum cost allowed as a tax deduction. An annual payment of 10 percent will require about 12 years to pay the entire cost, with interest on the unpaid balances, if mortality experience is normal and no terminations of employment have occurred.

Income tax regulations also require a minimum payment of past service costs in the plan so the total value of unpurchased past service benefits does not exceed the amount of such costs at the effective date of the plan*

In between these two annual rates at which past service may be funded there is a fairly wide range of choice to the employer in the amount he should pay in regular annual installments or in variable amounts in accordance with the state of business each year. In many union negotiated plans it is specifically agreed that the rate at which past service benefits shall be purchased is the level amount required to purchase the benefits over a period of 25, 30, or 35 years. Such a payment would be about 5 percent of the single sum cost.

The insurance companies have in the past required that the entire benefit for each employee be purchased on or prior to the date that the employee is retired or is eligible for normal retirement. Thus, if the plan included a substantial proportion of

---

* This limitation applies only if payments are suspended.

benefits on older employees eligible to retire or near normal retirement age, this rule might require the payment of more than 10 percent of the single sum past service cost in order to purchase in full the benefit for those employees before their respective normal retirement dates.

This requirement of full payment for an employee's annuity prior to the date on which he first becomes eligible to retire has in past years frequently resulted in exclusion from the plan of employees who are over 65 on the effective date of the plan. Relaxations of this requirement have made it possible to include the oldest employees in the plan without incurring extraordinarily high premium payments in the first years of the plan. This may usually be arranged to provide for the purchase of an employee's annuity over a minimum period of 5 or 10 years.

The contract will contain appropriate rates for the purchase of all benefits and state the due dates of the premiums and the methods of their calculations. Table 7 presents an illustration of the rates which may be used in a unit benefit type of plan.

The cost of the pure retirement income in column (2) of Table 7 is less than the total cost in column (3) when the employee contributes. This is because the employee contributions are returned to him or his estate at death prior to retirement, with the result that at retirement the contributions from employees who have previously died are no longer available to provide retirement incomes for those who remain to retire. The extra cost in column (3) is the cost of returning the employee's contributions at death.

The amount in column (6) represents the average portion of each dollar of employee contributions that remains available to provide retirement income benefits. In a normal distribution of employees by age, the portion of the aggregate employee contribution available for retirement incomes is about 80 percent. Therefore, each dollar of employee contributions will reduce the employer cost of retirement incomes by about $.80. The proportions or percentages in column (6) are approximately the respective probabilities of surviving from the date of purchase to the normal retirement age.

The illustrative rates and factors which are shown for group annuities are the current rates used by one company and technically described as based on the assumptions of (1) the 1951 Group Annuity Mortality Table with Projection C assuming the

TABLE 7

Group Annuity Unit Benefit Rates for $1.00 of Monthly Income
Males—Retirement Age 65

Age at Beginning of Year	Non-Contributory Rates		Contributory Rates Employee paying $2.00 Monthly			Amount of Reduction in Employer Cost Per $1.00 Employee Contribution $(5) \div 2$ (6)
	Past Service Single Premium (1)	Future Service Monthly Premium (2)	Total Monthly Premium (3)	Employer Monthly Premium (4)	Reduction in Employer Premium $(2) - (4)$ (5)	
25	$33.78	$2.86	$3.34	$1.34	$1.52	$.76
35	46.92	3.98	4.42	2.42	1.56	.78
45	65.79	5.58	5.98	3.98	1.60	.80
55	95.86	8.16	8.45	6.45	1.71	.86

purchase in 1960 with (2) 3¼ percent interest and (3) a loading of 5 percent of gross for expenses and contingencies.

Rates quite similar are used by a number of large companies underwriting group annuities. Other rates in current use, with an illustration of their relative values, are shown in Table 8. The price per unit is the single premium at age 45 to purchase for a male employee an annuity of $1 per year payable monthly starting at age 65 with no death benefit.

TABLE 8

Group Deferred Annuity Rates

Mortality*	Interest	Loading	Price Per Unit	Relative Price
GA 1951 Projection C-1960	3⅜%	5%	5.57	102
GA 1951 Projection C-1960	3¼%	5%	5.48	100
GA 1951 Projected	3½%	5%	5.60	102
GA 1951 Projection C-1964 (-1,-6)	3¼%	5%	5.52	101
GA 1951 Projection C	3¼%	5%	5.77	105

The rates initially used in the contract are usually guaranteed only for premiums received during the first five years of the contract. Thereafter, the insurance company reserves the right to specify a new set of rates which will apply to the premium payments after the fifth anniversary and for each succeeding plan year thereafter.

The insurance companies are required by the state legislation in certain states in which they operate to use a uniform set of premium rates for all group annuity contracts. Since these rates will be applied to a very large group of 1,000 or more employees or a small group of less than 25 employees, it is impossible to justify a uniform percentage expense loading. The companies have therefore developed a policy or contract charge that is usually between $500-$750 per year to be payable by all group annuity policies. If the policy covers a large group of employees, this policy charge is reduced by a percentage of the annual premium in excess of a minimum limit. The result is that the expense

---

* There are variations in the method of making and naming the projections of the mortality table.

charge for the small group is equal to the policy charge plus 5 percent of the premiums otherwise payable. For larger cases the expense charge may be just the percentage of gross premium, since the policy charge may become zero.

The administration of the group deferred annuity contract on the wholesale basis for a very large group of employees can be handled by an insurance company at a very small percentage of the annual premium income. On a very large group of employees this percentage may be as little as 3 percent, or even less. In the light of this small percentage expense charge for operating the plan, the premium tax levied on group annuity premiums by certain state jurisdictions may loom very large in relation to the total cost of the administration. State premium taxes on group annuity premiums may be as high as 2 percent. In fairness to those employers operating in states which have no premium tax, some insurance companies have a special charge to offset the state premium tax on group annuity premiums. This charge would be based on state of residence of the employees of the employer, and the total charge to the employer would be the estimated amount of premium tax payable by the insurance company to the states in which the employees live.

Financial Operations

Most of the insurance companies offering group annuity coverage will keep exact records for the premium receipts under each contract and of all benefit payments disbursed or credits allowed. They will also allocate to each contract interest earnings at an appropriate rate based on the actual investment earnings of the insurance company. They will charge each contract with the appropriate expenses for the administration of the contract in accordance with accepted cost accounting methods for allocating such expenses. This record will therefore show the cash position of each group annuity contract standing by itself.

The record of income and disbursements for each contract is subject to ready verification on the part of the policyholder. The policyholder can verify the cash payments to the insurance company and by appropriate examination of the individual employee records should be able to verify exactly the disbursements to employees or former employees for benefits paid under the plan.

The charges for expenses and the credits for investment earnings cannot, of course, be verified without reference to outside sources. However, these amounts are relatively small in proportion to the total premium and the approximate amount of charge or credit can be estimated and reasonably verified.

The insurance company at the end of each year will value the benefits which have been purchased and are still effective under the contract. The minimum basis for this valuation is usually specified in the contract, but the actual valuation basis may be higher than this minimum and will be uniform for all classes of similar contracts within any one insurance company. The company may also establish by formula a contingency reserve which will add to the safety and financial stability of the group annuity operations.

The difference between the cash balance of any contract and the sum of the liabilities and contingency reserves will indicate whether the contract shows a gain or loss from its operations. If there is a gain so computed, all or some part of this gain will be the basis of the return to the employer in the form of a dividend or a rate reduction. The amount of this return will depend on the size and length of experience of the contract and also on general conditions of the entire group annuity business of the insurance company.

Two things should be clearly evident from this description of the financial basis for dividends and rate credits. The result of the actual operation of the plan would depend not on the assumed basic rate of interest used by the insurance company in calculating the premium rates, but on the actual rate of interest credited to the group annuity contract fund. Similarly, the expense charge is determined by an actual cost accounting process and may be different from the assumed rate of expense represented by the percentage of premium loading plus the contract charge.

An important element of the cash position of each contract is the amount of investment earnings on the accumulated fund balance in the contract. In the past, each group annuity contract was combined with all the other business of the insurance company for the purpose of investments and distribution or allocation of investment earnings. Thus, each new contract and each new premium payment bought into the total investment portfolio of the insurance company.

Payments into the plan during a period of low investment return on high-grade securities participated in the higher yield of investments held by the insurance company from purchases made in a higher market. Conversely, of course, during a high yield market new premiums invested shared in the lower yield of securities purchased at less favorable times.

Some insurance companies have recently developed a method of crediting interest called the "investment generation" method or "new money" method. Under this method the amount of interest credited to an individual group annuity contract would depend upon the years in which the funds of the contract originated as premium payments or credits, less disbursements. This system has the effect of eliminating the possibility of one contract holder buying into an investment portfolio at a lower or higher yield than the current market rates justify.

During most of the 1930's and 1940's, the trend of investment yields on high-grade securities was downward. During the 1930's, the insurance companies made several successive increases in rate schedules in expectation of lower and lower interest earnings. At the same time, insurance companies with annuity contracts issued at the lower rates, with the high assumed interest of earlier years, strengthened their valuation bases. The result was a history of practically no dividends or rate reductions from 1935 to 1950. Since then, investment yields and the total dividends allowed by the companies have grown rapidly.

There will generally be no dividends during the first few years of the contract's existence because the higher initial expense of establishing the contract must be overcome by any surplus earned during this period. The existence of a dividend and its amount will depend on the kind of plan and the experience which has developed.

Administration of the Plan

After the employer has decided on having a group annuity plan, the insurance company will assist in putting the plan into operation and guide the administration.

The first step is the preparation of announcements for the employees. An employer may exercise his choice in the format of the booklet describing the plan to the employees or any other literature that is distributed. The insurance company will want to review any such literature for accuracy of wording before its distribution. On the other hand, the insurance company will be prepared to assist in the preparation of this material.

The insurance company will also prepare and assist in the campaign for enrollment of employees in a contributory plan. A carefully planned and executed campaign of presentation to the employees should normally secure practically 100 percent enrollment.

The employee and employer will file with the insurance company a statement of the information required to determine each employee's age, service, and amount of benefit under the plan. If the plan is contributory, the employee will name a beneficiary to receive the death benefits, if and when they become due, and also will execute an authorization for the employer to deduct the proper contribution to the plan from the employee's regular pay.

After the enrollment, the insurance company will prepare a statement of the premiums due on whatever basis of payment has been selected by the employer. The insurance company will also furnish the employer with an appropriate set of record cards for keeping individual membership records and with instructions and forms for the necessary periodical reports of changes in the coverage of employees under the plan.

Each employee covered by the plan will receive a certificate which will describe briefly the benefits of the plan to which he may be entitled and the principal conditions. This certificate is not a contract but a statement of the employee's rights under the master contract between the employer and the insurance company.

The group annuity contract that is delivered by the insurance company and accepted by the employer, and the certificates issued by the insurance company for distribution to the employees, are reviewed and approved by the insurance department of the state in which the contract is to be issued.

Group Deposit Administration

Deposit administration is a form of group annuity contract under which the premiums paid are not allocated to purchase benefits for any individual employee until his date of retirement. The premiums are accumulated in a deposit fund. If employees contribute, individual contributions account records are kept and the fund must be, at all times, adequate to cover the aggregate of contribution accumulations plus a margin of employer contributions. Upon retirement, the necessary single premium to provide the employee's total benefit is transferred from the deposit account to the purchase of an annuity for the retiring employee.

This type of contract has developed greatly in recent years to meet the competition of the self-administered trusteed plan in which the employer has more control of his contributions to the plan. It may be used for negotiated pension plans where contributions to the plan are fixed by negotiation or where it is desired to commit the least possible amounts of employer money. Administrative economies are more effective in a noncontributory plan where there is no need to keep individual records for each employee.

Plan Characteristics

The deposit administration contract may be used for a plan with the same benefit characteristics as a group deferred annuity plan. One of its advantages, however, is a capacity to provide a wider range of benefit formulae and plan provisions. For example, it is not necessary to have a fixed normal retirement age. No annuity is purchased until the employee retires.

Benefits may be based on final average salary, which cannot be determined accurately until retirement. Also, the benefits payable at early retirement can be larger than the actuarial equivalent of the accumulation under the regular group annuity contract. The plan may also provide disability payments to be paid directly from the deposit fund. Thus, such a plan need not follow any of the particular group annuity patterns as to plan provisions.

Since there is no purchase of annuities prior to retirement, there will be no credits to the employer on termination of employment or on account of deferred retirement. Such credits may be estimated in advance and allowance made in determining the employer's contributions to the deposit account.

The provisions for discontinuance of the plan must contain a formula for allocating the balance in the deposit account to the purchase of annuities at the time of discontinuance. Since these funds are not allocated to individual accounts during the life of the contract, there must be provision for their distribution to the credit of individual employees on the termination of the contract. The contract may provide for the transfer of a cash value of the remaining deposit fund to a continuing plan.

How Costs are Figured

The insurance company premium rates for the purchase of an annuity enter into the operation of this type of plan only at the employee's retirement. The premiums required for normal use, therefore, will be only the single premium cost of annuities to commence immediately. These rates will be guaranteed for the purchases made from all money arising from deposits within the first five years of the contract. The insurance company will also guarantee the minimum rate of interest to be allowed on the deposit fund. This interest rate will usually apply to the money deposited in the first five years until such money is completely used up for the purchase of annuities at retirement.

The employer's cost or contributions to this type of plan may be calculated under one of the standard methods of cost calculations for pensions. Allowances may be made for terminations of employment, for salary increases, for early or late retirement, and for any other factors considered pertinent. The insurance company, if desired, will furnish the actuarial services for these calculations or the employer is free to secure independent actuarial assistance. No minimum standards for valuation under the accumulation period of such a contract have been established. Presumably any reasonable standards that can be justified on the basis of the employer's past experience and likely future experience would be acceptable to the insurance company.

Obviously the employer secures through this type of contract immediate credit for any gains from operations during the accumulation period or conversely assumes the cost from any loss in such operations. In contrast to the group deferred annuity contract, the employer has more control and assumes some of the risks of his experience under this form of financing.

An extension of this form of contract for very large groups now permits the employer full credit for his own experience year by year including the actual experience on retired lives. This variation is called an "immediate participation guarantee" (I.P.G.) contract or "pension administration" contract. The insurance company offers technical and investment services, pooling the premiums under the contract with all other funds for investments. The result is that the insurance company is, in effect, acting as a trustee in a self-administered plan. This type of contract is limited to very large groups, usually 10,000 or more.

Ordinarily the funds under a deposit administration contract are commingled and invested with the total assets of the insurance companies. Recently some companies have established separate accounts composed entirely of equity investments in which the funds under a deposit administration contract may be invested. The incentive for separate accounts in equity investments is the potential appreciation of the equity investments. The insurance company limits the amounts which may be invested in the equity account, sometimes to 50 percent of the total premium deposits, to maintain some balance between fixed and equity investments. The funds invested in the separate account are credited with investment income and with appreciation and depreciation of asset values based upon the performance of the separate account.

Group Permanent Life Insurance

Group permanent insurance is a form of life insurance with cash values written on a group basis. Such life insurance with retirement income provisions or options issued under a group contract enable the employer and the insurance company to provide the benefits of a retirement plan. It is particularly appropriate when substantial amounts of death benefit are desired which are directly related to the retirement income benefits. The contract contains the entire plan. The employer pays premiums to the insurance company. The insurance company pays all the benefits of the plan.

Since this is a group life insurance coverage, it will be subject to state laws providing the minimum number of lives acceptable, usually 10. The form of coverage and administration is somewhat more complex than for group deferred annuities. Therefore, the minimum acceptable premium may be higher. It is desirable to avoid the somewhat higher costs of termination of employment by using this plan only for the more stable employment groups.

This form of group coverage developed naturally from the use of individual insurance or annuity contracts to provide pension benefits. Insurance companies issuing individual life insurance and annuity contracts, but not issuing group annuity coverage, were called upon from time to time to underwrite the benefits of pension plans. The individual insurance contracts best adapted to the purpose were used through the vehicle of a pension trust to hold title to the contracts required.

Subsequently, the insurance companies interested in underwriting group annuities and group pension plans in general adopted the benefit provisions of these individual contracts in combination with the group method of administration. The group permanent contract was the result. Certain definite advantages over individual policies were obtained such as:

1. Automatic non-medical insurance coverage up to the prescribed limits, eliminating most of the medical examinations required.

2. A reduction in commissions to agents. The insurance being written in large blocks, the commission rates were reduced for such coverage.

3. A reduction in the expenses of establishing and administering the plan, such as the issuance of certificates rather than contracts for each individual employee's coverage.

4. The grouping of experience for dividend purposes in a separate class.

Plan Characteristics

Retirement Income

This form of coverage lends itself naturally to a benefit formula which provides a fixed amount of monthly income at retirement regardless of length of service under the plan. The salary class schedule (Table 9) is illustrative of this type of plan. It provides benefits of approximately 20 percent of the first $4,800 and 40 percent of the excess over $4,800 of the final average salary.

The insurance and annuity form of coverage provides, for example, $1,000 of life insurance with each unit of $10 of monthly retirement income. A few companies offer some variations in the relative amount of insurance such as $500 or $1,500 with each $10 of monthly income. Other variations may be worked out with other forms of contracts by combining two or more forms.

TABLE 9
Salary Class Schedule for Insurance and Annuity Benefits

Class No.	Annual Salary Range	Monthly Retirement Income	Employee's Monthly Contribution	Amount of Death Benefit
1	Under $1,950	$ 30.00	$ 3.00	$ 3,000
2	$1,950 - 2,249	35.00	3.50	3,500
3	2,250 - 2,549	40.00	4.00	4,000
4	2,550 - 2,849	45.00	4.50	4,500
5	2,850 - 3,149	50.00	5.00	5,000
6	3,150 - 3,449	55.00	5.50	5,500
7	3,450 - 3,749	60.00	6.00	6,000
8	3,750 - 4,049	65.00	6.50	6,500
9	4,050 - 4,349	70.00	7.00	7,000
10	4,350 - 4,649	75.00	7.50	7,500
11	4,650 - 4,949	80.00	8.00	8,000
12	4,950 - 5,399	90.00	9.00	9,000
13	5,400 - 5,999	110.00	11.00	11,000
14	6,000 - 6,599	130.00	13.00	13,000
and so on by steps of $600		$ 20.00	$ 2.00	$ 2,000

The use of group permanent ordinary life insurance with an auxiliary fund is discussed in a later section.

A unit benefit per year of service may also be used as the formula for retirement income benefits in a group permanent plan. Where the death benefit is $1,000 for each $10 of monthly retirement income, and a unit benefit formula is used to determine retirement income, then it follows that the death benefits will vary with the age at the time the employee enters the plan or receives an increase in benefit under the schedule. The resulting death benefit may be considered undesirable.

The benefit formula illustrated in Table 9 provides a death benefit of 167 percent of the first $4,800 of salary plus 333 percent of salary in excess of $4,800. Such substantial death benefits may be arranged to provide the surviving widow of the deceased employee with a significant amount of monthly income for her future lifetime, either by terms of the plan or by provisions available through options in the plan.

Retirement Date

There will be only one normal retirement date in each year on which all of the annuities will normally mature. This will be the earliest date at which the employee will be able to retire on his full normal amount of income. It will generally be the contract anniversary nearest age 65.

Early retirements may be permitted. At early retirement the usual procedure will be to apply the then accumulated cash value to purchase whatever it will yield in the form of annuity desired. In effect, the procedure is the same as in a group deferred annuity contract. The steps in determining the amount payable are different. The cash value is determined according to the age at entry and age attained by the employee. The cash value is applied to purchase an immediate annuity according to the age attained at the time of retirement. (See the yields in Table 11.)

Because of the large death benefits after retirement in this form of coverage, the plan does not lend itself to delaying retirement and crediting the employer with the values of the benefits not received by the employee, though this procedure can be worked out if desired. The normal practice will be to commence annuity payments at normal retirement date regardless of the employee's actual retirement. The employer may then adjust the compensation of an employee who continues to work or make new employment arrangements with him.

Death Benefits Prior to Retirement

Two types of coverage are usually used in group permanent contracts, one with and one without insurance. The normal form, as indicated, will have a face value of $1,000 of insurance for each $10 of monthly retirement income benefit. The capital value required to provide the monthly income will generally exceed the face amount of insurance. This means that the accumulating reserves for each employee covered will exceed the face amount of his insurance during the last few years immediately prior to retirement date. For this period the amount payable at death of the employee will be the cash value of his coverage.

Table 10 illustrates for various ages of entry into the plan, or ages at issue for increases in benefits, the ages at which the cash value and death benefit exceed the $1,000 face amount of insurance.

TABLE 10

Males—Retirement Age 65
Normal income 5 years certain and life

Age at Issue	Age at Which Cash Value Exceeds $1,000
20	57
30	58
40	60
50	62
60	64

As indicated, the amounts of death benefit under this type of plan are substantial. These insurance coverages will be issued under the group contract without medical examination automatically as the employee becomes eligible for them, provided only that he be at work when the insurance becomes effective. The amounts of insurance which the insurance company will issue on this automatic basis are limited by underwriting limits similar to those that apply to group life insurance on the term basis.

Beyond the nonmedical limits determined as applicable under the group permanent contract if an employee would be entitled to more insurance by the benefit formula, he must pass a medical examination prescribed by the insurance company in order to secure the coverage.

There will frequently be employees who will fail to pass the medical examination, and there may be some employees whose retirement incomes under the formula would entitle them to more than the maximum amount of insurance which the insurance company will permit under any group permanent plan. In order that these employees may not be deprived of their retirement incomes because they cannot secure the insurance coverage, a second form of coverage comes into play. This form, generally called "retirement annuity," provides for the accumulation of the sum necessary to provide the retirement incomes in excess of those provided with insurance. This form of contract has a death benefit equal to the cash value or the accumulated premiums at the date of death, whichever is greater. During the early years under any policy, for about 10 years, the cash value is less than the total premiums which will have been paid. During this period, the death benefit is the total amount of the premiums paid.

The maturity values at retirement age for these two types of coverage are identical, the only difference being the amount payable at death prior to retirement.

The insurance contract may provide for the payment of these death benefits in a single sum. It will usually provide, however, for the payment under any one of several options or settlement methods available in individual contracts. These optional settlements will usually include the following forms:

> 1. Payment of interest on the capital amount of the death benefit at a guaranteed minimum rate with the capital sum at some future date.
> 2. The payment of the capital and interest in installments over a fixed period of years such as 5, 10, 15, or 20 or, alternatively, the payment of a fixed amount of income for as long as capital and interest will last.
> 3. Payment of a life annuity for the lifetime of the beneficiary. The amount of annuity depends on the age and sex of the beneficiary. The option may also contain a guarantee of payments for a fixed minimum period of years.

Death Benefits After Retirements

Normally the maturity value would be payable to the employee in the form of retirement income for life with a minimum guarantee period of five or ten years. There will, however, be available to the employee one of several optional forms of retirement income. The forms of income generally available would, in addition to the five- or ten-year guarantee periods, include a life annuity and a joint and survivorship or contingent annuity, which would pay the same or a reduced monthly income to the contingent annuitant named by the employee, if she outlives the employee.

Since these optional forms of annuity all involve a death benefit in some form, the employee in making an election exchanges part of his annuity for a death benefit, or a part of his death benefit for a larger annuity. Obviously, if the employee is in poor health, it will be to his advantage to elect a form of annuity which will provide a larger death benefit. As a consequence, these optional elections involve, in effect, the issue of insurance for the employee.

They should be subject to evidence of the employee's insurability at the time he makes the election. It is considered impractical to require a medical examination for one of these elections. Therefore, general practice is to require selection of the option several years before actual retirement or to provide for the reduction of the amount of annuity payable by an amount which may be called a selection charge. This selection charge takes the form of providing annuities under the option that would be appropriate for an age one year younger than the actual age of the employee making the election. The result is a charge of about 3 percent of the maturity value when making such an election.

Tables 11 and 12 illustrate the yields per $1,000 of cash value or maturity value under the various forms of annuity.

TABLE 11

Group Permanent Insurance
Monthly Income per $1,000 of Cash Value

Male	Female	Life Annuity (No Death Benefit)	5 Year Certain And Life	10 Year Certain And Life
50	55	$4.74	$4.72	$4.67
55	60	5.27	5.24	5.15
60	65	6.01	5.95	5.77
65	70	7.04	6.92	6.55

TABLE 12

Group Permanent Insurance
Monthly Contingent Annuity for Male Employee Age 65
per $1,000 of Cash Value

Female Contingent Annuitant Age	Percentage of the Employee's Annuity Payable to Contingent Annuitant		
	100%	66⅔%	50%
55	$4.50	$5.18	$5.58
60	4.86	5.55	5.97
65	5.25	5.96	6.40
70	5.64	6.42	6.92

Termination of Employment

The total value available to an employee and employer together on termination of employment under this coverage will be determined by the cash value which is similar to the cash value on an individual insurance policy. The amount depends upon the age at issue of the coverage, the number of years the premium is paid, and sometimes upon the year of issue or year of normal retirement. Table 13 illustrates the total termination values which may be available at the end of a specified number of years and in accordance with the age at issue of each unit of coverage. This table illustrates the full termination value which would be credited against future premiums under the plan. Any part of this termination value which is paid in cash to the employee as his withdrawal value would result in a surrender charge based on the employee's cash value, but deducted from the remaining portion creditable to the employer.

TABLE 13

Illustrative Termination Values
*Group permanent insurance of $1,000 and income of
$10 per month at age 65—male*

(*Normal income 5 years certain and life*)

	Age at Issue		
	25	40	55
Annual Premium	$ 29.53	$ 53.79	$ 150.89
Termination Values End of Year			
1	15.00	35.00	115.00
3	57.00	120.00	367.00
5	102.00	208.00	640.00
10	226.00	449.00	1,428.00
Age 65	1,428.00	1,428.00	—

The employee's cash values on termination of employment may be provided out of the termination value. The employee's share may be his accumulated contributions with interest which will assure the employee the return of all his own money. An alternative employee return on withdrawal, sometimes used, gives him a proportionate part of the total termination value equal to the proportion of the employee's contribution to the total premium for his coverage. In any case, the balance of the termination value not allowed the employee would be available to the employer as a credit against future premiums required by the plan.

At termination of employment, an employee may convert his coverage under the group permanent plan to an individual annuity or life insurance contract on which he would thereafter pay the full premium. The employee receives a paid-up contract for a reduced amount of benefits provided by the withdrawal value at the time of termination of his employment. He may then convert the remainder of his insurance coverage to a new policy. The conversion of this reduced amount of insurance coverage at his attained age will usually result in the continuing premium, which is approximately the same as the premium which would have been applicable had he purchased the individual contract for the full amount of his coverage as of the original date of his coverage in the group permanent plan.

Premiums and Rates

Costs are relatively rigid under a group permanent contract. Each unit of benefit is purchased by a fixed level annual premium payable from the date of the employee's entry or increase in benefits to his normal retirement date.

Premiums are payable annually in advance. If the employees contribute, the employer is expected to advance the employee's contributions and reimburse himself from the monthly payroll deductions through the ensuing year.

The contract will contain all the necessary rates and the method of applying these rates to determine the total annual premium payable. The contract rates are guaranteed for a specified period such as three years. This means that the rates will be fixed for the lifetime of each unit of benefit on which the first premiums are paid during the period of this guarantee. New rates, if specified by the insurance company, will apply to new employees becoming eligible and to any increase in benefits for employees previously covered.

The contract may be continued at the pleasure of the employer (subject to any restrictions of Internal Revenue Service or a union agreement) and may be discontinued by the nonpayment of any premium due. The insurance company may discontinue the contract

> (a) if the number of employees covered is less than 75 percent (in a contributory plan) of those eligible or less than 10 lives in any event, or
> (b) if the employer fails to pay any premium when due.

The cost for each employee's benefit is so determined that the same amount of annual premium paid for each year from the employee's entry into the plan to his normal retirement date will accumulate a sum sufficient to provide the retirement income benefits and, in addition, pay for the cost of the insurance benefits in excess of the amounts of accumulation during the accumulation period. The annual premiums in Table 14 are illustrative of the rates which would be used for the purchase of a unit of $10 monthly income starting at retirement age 65.

TABLE 14

Group Permanent Insurance
Annual Premiums per $1,000 of Insurance and $10 of Annuity
Retirement Age 65

Normal income 5 years certain and life

Age at Issue	Insurance and Annuity		Retirement Annuity	
	Males	Females	Males	Females
25	$ 29.53	$ 32.76	$ 27.43	$ 30.94
35	42.86	47.88	40.37	45.79
45	70.22	79.02	66.71	76.08
55	150.89	171.61	144.85	166.58
65	1,647.13	1,909.20	1,647.13	1,909.20
Maturity Value	1,428.00	1,656.00	1,428.00	1,656.00

For illustration, assuming a male employee is age 35 when he enters the plan and is entitled to $100 of monthly income and $10,000 of insurance under the formula, his premium for this coverage would be 10 times $42.86 or $428.60 per year for each year until he reaches retirement age 65 (30 premium payments).

If the automatic insurance limit is $8,000 and he fails to pass the medical examination, his premiums would be 8 times $42.86 or $342.88 plus 2 times $40.37 or $80.74 making a total of $423.62. If when he reaches age 45 this coverage is increased by two units, $20 of monthly income and $2,000 of insurance, an additional premium would be payable from that point on of $140.44 with insurance or $133.42 without insurance.

The dividend and the rate credit practice of group permanent life insurance follows the methods used for group annuity accounting or dividend and rate credit treatment.

Individual Contract Pension Trust

An individual contract pension trust plan is operated through a trust, with either a corporate trustee or individual trustees, established for the purpose of holding title to, and possession of, the individual insurance or annuity contracts providing the benefits of the plan. The trustee receives the premium payments from the employer and transmits them to the life insurance company. The insurance company will generally pay the benefits directly to the employees. Payments may alternatively be made by the insurance company to the trust for transmittal to the employee.

This type of financing is particularly appropriate for a small group of employees not large enough to warrant the use of a group annuity or group permanent life insurance contract on an economical basis. Some insurance companies limit the maximum number of people covered in a plan using individual contracts to 100 or 200 lives. The plan may be used for larger groups when there is a particular reason for the additional expenses and administrative work involved in using individual contracts. Individual contracts will generally be issued only for a minimum initial amount of at least $10 monthly income and for minimum additional units of at least $5 monthly income on any one employee.

The additional administrative expense will include such items as the issue of an individual contract for each unit and for each member of the plan, the payment of commissions appropriate for individual contracts rather than group or bulk contracts, the problem of custody and safe-keeping of the contracts themselves, which must be kept by the trustee, and the computations of individual premiums for each unit of coverage and each employee covered.

The trustee will apply for the insurance or annuity contracts required on the life of each employee. If insurance is involved, there may be a requirement that each individual for whom a contract is purchased shall furnish evidence of his insurability satisfactory to the insurance company. In general, this means a medical examination for each new employee as he enters the plan and for each employee who receives an increase in his benefits under the plan. Most companies will issue this type of coverage without requiring medical examination or on the basis of a so-called "short form" of questionnaire concerning the individual's past medical history and the present condition of health. If the short form indicates any questionable condition, a medical examination would be required.

Most companies will issue these contracts within specified limits without medical examination under a practice which is commonly called "guaranteed issue."

When evidence of insurability is required, those who are uninsurable at standard rates (a) may have a retirement income policy issued charging a substandard extra premium, or (b) may have a retirement income policy issued at the regular premium providing the same amount of retirement income but with a smaller death benefit, or (c) may have a retirement annuity contract issued providing only the cash value as a death benefit prior to retirement.

There is no necessary maximum amount of income or death benefit under such a plan. If the amounts exceed for any individual the amount of insurance the company would be willing to underwrite, the additional amounts provided by the formula may be purchased from one or more additional insurance companies or arranged for through reinsurance contracts.

Plan Characteristics

It is common to provide that employees age 55 to 60 inclusive on the effective date of the plan will retire on the tenth anniversary of the plan, and employees age 61 and over will retire at age 70. This arrangement of retirement ages arises from two factors. The first is that the insurance companies do not ordinarily issue individual insurance and annuity contracts to run for shorter periods than 10 years. The second is that the use of a uniform retirement age 65 might involve a very large premium for a short period of time to provide the annuities for the older employees. The general result of such retirement ages is to delay the effectiveness of the retirement plan while it decreases the company's annual cost. It may be 10 years before any older employee can retire in such a plan. If some employees ought to be retired within that period, the plan to that extent will not serve its full purpose.

In most respects, this type of plan will be similar to the group permanent insurance plans already described.

It is not essential in the individual contract pension plan that the insurance or annuity contracts used provide the identical benefits of the plan. If the contracts provide more benefits than the plan calls for, the excess benefits may be paid to the trust and used as a credit against subsequent premium payments under the plan. To the extent that such excess benefits exist, the features of the insurance contract become, in effect, an investment of the trust fund. Whether they are desirable or practical may be weighed in the light of their nature as investments.

Premiums and Rates

The cost of this type of a plan providing benefits similar to a group permanent insurance plan should be substantially the same as the group permanent plan. The use of individual contracts, however, would tend to make the cost somewhat higher. The premiums, for instance, illustrated in Table 15 should be higher because of the additional sales and administrative expenses under this type of plan. Cash values on termination of employment will generally be lower in the early years as appears in Table 16. This higher cost may be offset by mortality savings arising from the medical examination required for insurance coverage and the elimination of the poor insurance risks from the plan.

In general the rates applicable to any contract are guaranteed for the lifetime of that contract, but no guarantees are made by the insurance company as to rates which will apply for contracts to be issued under the terms of the plan at any future date for new employees or increases in benefits.

TABLE 15

Individual Contracts
Annual Premiums per $1,000 of Insurance and $10 of Annuity
Retirement Age 65

Normal income 10 years certain and life

| Age at Entry | Insurance and Annuity || Retirement Annuity ||
	Males	Females	Males	Females
25	$ 31.39	$ 34.07	$ 26.49	$ 30.02
35	45.68	49.97	40.77	46.19
45	75.74	83.31	70.37	79.74
55	165.63	183.73	162.87	184.50

TABLE 16

Individual Contracts
Termination Values For $1,000 of Insurance and $10 of Annuity
Retirement Age 65—Male

(Normal income 10 years certain and life)

| End of Year | Age at Issue ||||
	25	35	45	55
1	$ 9	$ 21	$ 44	$ 119
2	34	58	107	259
3	60	97	171	405
5	114	177	304	715
10	261	395	673	1,610
Age 65	1,610	1,610	1,610	1,610

There will normally be no record of the aggregate financial position of a plan of this type as to premiums, interest earnings, and benefit payments. The contracts under this type of a plan are individual contracts and will be combined with similar contracts by the insurance company for the determination of experience and dividends which may become payable. Each plan receives the benefit of the average rate of dividend regardless of the plan's own experience. Thus the cost of this type of plan will generally be lower than the cost of a group permanent plan, if in actual experience the plan has more deaths prior to retirement than would normally be expected or if it has fewer deaths after retirement than would normally be expected. Conversely, if a plan of this type has fewer deaths prior to retirement and more deaths after retirement than would normally be expected, the plan will not receive full recognition for its own good experience and the cost would normally be higher than a group permanent contract.

Table 17 illustrates the monthly income that can be provided by $1,000 of cash value in various forms of annuity.

TABLE 17

Individual Contracts
Monthly Income per $1,000 of Cash Value

Retirement Age		Life Annuity	10 Years	20 Years	Cash
Male	Female	(No Death Benefit)	Certain and Life	Certain and Life	Refund Annuity
50	55	$4.32	$4.27	$4.07	$4.01
55	60	4.92	4.81	4.40	4.40
60	65	5.75	5.48	4.71	4.88
65	70	6.81	6.21	4.96	5.45

Administration of the Plan

The administration of the plan will be left to the employer, with the assistance of the consultant or the insurance agent or broker who is placing the insurance contracts. It may be expected that the commissions on the insurance contracts will be sufficiently large to justify the expectation that the agent will bear a large portion of the responsibility for keeping necessary records and furnishing other administrative services to the plan. It will also justify giving specialized individual service to the members of the plan that would not be practical in a larger group or a plan governed by a group contract.

Ordinary Life Insurance With Supplemental Fund

This type of plan is a combination of insurance with a trusteed self-administered plan or an auxiliary fund held by the insurance company. The insurance contracts used are the ordinary life or whole life plan of coverage which provides the amount of death benefits under the retirement plan. The policies are held by, and the premiums are paid through, the trustee. The insurance coverage is maintained until the employee reaches retirement age and the cash value then used to provide a part of the pension. The trust or insurance company will also accumulate in an auxiliary fund the additional sums necessary to purchase at retirement the balance of the retirement income benefits of the plan. Upon retirement enough cash is taken from the auxiliary fund to buy an annuity which, when combined with the annuity obtained from the ordinary life insurance cash value, will provide the total retirement income benefit of the plan. The insurance company may provide for the conversion of life insurance coverage to an annuity contract on or prior to the employee's retirement. It may also provide for the purchase of additional income at maturity at some advantage under the then current market cost of such retirement annuities at date of retirement.

The ordinary life coverage in this type of a plan may be had through individual contracts if the number of employees is small, or through a group permanent ordinary life contract. The group contract will, of course, have the advantages of group coverage including the automatic non-medical insurance. Since either individual or group insurance is available, this type of plan can be used for any size of group.

Plan Characteristics

The benefits under this type of plan are essentially similar to those of a group permanent plan or an individual contract pension trust using insurance and annuity coverage. The death benefits of the plan will be provided by the ordinary life insurance and the retirement incomes by the auxiliary fund accumulations plus the cash values of the ordinary life insurance at the employee's retirement date.

In contrast with insurance and annuity coverage where the death benefits for a few years prior to retirement exceed the face amount of insurance coverage, the death benefits under this type of a plan will be the face amount of insurance up to the date of conversion of the policy. The conversion will generally be at the date of retirement or as required by some companies the policy anniversary one year prior to retirement.

Termination values under this type of a plan will also differ from those in the group permanent coverage. Cash values are those of the ordinary life insurance and will be available on terminations. In addition there may be an accumulation in the auxiliary fund all or a part of which may be paid as a termination benefit. It is important to note, however, that the accumulations in the auxiliary fund are similar in nature to employer contributions to a group annuity plan. The accumulations may have been made on the basis of rates discounted for mortality. In that case there are theoretically no values available from the trust accumulation unless the employee is in good health.

Normally the cash values available under the life insurance would be available to provide paid-up insurance benefits after termination of employment. However, unless these cash values are converted into paid-up retirement annuities with death benefits not exceeding the amount of cash value, there will result from the termination a tax liability on the individual employee for the value of the life insurance coverages which he receives.

Premiums and Rates

The employer's cost under this type of plan will be a combination of the cost for the ordinary life insurance and the amount set aside for accumulation in the auxiliary fund. For the insurance portion of the plan, the insurance company's rates for regular life insurance will apply.

The amounts to be contributed to the auxiliary fund have no necessarily fixed method of computation. There is considerable freedom of choice on the part of the employer with the advice of his consultant or actuary to determine the method used in calculating these amounts and to permit flexibility in the employer's contributions.

Some insurance companies will hold the auxiliary fund for the employer, and will furnish all the necessary calculations of costs and liabilities under such a fund.

Typical rates for ordinary life insurance and for such accumulations on the basis of level premium costs to provide $1,000 of insurance are illustrated in Table 18. Contributions to the auxiliary fund provide an amount which, when added to the ordinary life value at age 65, produces the total maturity value for males $1,610 and for females $1,825.

TABLE 18

Ordinary Life Insurance
Illustrative Rates and Values
Annual Premiums and Cash Values

Age at Entry	Premiums	\multicolumn{6}{c}{Policy Values at End of Year}
		1	2	3	5	10	Age 65
25	$19.84	$ 0	$12	$26	$ 56	$134	$622
35	25.59	2	21	40	78	179	565
45	36.13	8	33	58	108	237	471
55	55.95	16	49	81	147	308	308

The insurance company will guarantee the rates for ordinary life insurance only with respect to policies which have already been purchased. Contracts to be purchased in the future would be subject to any change in the insurance company rates. With respect to the amount required to purchase an income upon retirement of the employee, the insurance company may offer a guarantee limited to a specific amount of annuity for each unit of face value of an ordinary life insurance in force. In the absence of this guarantee, the annuities may be purchased in the open market from the same or other insurance companies at the then current rate.

The rates and values for the auxiliary fund accumulations may be furnished by the insurance company. These would probably show the accumulations which should be in the fund at the end of each year with respect to each unit of retirement income. When the aggregate amount required to be in the fund has been calculated, the actual amount of the fund is deducted and the remainder is the amount which must be contributed by the employer that year. The result of this process is that the gains and losses for any source are adjusted each year to the correct theoretical amount that should be in the fund. The employer thus receives credit directly and immediately for any gains and also makes up immediately any losses with respect to the auxiliary fund.

Administration

In general, the administration of this type of plan is entirely in the hands of the employer with the assistance of his consultant, actuary, or insurance agent. If the standard level premium method of funding for an auxiliary trust fund is used, then the insurance company may furnish the necessary factors for the appropriate valuation. The insurance company or the consultant will presumably make the necessary calculations, if desired.

Alternate methods of funding for the auxiliary trust fund are available which will accelerate or retard the accumulation rate or give the employer flexibility in the amount of payments to be made from year to year. If the employer desires to make use of this opportunity for flexibility, he will want the assistance of an actuary for advice on how to obtain his objectives and assistance in making the necessary calculations.

Self-Administered Trust

As the name suggests, this type of plan is administered by the employer, by a committee appointed by the employer, or by a joint board of trustees for a plan covering the employees of more than one employer through the instrumentality of a trust. The fund is deposited with a trustee for the purpose of investment and accumulation with interest and payment of benefits to employees under the terms of the plan. The trust indenture is the formal document under which the plan operates. It is primarily a statement of the responsibilities of the trustee and the employer in the administration of the fund. It may include explicitly all the terms and conditions of the plan itself or the plan may be included only by reference. The plan is put into effect by the execution of the trust indenture by the employer and the trustee who may be either a corporate trustee or a group of individual trustees. The preparation of the trust indenture will require the assistance of legal counsel in drafting the language and acceptance of both the employer and the trustee.

In general there are no rules or restrictions as to the availability of this form of plan for financing retirement benefits. The absence of such restrictions obviously involves the employer, his legal counsel, and his actuarial counsel with more responsibility for the soundness of the plan and its operations. For larger groups having enough exposure to produce average mortality experience over a period of years, the same mortality discount may be assumed as in the group annuity type of plan. If the group is smaller, however, larger margins of safety should be used in determining the cost to allow for the absence of the average mortality experience from year to year.

Plan Characteristics

Retirement Income

Unit benefits per year of service may follow the same pattern as the group deferred annuity benefits, expressing the benefit as a percentage of earnings or a fixed dollar amount for each year of service. This type of plan sometimes expresses the unit benefit in terms of a fraction of the final average earnings such as 1/60th or 1/70th of the earnings for each year of service.

Employee contributions in a contributory plan are sometimes treated on the money-purchase basis while employer contributions may buy unit benefits. Employee contributions on this basis are in effect individual savings accounts for accounting purposes. Each employee's account is credited with his contributions and appropriate interest earnings at the average rate actually earned by the fund or at a stipulated rate declared by the fund management. Upon retirement, the employee's contributions will be used to provide an annuity on the basis of the capital value established for this purpose.

Date of Retirement

A normal retirement date may be established similar to the group deferred annuity plan, but the self-administered plan may have no specific normal retirement date, or may for cost purposes assume retirement at a different age. The benefits in accordance with the formula may be payable at retirement or at any age after qualification. The assumption might be made in such case that employees will retire on the average at age 67. The costs and liabilities might be determined as if age 67 were the normal retirement age.

Death Benefits

Death benefits may be provided under the plan by any reasonable or practical formula. If the plan is contributory, the death benefits might be the total accumulations of the employee's account at the date of death. Or the benefit might be a larger sum determined independently of the employee's contributions, such as one year's salary.

It is possible to provide substantial death benefits in excess of the employee contribution accumulation—as, for example, a flat amount of $1,000 or more, or an amount equal to one year's pay or a multiple of that amount. Such benefits involve an element of insurance risk which in the case of bad experience might draw heavily on the funds of the plan. In general, however, this is not a serious objection to death benefits if the group is large enough so that average experience may reasonably be expected. The risk of loss through heavy mortality is substantially offset or hedged by the possible gain in the annuity funds at the higher ages where the heavy mortality usually occurs.

Disability Benefits

It is common practice to include a monthly disability benefit in a self-administered plan. Because of the administrative difficulties in determining when and if the individual has qualified for disability benefits, insurance companies have been generally reluctant to underwrite this type of benefit. If the employer, however, understands that he is involved in any administrative difficulties that may arise, such benefits may be included in this type of plan.

Under the group deferred annuity type of plan, disability benefits are generally not made a part of the plan. Some insurance companies will underwrite a disability income benefit as a separate group insurance. In a deposit administration group annuity contract, disability benefits may be paid from the deposit fund at the instructions of the employer.

Benefits on Termination of Employment

On termination of employment, the employee will generally be assured of the return of at least his contributions with or without interest. It is not so common under a self-administered plan trust to provide for the vesting of benefits purchased by the employer contributions. Frequently one of the reasons for adopting this type of plan is the savings, or discount, which may be obtained from termination of employment and other sources of credit.

Discontinuance and Modification of the Plan

There are no standard provisions for discontinuance and modification of this type of plan such as have been developed for group annuity plans. Current regulations of the Internal Revenue Service require some specifications for the allocation of funds on the termination of the plan. The employer has wide latitude in establishing the rights of employees in the event of discontinuance as long as the provisions are otherwise acceptable to the Internal Revenue Service as nondiscriminatory and equitable. The available funds may therefore be allocated for the protection of successive preferential classes defined by the plan so long as the classification is not discriminatory.

Premiums and Rates

The costs under a self-administered trusteed plan will normally be determined by the actuary or determined by the employer with the advice of the actuary. There is, therefore, a very wide latitude in establishing the method of calculating costs and the program for funding of this type of plan. The standard methods used by insurance companies for group annuity or individual contracts may be used in this type of plan.

The element of costs used by the insurance companies in determining their rates for fully insured benefits are limited to mortality, interest, and loading for expenses and contingency margins. In a self-administered trusteed plan other elements may come into consideration. Some of these elements are mentioned below with a brief indication of their effect on total costs.

> (1) *Rates of Retirement:* This factor will probably decrease costs on the assumption that the average age of retirement will be higher than a normal retirement age 65. If the assumed average age of retirement should be a lower age, the cost would of course be increased.

(2) *Salary Increase Factors:* If the benefits are based on final average salary over a period of years, this final salary will generally be higher than the current rate of salary for active employees at any point of time. An assumption that salaries will increase as the employees approach retirement will increase the cost of the plan. If a salary increase factor is used, a discount may also be used for turnover. These factors will in part offset each other.

(3) *Turnover or Withdrawal Discount:* Application of this factor assumes that no benefits or reduced benefits will be available to employees who terminate employment before retirement date. Therefore, the cost would generally be reduced by this element.

(4) *Death and Disability Benefits:* If death and disability benefits are provided, they will of course increase the cost of the plan.

All of these factors and others which may be taken into account in determining the cost of the self-administered trusteed plan will presumably be based on the company's prospective experience and will be determined by a study made by the actuary of the past experience of the employee group or based on his judgment as to reasonable expectations.

The actual experience of a particular group of employees included in the plan will be examined annually or periodically at intervals of say three or five years and appropriate adjustments will be made in future contributions to the plan for any gains or losses which derive from prior experience. A self-administered plan permits the direct and immediate recognition of gains or losses in the operation of the plan based on the group's experience. In effect, the self-administered plan is an insurance operation in itself. The employer assumes the obligation of making up any losses and gets the advantage of any gains. The determination of the basis of financial operation is up to the employer with the advice of his actuary.

Administration of the Plan

In general, the necessary forms and procedures to be used in the administration of the plan are similar to those which would be required for group deferred annuity plans. All of the materials and methods for the administration of the plan will have to be established by the employer with the advice of his consultant or actuary or the trustee.

Underwriting

Since there is no insurance company involved in any of the risk or the administration of this plan, there are no established rules for minimum or maximum benefits in regard to proper terms and procedures. The employer, therefore, relies heavily on the advice of his consultant and actuary in the establishment of all the elements of the plan which may contribute to its success or failure.

For example, there is no limit on number of lives that would be appropriate for such a plan. Theoretically, there is no objection to the establishment of a self-administered plan for a small group of employees, if such a plan can be established with reasonable safety to the employer and employee and provided adequate margins are used in determining the appropriate contributions to the plan.

Variable Annuities

Variable annuities are a relatively late development in the pension field. The earliest plans have now been in existence for just over 10 years. The experience of the earliest plans may now be said to have continued for a long enough period to have established the validity and practicality of variable annuities.

Two basic types of variable annuity plans are in existence. In one type, the amount of benefit payable to an employee upon retirement is geared to the changes in the Bureau of Labor Statistics cost-of-living index. The amount payable at retirement is the amount purchased or allocated for the employee during his active membership with each purchase or allocation increased or decreased in proportion to the change in the cost-of-living index between the date of the allocation and his retirement date. Subsequent to retirement the amount payable is adjusted periodically, at least once a year, for any significant change in the cost-of-living index.

This type of plan could be established and operated exactly as any other self-administered trusteed plan. The effect of the change in the cost of living is just another factor in determining the amount of benefit and costs under the plan. The employer, who pays the basic or residual costs of the plan, will bear the cost or risk of increases in benefits that result from changes in the cost-of-living. The insurance companies, under the new separate accounts procedures, are or will shortly be prepared to handle this type of variable annuity plan.

The other type of plan is one in which part of the retirement income is payable to the employee in a fixed amount and part of the income is payable in the form of an equity annuity, the amount of which is determined by the performance of a common stock investment fund. The amount of equity benefit would be determined by a revaluation of the investments of the fund and will reflect increases in the market value of the underlying investments as well as investment income in excess of the assumed interest rate. The combined income for an individual might be variable depending upon the results of a single balanced investment fund with an appropriate balance between fixed dollar and equity investment.

The equity benefit type of plan can only be administered through a trust fund. The insurance company, under the separate accounts procedures, would be able to furnish the equity investments, but as yet they are not generally able to automatically adjust the benefit payments under the plan in proportion to the underlying common stock investment fund results.

Based on historical analysis, there has been shown to be a substantial long-term correlation between the income from an annuity based on a common stock fund (adjusted for both investment income and market appreciation or depreciation) with the corresponding trend in the cost-of-living index. Changes in the value of the common stock fund investments from year to year have been much larger than the corresponding changes in the cost-of-living. Therefore, a balanced combination of two incomes, one a fixed income and the other an income based on an equity fund, is required to produce variations from year to year, which are not only comparable in direction but roughly comparable in size to cost-of-living changes.

A reasonable balance between fixed dollar and equity dollar income is required in order to produce reasonably good results. If there were too much in fixed dollar benefits, the changes in total income would not be sufficient to match cost-of-living changes. If there were too much in common stock or equity benefits, the changes in total income would be too large to produce a satisfactorily stable income for a retired person.

Historical analysis has also shown that over a sufficiently long period of time, say 20 years or more, the yields from the common stock investments have been significantly higher than the yields from fixed dollar securities such as bonds or mortgages. If this trend continues in the future, a fund invested in diversified common stocks as a supplement to the fixed dollar fund or a single balance fund should produce substantially lower costs to the employer for the same benefits.

As between the two types of variable benefits, the benefits based on the cost-of-living index places the burden of the investment risk on the employer and guarantees the employee an income directly related to the cost-of-living changes. The equity type of benefit on the other hand, relieves the employer of all investment risk and may or may not produce for the employee a close correlation between his retirement income and cost-of-living changes. On the other hand, it may give the employee substantially more income.

Certain practical considerations seem to be essential to the satisfactory operation of an equity type of variable benefit plan. The amount of benefit payable depends on the changes in value of the underlying investment fund. The equity plan, therefore, requires that benefits be funded as they accrue to the employee during his active membership in small units over a number of years. Without the funding, there would be no possible market appreciation and hence no possibility of adequately reflecting changes in the cost of living.

In order to produce a reasonable benefit for each member of the plan, there must be a balance or division of his benefits for both past service and future service in reasonable proportions between fixed dollar benefits and equity benefits. Satisfactory results cannot be obtained by providing for a portion of future service benefits only to be in equity annuities. It would take too long before the employee would have an adequate portion of his total income in such annuities.

It is necessary to avoid funding or investment for any one individual at one time in the equity market, which might be at either a high or a low extreme in the market. For the funding of large amounts of income such as the accumulated past service benefits, the funding should be spread over a minimum period of five years in order to get a reasonable amount of averaging of the market.

In an equity type of benefit, the amount of benefit already funded will vary from year to year following the changes in the value of the underlying investment fund. The accounting can be conveniently established and carried in terms of units or shares in the fund. This would generally be more practical than adjusting the dollar benefits for members each year.

Mechanically, it would be quite possible to distribute among employees any credits which are usually considered employer credits arising from other sources such as deferred retirement, termination of employment, and mortality experience. Since such credits arise from persons who have left the membership group, it may be considered undesirable to distribute such credits among persons remaining in the plan. On the other hand, if the potential gain or loss from any such source of credit is not large, as in the case of mortality gains or losses in a large group of employees, such an element may be included with the investment element in the distribution to employees without material effect.

It is of vital importance that the employee covered by such a variable annuity plan fully understand the characteristics of the plan and the results that might develop. It is essential that the employee be prepared to accept decreases in benefits resulting from market depreciation as a normal result to be expected from the operation of this type of plan.

ANALYSIS OF FINANCING METHODS
Reflecting the Most Common Practices for Each Method

Elements of Plan	Group Deferred Annuities	Group Deposit Administration	Group Permanent Life Insurance	Individual Contract Pension Trust	Ordinary Life & Supplemental Fund	Self-Administered Trust
Underwriting						
Size of group	10 or more	10 or more	10 or more	No limit, usually less than 100	Any size	Generally 100 or more, smaller number with due allowance for safety factors.
Formal Documents Used						
Descriptive booklet for employees, plus	Group Annuity contract. Employee certificates.	Group Annuity contract. Employee certificates. Plan.	Group insurance contract. Employee certificates.	Plan Trust indenture. Insurance contracts.	Plan Trust indenture. Insurance contracts.	Plan. Trust indenture.
Plan Characteristics						
Retirement benefit formula	Unit benefit per year of service Money purchase	Any form	Fixed Amount Percent of final pay Unit benefit per year	Fixed amount Percent of final pay Unit benefit per year	Fixed amount Percent of final pay Unit benefit per year	Any form
Death benefits before retirement	Return of employee contributions	Return of employee contributions	$1,000 per $10 monthly income.	$1,000 per $10 monthly income.	$1,000 per $10 monthly income.	Any form or amount
Death benefits after retirement	None Modified cash refund	Any form	5 or 10 years certain and life	5 or 10 years certain and life	5 or 10 years certain	Any form
Disability benefits available	Early retirement benefit Possible separate insurance plan	Any amount	Early retirement benefit	Early retirement benefit	Any amount	Any amount

FINANCING A PENSION PLAN

Vesting of benefits on termination of employment	All or part of benefits purchased	All or part of benefits accrued	All or part of benefit provided by cash value	All or part of benefit provided by cash value	All or part of benefit accrued	All or part of benefit accrued

Costs and Experience Factors

Initial premiums or payments to plan	Fixed by insurance company.	Determined by employer and actuary.	Fixed by insurance company	Fixed by insurance company	Insurance premiums fixed by insurance company. Fund payments determined by employer and actuary.	Determined by employer and actuary.
Interest earnings credited	Averaged	Averaged	Averaged	Averaged	Insurance-averaged Fund —own or averaged	Own earnings solely
Mortality experience credited	Own weighted by size of group	Own experience solely	Own weighted by size of group	Averaged	Insurance-averaged Fund —own	Own experience solely
Expenses incurred	Partly averaged and partly own	Partly averaged and partly own	Partly averaged and partly own	Averaged	Partly averaged and partly own	Own expense solely

Responsibility for Reserves, Contingency Funds and Investments

Responsibility rests in	Insurance company.	Insurance company and employer.	Insurance company.	Insurance company.	Insurance company and employer.	Employer only

Administration of Plan

Procedures furnished by	Insurance company.	Insurance company and consultant.	Insurance company.	Insurance company.	Employer and agent or consultant	Employer or actuary

CHAPTER 4

PENSION COSTS AND COST EXPERIENCE

By WILLIAM W. FELLERS

Reducing Pension Costs

The "cost" of a pension plan depends on what benefits are payable, when the benefits are payable, and the expenses that arise in connection with the actual payment of these benefits. One method utilized to reduce an employer's outlay for a pension plan below the so-called true "cost," determined as actual benefits plus actual administrative expenses, is through building up a retirement fund.

By putting into the fund an amount each year to pay for pensions when they come due, a company is able to take advantage of the interest earned by the fund to reduce its cost for the eventual pension benefit, and the interest earned can become a sizable amount. To illustrate, let us consider the case of a certain mythical Mr. X. He may be considered to be fairly typical of the average person covered under a pension plan. In particular, we know that Mr. X will live about fifteen years after retirement. If he is going to receive a pension of $100 a month, the total outlay in pension benefits comes to $18,000 ($100 monthly, times 12, times 15). But let us set up a fund for Mr. X when he retires, so that the fund together with the interest on the fund will be sufficient to pay out his $100-monthly pension benefit. If the fund can earn 3 percent interest, the amount required in the fund for Mr. X would be about $14,600. Hence, the outlay for pensions or the "cost" would be reduced some 19 percent because of setting up such a fund. Also, there is another step that may be taken to utilize this factor of interest even more, and that is to make payments into the fund before Mr. X retires, so that when he retires these payments together with interest thereon will have accumulated to the $14,600 amount noted above. If equal annual payments (with interest compounded at 3 percent) were to be put into the fund on behalf of Mr. X over a period of 30 years, the annual payments would be approximately $300 a year, and thirty of them would amount to some $9,000. This would reduce the outlay or "cost" by 50 percent (going from the $18,000 of potential benefit payments down to the $9,000 outlay for those benefit payments). Consequently, this factor of interest, that is made possible by building a fund, can have a considerable effect on the cost of the pension benefits.[1]

Another way, and probably a more important way of reducing costs, is in the tax advantages gained under a qualified plan. This involves the company securing approval of the plan under Section 401(a) of the Internal Revenue Code and then being able to claim as a tax deduction company contributions made within certain limits, under Section 404. For example, in the case of a company which pays 50¢ out of every dollar of income in taxes, this means that the contributions made towards a qualified pension plan would only cost the company 50¢ for each dollar contributed. By the same token, from an individual's standpoint, if he wanted to purchase an equivalent pension benefit in the open market (usually by purchasing an annuity from an insurance company), he would have to buy this benefit from his net income after taxes. Consequently, there is a savings in taxes from the individual's standpoint if his company makes available the contributions to provide for him a pension benefit, not to mention the savings involved because the company can do the job on a wholesale basis rather than on the more costly retail basis. In this connection it should also be noted that the interest earned by the fund (as well as any capital appreciation in trust fund assets) is tax-free under a qualified funded plan. Of course, when the pension becomes payable, it is then subject to the income tax, but the tax effect thereof is minimized, first to the extent that the pensioner is in a lower tax bracket than the company for which he worked, second to the extent that the pensioner is in a lower tax bracket *after* retirement than *before* retirement, and third to the extent that the pensioner over a certain age may receive a larger personal allow-

---

[1] It might be argued by some that the interest earnings should not be considered as a cost-reducing factor in a pension plan since if the funds had been invested elsewhere they would have earned interest.

ance before his income is subject to tax than he did before he attained that age.

In the last paragraph we mentioned the idea of "costs" in a different way than the idea of "contributions" being made to a fund, and it may be well at this point to make a distinction between the two concepts involved. To repeat again what has already been indicated earlier, the "cost" is the outlay for benefits provided under a plan, plus administrative expenses and *less* any interest earned by a fund. Consequently, the larger the fund available to earn interest, the lower the "cost"; by the same token the larger the "contribution" initially to build up such a fund, the lower the long-range "cost" of the benefit program. Therefore, the level of contributions is not necessarily an indication of "costs," unless there is no fund. On the other hand, as a practical matter from the standpoint of a company contributing towards a benefit program, the level of "contributions" is thought of as the current level of "costs," and so, throughout the balance of this chapter, these two words will be used interchangeably, but the meaning will generally be that of "contributions" as described in this paragraph.

There are many other factors involved in the determination of the costs of a pension plan, such as the age assumed at which employees may retire, how long employees may live after retirement (involving mortality tables and life expectations), terminations from employment other than for retirement (involving withdrawal rates), and future rates of earnings (where pensions are based on average earnings and/or when the Social Security benefit is involved in the benefit formula). These factors all enter into the problem of determining pension costs and will be discussed later on in this chapter. But first we will examine some of the methods used in deriving the level of costs and then review some concrete examples based on fairly recent experience.

Funding Methods

There have been adopted a number of labor agreements that set forth a specific method of determining the level of contributions for the pension plan which is provided by the agreement. These and other actuarial cost methods are respectively called "terminal cost," "unit cost," "entry-age-normal-cost," "aggregate cost," etc. Some of these are described as follows:

Terminal-Cost Method

The actuarial mechanics of this method are: (1) determine the present value of future benefits payable to the pensioners; (2) subtract from this actuarially determined amount the value of the assets on hand; and (3) contribute to the fund (held by a trustee or insurance company) the amount needed to keep the assets on hand at least equal to the value of future pension benefits currently being paid to pensioners. To simplify, on the assumption that the interest and mortality factors used by the actuary conform to the actual experience, this method involves essentially contributing an amount equal to the one-sum value of the employee's benefits at the time he terminates active employment by retirement. This is where the designation "terminal cost" comes from, since contributions may be thought of as being made on behalf of the covered employees at the time they terminate employment by retirement.

With respect to the characteristics of the method itself, it should be noted that in good times, when money is more plentiful and when jobs are plentiful, the tendency is to dissuade people from retiring, but this is usually the time the company could best afford to pay for the retirements which are not, however, occurring. On the other hand, when jobs become less plentiful and money is harder to get in order to pay for retiring employees, the pressure from many sources is—to the extent seniority rules permit—to retire those employees who are eligible in order to make available their jobs to the younger employees who would otherwise be laid off. This is a major criticism of the terminal cost method. Another criticism of this method is that no advance provision is being made in the fund for employees before their retirement.

Unit-Cost Method

By this method, a unit of pension, such as 1 percent of salary, is assumed to accrue each year, and a contribution is made, equal to the value of the unit of pension. This method is also used in the "fixed contribution" or "money purchase" type of plan and is frequently used in the funding of insured group annuities, as well as occasionally in trust fund plans. A disadvantage of the method may lie in the fact that the cost for each individual employee increases each year because of his advancing age and decreasing period to retirement, although for a given group of employees, the replacement of the older employees, who retire, by younger employees, may offset, on the average, this disadvantage when viewed for an individual employee in the group.

Entry-Age-Normal-Cost Method

The costs under this method are separated into two parts, one part attributable to service after the effective date or anniversary of the plan, and another part attributable to service prior to the effective date or anniversary of the plan. The portion of costs attributable to service after the effective date of the plan is designated as the "current cost" or "normal cost," and is actuarially determined to represent the going annual cost of the plan on the assumption that funding for the plan had been in effect for many years in the past. Therefore, the portion of cost attributable to service prior to the effective date of the plan (over and above assets on hand) represents an unfunded accumulation of normal costs from past years which were not paid in those years because there was no plan.

Level-Cost Method

By this method, the ultimate pension for each employee is determined, based on his present earnings, and a level cost is paid each year until retirement, of sufficient amount to provide the total ultimate pension. This method, by level annual premiums, is in general use for individual insurance policies and group permanent insurance with retirement income features; a few trust fund plans also follow the level-cost method. A main disadvantage of the method is that when a plan is being initiated, it involves very high annual premiums for the employees at the older ages, with only a few years in which to meet the whole pension liability.

Aggregate-Cost Method

By this method, the present value of all future benefits less accumulated funds, and the present value of all future salaries (or employee years, or benefits weighted by annuity-to-retirement factors) are ascertained. Dividing the first amount by the second gives the "percentage" of salaries (or years or benefits) required to be contributed to provide the benefits. The method is used for some deposit administration contracts and some trust-fund plans. Under this method: (a) there is no usual subdivision of past-service cost and normal cost; (b) it is in the nature of level-cost funding, but on a collective basis rather than on an individual basis, with the "percentage" used in deriving the contribution level tending to decrease very gradually as the undefined past-service cost becomes funded.

Cost Examples

Now let us turn to some examples which should help to illustrate some of the actuarial cost methods described above, as well as the level of initial contributions (designated as costs) for certain typical benefit formulae.

In Table A the illustrative costs are set down for a particular group of employees. These results are on the "entry-age-normal-cost" method for a number of different benefit formulas to illustrate the average annual cost per employee involved. While the group of employees you are particularly interested in may have some of the characteristics of this group, it is very unlikely that your group would have all of them. The main determining characteristics for initial cost considerations are the age composition, the service composition, the composition by sex and race, frequently the level of earnings, and what the probable future might hold for the particular group involved because of the changing economic picture.

In Table A illustrative costs have been shown for four different types of benefit formulas. Formula 1 is basically the automotive type of negotiated benefit formula providing a monthly pension of $2.80 per year of service. Formula 2 is the flat $50 monthly pension, with the amount of benefit reduced pro rata for less than 25 years of service at retirement. Formula 3 is the Steel type of negotiated benefit formula of 1 percent of final ten year average compensation per year of service less $80 per month, with a minimum monthly pension of $2.50 per month per year of service up to 35 years of service.

Formula 4 has not been generally followed by any of the labor settlements. It is the more traditional or classical type of benefit formula without any Social Security offset and based upon 1 percent of earnings (career average) per year of service. Without

TABLE A

Illustrative Costs of Certain Pension Formulas
Determined by Entry-Age-Normal-Cost Method

	Formula 1		Formula 2		Formula 3		Formula 4	
A. Formula	$2.80 monthly per year of service[1]		$50 monthly[1]		1% of earnings per year of service less $80 per month[2]		1% of earnings per year of service	
	Annual amount per capita	Cents per hour[3]	Annual amount per capita	Cents per hour[3]	Annual amount per capita	Cents per hour[3]	Annual amount per capita	Cents per hour[3]
B. Initial total annual cost ("normal cost" plus budget for "past service")								
(1) If "past service" is amortized at 10% per year	$425	21.3¢	$230	11.5¢	$380	19.0¢	$510	25.5¢
(2) If "past service" is amortized over a 30-year period	290	14.5	160	8.0	260	13.0	350	17.5
(3) If interest only is paid on "past service"	240	12.0	130	6.5	220	11.0	290	14.5

PENSION COSTS AND COST EXPERIENCE 153

C. Basic assumptions

(1) Composition of employee group:

Age group	Proportion of employees in age group	Average annual earnings	Average years of service
Under 35	42%	$3,800	1
35-50	33	4,100	10
50-65	25	4,200	25
65 and over	—	—	—
All ages	100%	$4,000	8

Average age: 40
Average age at hire: 32

(2) 1965 Projected Annuity Mortality Table—a table prepared from the basic Ga-1951 table with loading removed and then projected 14 years by scale C.
(3) 3% interest compounded annually.
(4) Normal retirement at age 65. If retirement is, on the average, at age 66 in the future, the above costs would reduce by about 7%.
(5) A moderate rate of withdrawal was used for ages under 50.
(6) A 6% margin was included for disability. Whether a strict or loose method is used in administering this benefit will determine its ultimate cost.
(7) No margin included for administrative expenses. The appropriate margin might be 4% of the net costs for groups of sufficient size.

[1] Benefits commence at age 65, or earlier under certain conditions (after 15 or more years of service, subject to total and permanent disability).
[2] Subject to a minimum of $2.50 per month per year of service to 35 years. Since the average earnings are $4,000 per year, 1% of this is $40 which comes to $1,320 for 33 years of service at retirement (assuming age 32 at entry), from which is deducted $80 per month to result in a net annual pension of $360 by the 1% formula. Hence the $2.50 minimum formula would control, producing an annual pension of $990 ($2.50 × 12 × 33). In fact, the minimum formula would generally control until the level of annual earnings exceeds $5,900 for the person with 33 years of service at retirement.
[3] On the basis of a 2,000-hour work year. If the work year were only 1,800 hours, these costs-per-hour results would be more than 10% higher than those above.

taking into account the Social Security benefits as an offset, it is interesting to note that the level of cost for Formula 4 is higher—under the assumption for Table A—than the level of cost for any of the other three benefit formulae.

An important element in the initial levels of cost is the method adopted for funding the "past service." In Section B of Table A the costs have been shown on three bases (1) on the assumption that "past service" is amortized at 10 percent per year (the maximum permitted as a tax deduction by one criterion used by the Internal Revenue Service); (2) on the assumption that the "past service" is amortized over a 30-year period (the funding basis found in many agreements negotiated with the United Automobile Workers); and (3) on the assumption that "interest only" is paid on the "past service liability" so that there will be no increase because of imputed interest on this item.

The cents-per-hour result has been a popular cost index for the purpose of union negotiations. Consequently, the cents-per-hour results are shown beside the annual per capita costs. However, it should be appreciated that the cents-per-hour index is not a very stable relationship. It can only reflect the situation at a particular time on the basis of a given average work year involving a certain number of hours. 2,000 hours has been used for purposes of illustration in Table A, but if the work year is only 1,500 hours in some future year, for example, the cents-per-hour results could increase by as much as one-third. A generally more stable cost index is the average per capita cost which is also shown in Table A.

Table B has been prepared to show in the form of a graph the annual costs of a pension plan on the basis of two different actuarial cost methods as well as by paying for pensions only as due (i.e., "pay-as-you-go"). The pension plan formula used as a basis for this graph is Formula 2 in Table A. It provides a pension benefit of $50 monthly. Also, it is assumed that there are 500 non-retired employees in the group, and the group was assumed to have the same characteristics as the group used for the purpose of determining the illustrative average per capita costs shown in Table A.

The dotted line (A) in Table B represents the amount of pension disbursements each year payable to employees who have retired from the original group of 500. In the first year, the level

TABLE B

Graph of Annual Pension Costs by Certain Actuarial Cost Methods

Basis: Benefit Formula 2, from Table A, $50 monthly from age 65 for 500 employees following age and service composition as indicated in Table A.

(A) .... Annual pension outgo on pay-as-you-go
(B) – – – – Terminal or funding-at-retirement method
(C) ———— Annual normal cost plus 30-year amortization of past service

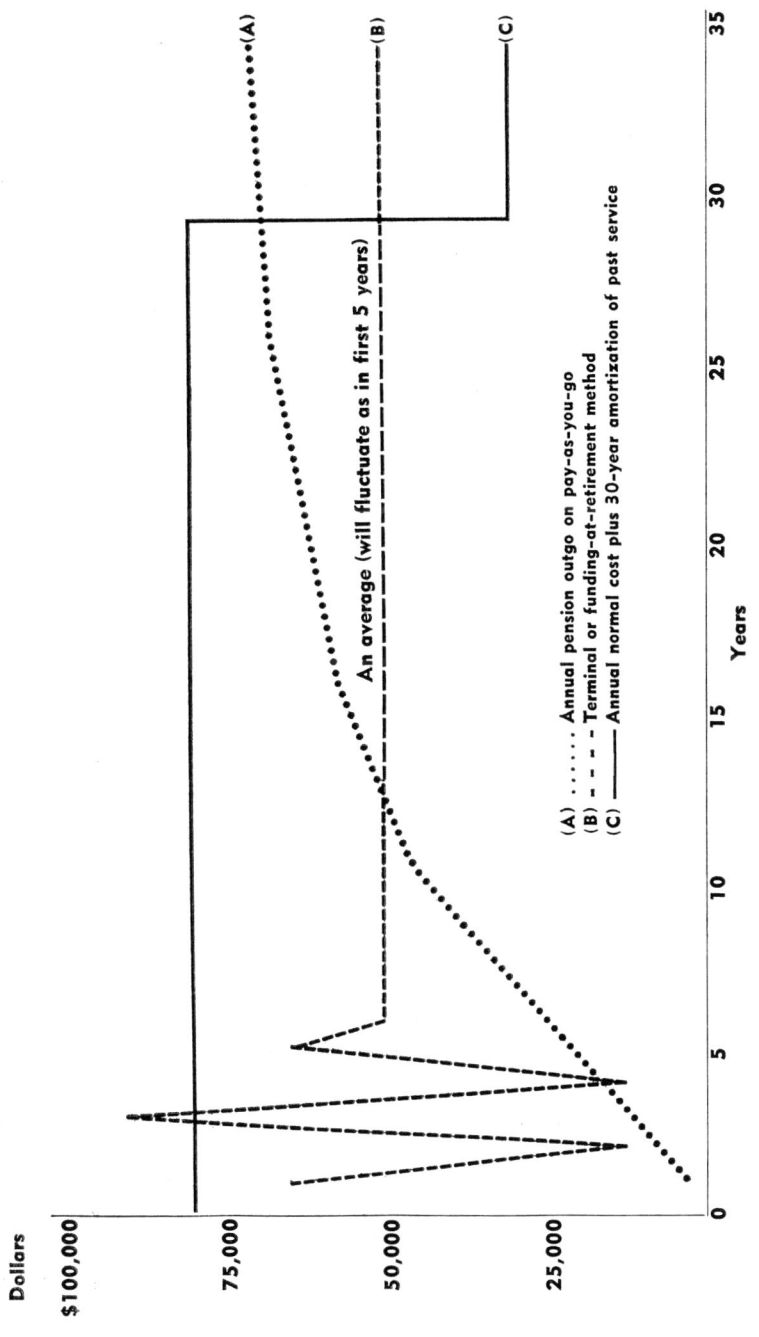

of annual pension payments is some $6,000; in the tenth year this will have grown to about $42,000; and in the 30th year it might become about $70,000. This might level off ultimately at about $75,000 to $90,000 a year or a cost of $150 to $180 per year for each of the 500 active employees. However, this is not considered an "actuarial" method since no fund is built up in excess of current benefit payments. It is simply a payment of pensions by the employer as they fall due, commonly referred to as the "pay-as-you-go" arrangement.

There is no assurance to retired employees in the form of a fund that benefit payments can or will be made in the future. The lack of security is a main reason why this pay-as-you-go method has not been followed in very many of the plans that have been initiated on a formal basis. There are many other reasons too; one apparent reason is that the costs on this basis are ultimately higher than they would be if some arrangement for advance funding is used. This is because under an advance funding arrangement, both the higher early contributions to the fund and the interest earned by the fund help to reduce the ultimate "cost" of the pensions, as emphasized earlier.

The broken line (B) on the graph illustrates the one-sum funding at retirement method or terminal cost method. This method, as a minimum, is being used by a number of steel companies. Under it, in essence, the one-sum amount necessary to pay the lifetime retirement benefit is determined for each person who retires. Then this amount is put into the fund. There is some assurance by reason of the fund thereby created that retirement benefits will be paid even though the company may go out of business, or terminate the plan. However, there is a major objection to this cost method which is brought out by the graph. Note how jagged this line (B) is indicated to be. The computation was made after the first 5 years by 5-year age groups, and so there is considerably more smoothing after the first 5 years than would actually be the case. Other difficulties of this method relative to the pressures of economic conditions have been discussed previously.

Now, let us look at solid line (C) in Table B. This represents the normal cost plus the 30-year budget for past service approach which is currently being used by many companies in funding their negotiated pension plans. We have again assumed a constant group of 500 active employees. After 30 years the "past service" is paid up, and the level of costs becomes lower than under the other two methods. The costs are lower because a larger fund than for line (B) has been built-up, and the interest from this larger fund is available to help provide the pension benefits. It should be noted, also, that this is an extremely flexible cost method. In good years, considerably more than the normal cost plus the 30-year budget towards past service may be put into the fund. In poor years, considerably less than the normal cost plus the 30-year budget may be put in the fund. The solid line is shown merely to indicate the level of annual costs if the 30-year budget were adhered to strictly.

In Table C another graph indicates the fund development on the basis of the two actuarial cost methods of advance funding from Table B. The fund that emerges after 30 years on the basis of the "terminal" method is from one-half to one-third of the fund developed on the basis of paying the normal cost and amortizing the past service over the 30-year period. The reason is primarily this: In the first case the fund represents reserve assets only in respect of retired employees; in the second case the fund represents reserves not only for the retired employees but also for active employees. Ultimately, on the basis of fully meeting the past service, the fund might level out at about $1,300,000. This would mean that the interest of about $39,000 (at 3 percent of $1,300,000) plus the normal cost of about $31,000 would exactly balance the ultimate pension outgo, on the average, of the possible potential of $70,000 per year. In other words, the interest from a fund can go a long way towards supporting the pension load, and the fund at the same time provides considerable assurance that the pension benefit payments will be met.

Now, let us follow through the changes of an illustrative negotiated pension agreement that was first settled in 1949 on the basis of a $100 monthly pension less the Social Security benefit. In 1950 the Social Security benefits were increased considerably, and so the cost of the pensions appeared to reduce; but in 1951 the pension agreement was renegotiated to the $125 monthly pension level less Social Security and this brought the level of pensions pretty much back into line with what was originally negotiated. Then in 1952 the Social Security benefits were again increased, and so in 1953 the benefit formula was changed to $1.75 per month

TABLE C
Graph of Fund Development by Two Actuarial Cost Methods

Basis: Level of benefits and costs shown in Table B for group of 500 active employees and retirements from the group. Retirement benefits of $50 monthly.

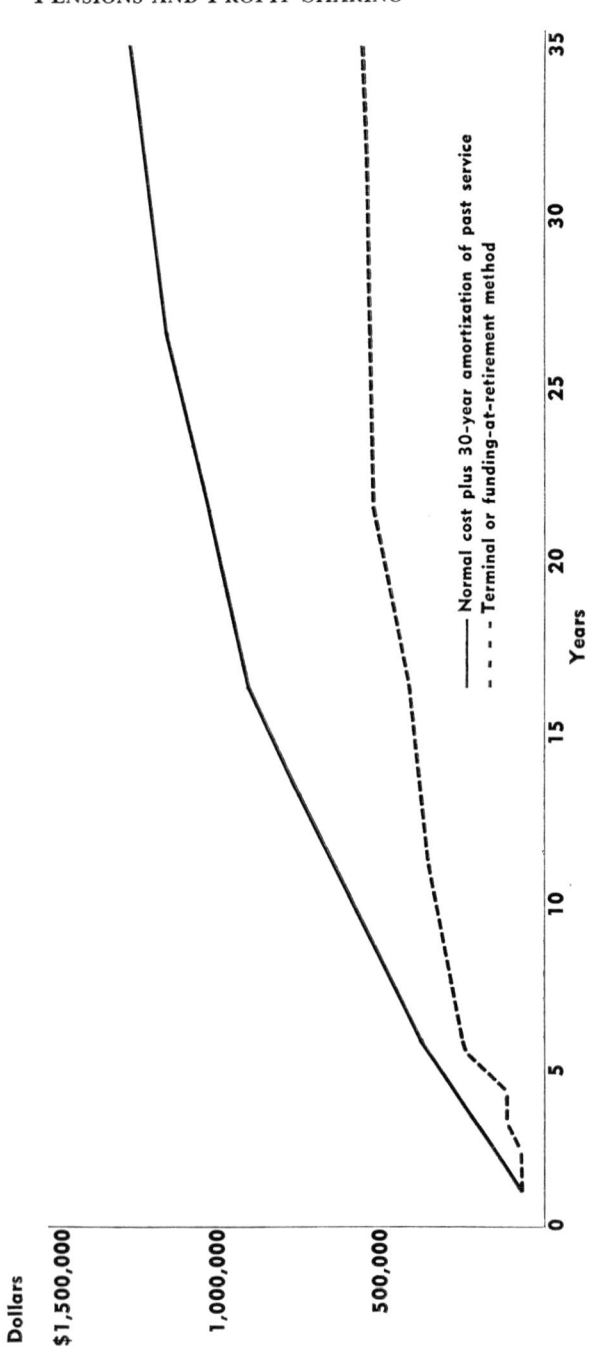

——— Normal cost plus 30-year amortization of past service
- - - Terminal or funding-at-retirement method

per year of service up to 30 years. You will note that this change meant that the level of pension under the formula became independent of the Social Security Act so that any future increases in Social Security would not reduce the amounts payable under the revised pension formula. Then in 1955 the $1.75 benefit unit was increased to $2.25, in 1959 it was increased to $2.40 for service through 1958 and $2.50 for service thereafter, and in 1962 the benefit unit was increased to $2.80 for *all* service. For those retired, however, the 1959 change only granted an increase in the benefit unit from $2.25 to $2.35, and no increase in benefit unit was given to those already retired in the 1962 benefit increase. Hence as the number receiving pensions increased, the cost of providing these ex-employees increased benefits became more significant and so was not negotiated. The more detailed cost results for this example are shown in Table D. The first six items of this table show the number of covered employees, their average potential pension benefit (including pensions being paid), the "actuarial deficiency" (or liability attributable to prior service, if no fund existed), the fund, the resulting net deficiency, and the normal cost for selected years 1949 through 1962.

Item 7 of Table D is a development of what is designated as the minimum contribution requirement, and this has been derived on the basis of paying the normal cost and budgeting the deficiency over a 30-year period. For example, the minimum amount came to $68,500 in 1949 and was made up of the normal cost of $50,000 and the 30-year budget of $18,500 for the initial deficiency. However, as noted in item 9, a contribution of $75,000 was actually made, and so this meant that an additional payment of $6,500 was made over and above the minimum first-year requirement which was taken into account in the development of the second-year minimum contribution. The $6,500 has been taken into account first by increasing the deficiency net by $6,500 (since $6,500 less would have been in the fund if only the minimum had been contributed in the first year), and second by deducting the $6,500 from the sum of the normal cost plus the 29-year budget for the net deficiency. The method involved would be the same if a different period had been used for funding the past service, and it should be noted that the two minimum requirements implied by the Internal Revenue Service of (1) keeping the deficiency from increasing and (2) having a fund at least equal to the

160   PENSIONS AND PROFIT SHARING

TABLE D
Illustrative Valuation Results for Selected Years 1949-1962
Basis: Active group of 500 employees and pensioners from that group
Applicable benefit formula and selected years

Item (1)	$100 monthly less Social Security 1949 (2)	$100 monthly less Social Security 1950 (3)	$125 monthly less Social Security 1951 (4)	$125 monthly less Social Security 1952 (5)	$1.75 monthly per year of service to 30 years 1953 (6)	$2.25 monthly per year of service 1955 (7)	$2.40 monthly per year of service thru 1958 plus $2.50 monthly per year thereafter 1959 (8)	$2.80 monthly per year of service 1962 (9)
1. Number of covered employees								
a. Non-retired	500	500	500	500	500	500	500	500
b. Retired	0	10	12	15	20	25	45	60
2. Average annual pension payable	$600[a]	$300[a]	$600[b]	$540[b]	$600	$900	$1,000	$1,150
3. Gross actuarial deficiency								
a. Non-retired	$400,000	$195,000	$475,000	$460,000	$560,000	$900,000	$1,110,000	$1,345,000
b. Retired		30,000	70,000	80,000	110,000	200,000	350,000	480,000
c. Total	400,000	225,000	545,000	540,000	670,000	1,100,000	1,460,000	1,825,000

4. Assets in fund	—	76,000	112,000	190,000	270,000	370,000	760,000	1,025,000
5. Net deficiency (3 minus 4)	400,000	149,000	433,000	350,000	400,000	730,000	700,000	800,000
6. Annual normal cost								
a. Total amount	50,000	25,000	50,000	45,000	50,000	67,500	72,000	80,000
b. Amount per non-retired employee	100	50	100	90	100	135	144	160
7. Minimum contribution								
a. Additional payments made[1]	—	6,500	14,800	22,800	39,100	—	9,600	7,600
b. Adjusted net deficiency (5 + 7a)	400,000	155,500	447,800	372,800	439,100	730,000	709,600	807,600
c. Requisite budget on 7b[2]	18,500	7,200	22,000	18,700	22,600	36,500	37,000	41,200
d. Normal cost of 6a + 7c − 7a	68,500	25,700	57,200	40,900	33,500	104,000	99,400	113,600
e. 7d as amount per non-retired employee	137	51	114	82	67	208	199	227
8. Maximum contribution per I.R.C. 404(a)(1)(C)								
a. Principal contribution toward deficiency	—	16,000	28,100	48,400	75,500	106,500	186,200	234,900
b. Adjusted 10% base (5 + 8a)	400,000	165,000	461,100	398,400	475,500	836,500	886,200	1,034,900

Item	$100 monthly less Social Security	$125 monthly less Social Security	$1.75 monthly per year of service to 30 years	$2.25 monthly per year of service	$2.40 monthly per year of service thru 1958 plus $2.50 monthly per year thereafter	$2.80 monthly per year of service
c. Normal cost of 6a plus 10% of 8b	90,000	96,100	97,600	151,200	160,600	183,500
d. 8c as amount per non-retired employee	180	192	195	302	321	367
9. Actual contribution made	75,000	80,000	90,000	125,000	125,000	125,000
10. Valuation rate of interest[3]	2¼%	2¼%	2¼%	2¾%	3%	3¼%

^a Annual benefits reduced from $600 in 1949 to $300 in 1950 because of 1950 Amendments to Social Security Act.
^b Annual benefits reduced from $600 in 1951 to $540 in 1952 because of 1952 Amendments to Social Security Act.

[1] Portion of contribution of item 9 in excess of prior years' minimum requirements of item 7d.
[2] On basis of 30-year funding of past service, and a new 30-year funding period for each increase in past service attributable to an increase in the benefit formula.
[3] Indicative of changes made in the valuation rate of interest assumption made since 1953 by reason of the investment experience and outlook at the respective years of the fund. A ruling by the Internal Revenue Service early in 1963 (Revenue Ruling 63-11) implies a minimum valuation rate of interest of 3½% for computing the maximum tax deduction under a trust funded plan, and so in 1963 the trend has been towards utilizing a 3½% rate of interest for valuation purposes.

liability for retired lives are met. (See I.R.S. mimeograph 5717, P. S. No. 57 and No. 64.)

Item 8 of Table D develops the estimated maximum contribution for tax deduction purposes under 404(a)(1)(C). Although this does not bring out an explicit determination of an experience "gain" or "loss," it may be noted that this has been taken care of implicitly by using as the basis the net deficiency, which reflects the past experience of the fund to the date of valuation as well as the experience of the group. To the net deficiency are added the principal payments (i.e., portion of contribution made in excess of the normal cost and interest on the net actuarial deficiency) made towards the unfunded deficiency in past years, in order to arrive at a new 10 percent base that reflects the experience of the fund and group up to the valuation date. In this connection it should be noted that this follows the limit as set forth under (C) of I.R.C. 404(a)(1) of the law, but there are two other limits that might be used for tax deduction purposes. These limits are (1) 5 percent of covered payroll and (2) the level annual cost or premium to retirement on behalf of each employee covered under the plan. The pertinent part of 404 spelling out these three limits is as follows:

"(1) Pension Trusts—In the taxable year when paid, if the contributions are paid into a pension trust, and if such taxable year ends within or with a taxable year of the trust for which the trust is exempt under section 501(a), in an amount determined as follows:

(A) an amount not in excess of 5 percent of the compensation otherwise paid or accrued during the taxable year to all the employees under the trust, but such amount may be reduced for future years if found by the Secretary or his delegate upon periodical examinations at not less than 5-year intervals to be more than the amount reasonably necessary to provide the remaining unfunded cost of past and current service credits of all employees under the plan, plus

(B) any excess over the amount allowable under Subparagraph (A) necessary to provide with respect to all of the employees under the trust the remaining unfunded cost of their past and current service credits distributed as a level amount, or a level percentage of compensation, over the remaining future service of each such employee, as determined under regulations prescribed by the Secretary or his delegate, but if such remaining unfunded cost with respect to any 3 individuals is more than 50 percent of such remaining unfunded cost, the amount of such unfunded cost attributable to such individuals shall be distributed over a period of at least 5 taxable years, or

(C) in lieu of the amounts allowable under Subparagraphs (A) and (B) above, an amount equal to the normal cost of the plan, as determined under regulations prescribed by the Secretary or his delegate, plus, if past service or other supplementary pension or annuity credits are provided by the plan, an amount not in excess of 10 percent of the cost which would be required to completely fund or purchase such pension or annuity credits as of the date when they are included in the plan, as determined under regulations prescribed by the Secretary or his delegate except that in no case shall a deduction be allowed for any amount (other than the normal cost) paid in after such pension or annuity credits are completely funded or purchased."

It is of interest to note from item 1b in Table D that for this hypothetical Pension Plan covering 500 active employees, the number retired has increased gradually from year to year so that there are 60 on the pension roll in 1962. The liabilities for their pensions, indicated by the gross actuarial deficiency for the retired, has increased to $480,000 in 1962 per item 3b, and the total assets have accumulated to amount to somewhat in excess of $1,000,000 per item 4. Hence the assets in 1962 are more than double the liabilities for those on the pension roll. However, the net deficiency of item 5 represents the unfunded liabilities attributable to prior service, and this has increased from $400,000 as of the effective date of the Plan to $800,000 in 1962, the last increase having been brought about by the retroactive increase in the benefit unit in 1962. Though the normal cost of item 6 and the minimum contribution of item 7 have increased from 1949 to 1962, these amounts have not increased by as much as the average annual pension being funded. The main reason has been in the changes made from time to time in the assumed valuation rate of interest, as indicated by item 10. This was increased from 2¼ percent to 2¾ percent in 1954, from 2¾ percent to 3 percent in 1959 and then to 3¼ percent in 1962.[2] As will be indicated later, an increase in the valuation rate of interest (reflecting increased earnings of the fund) means a lower actuarial cost.

---

[2] Would increase again to 3½% in 1963 because of Revenue Ruling 63-11. See footnote [3] of Table D.

Factors Affecting Costs

Now that we have seen certain examples of illustrative costs, let us examine some of the basic factors that enter into their determination.

Mortality

First, to illustrate the mortality principle involved let us say that we had the complete mortality experience of 100 mice. Suppose that 25 of them have died each year. This means that the rate of mortality in the first year is the 25 deaths divided by the 100 alive at the beginning of the year, or one-quarter. Similarly for the second year the rate of mortality is the 25 deaths divided by the 75 mice alive at the beginning of the year, or one-third. This development is shown in the following "Mouse Mortality Table," Table E. In the third year, the rate of mortality is one-half and, of course, in the fourth year, all of the remaining mice have died with the rate of mortality being unity.

TABLE E

Mouse Mortality Table[1]

Year of Life (1)	No. Living Beginning of Year (2)	No. Dying During Year[2] (3)	Annual Rate of Mortality Per Mouse (3) ÷ (2) (4)	Years of Complete Expectation of Life at Beg. of Yr. in Col. (1) (5)
0-1	100	25	¼	2.00
1-2	75	25	⅓	1.50
2-3	50	25	½	1.00
3-4	25	25	1	.50

[1] Not based on any actual experience.
[2] Deaths assumed to occur uniformly over the year.

A little more difficult is the determination of the life expectation of a mouse. During each year let us assume that all of the mice who died have lived an average of one-half of that year; and so, for example, their life expectation is one-half a year when they are 3 years old. When 2 years old, one-half of them survive a year, and to this we add the other one-half that they all live in their respective year of death, making the average life expectation of a 2-year-old mouse exactly one year. In a similar manner, the life expectation of a mouse at birth may be shown to be exactly 2 years, for we can see that 75 out of 100 survive the first year, 50 out of 100 the second year, and 25 out of 100 the third year. Adding together 75/100, plus 50/100, plus 25/100 plus the half year on the average that all live in the year of death, we have the two-year life expectation that a mouse of this particular fictional experience has at birth.

Application of Mortality Rates

The same principles are followed in making a mortality table for humans. The essential thing is to determine first the rate of mortality for each age. With our mice, we noted that 25 out of the 100 died in the first year of life. Similarly, for each age with humans, we determine the proportion dying in each age group. This proportion represents the "crude" mortality rate for each age group. The crude mortality rate is then refined by a smoothing process called "graduation" in order to take out any special kinks in the data that the actuary feels may not be indicative of the "true" rate of mortality for the use to which it is to be put. Then, once a set of mortality rates is made up, they are applied successively by age to a given group of entrants, (such as another family of mice than those in the "Mouse Mortality Table") to estimate the number of deaths each year and the number of survivors from the original group in each year of life.

The life expectation is obtained in the same manner as described for the mice above, and it may also be noted that this life expectancy is also the same as the value of a life annuity with a zero rate of interest. When the interest factors are then included, the value of an annuity or insurance at an applicable rate or interest may be determined. The more extended actuarial techniques of showing how the interest function is tied in with mortality are necessarily too long and involved for detailed treatment here; the purpose served in going this far has been merely to indicate the mortality principles involved.

Mortality Tables

Probably the mortality table that is still best known in this country is the "American Experience Table," which was first published under its present name in 1868, although it was used as early as 1861. Prepared by Sheppard Homans, actuary of the Mutual Life Insurance Company of New York, it was based in general upon the insurance experience of the Mutual Life Insurance Company during the years 1843 to 1860, but was also to a certain extent based upon Mr. Homan's personal opinion of what would probably represent the future death rates among insured lives, together with a margin for future fluctuations in mortality because of possible epidemics, etc. One reason that this table became well-known is that it was generally prescribed by state law for life insurance valuation purposes from about 1901 to January 1948, when many states prescribed a new mortality table. According to this old table, a person who attained age 65 might be expected to live 11.1 years.

Life Insurance vs. Annuity Tables

However, the type of mortality experience from a group of people who buy insurance and who, in a sense, are betting that they are going to die "before their time" is naturally different from the type of mortality experience from a group of people who buy annuities and so are, therefore, betting that they are going to live "beyond their time." Therefore, insurance companies generally use different mortality tables, reflecting their actual respective experience, for people who buy annuities as compared with people who buy insurance.

The Combined Annuity Mortality Table was published in 1928 and is representative of annuity experience at the older ages during the ten-year period ending 1928. The number of years that a male may expect to live, on the average, at age 65, in accordance with this table, is 12.74 years, or almost 2 years longer than he might expect to live according to the American Experience Table. Following this a step further, because of general improvement in medical practice and facilities and in our health standards of living, we have found that people buying annuities are living even longer, and so the 1937 Standard Annuity Table shows that a male aged 65 can expect to live 14.40 years on the average, another 2 years over and above the average duration according to the Combined Annuity Table. This illustrates the decrease in mortality rates among annuitants, as well as the difference between a mortality table which was widely used for life insurance as compared with a mortality table used for annuities. Generally, the use of the Combined Annuity Mortality Table may result in estimated costs some 10 percent less than the 1937 Standard Annuity Mortality Table, depending on the age distribution of the group involved and the nature of benefits being provided.

A statement above indicated that the average number of years a male aged 65 might live under the 1937 Standard Annuity Table was 14.40 years. It has been found that for a wide range of ages, a female seems to have the same number of years to live, on the average, as a male 5 years younger. This means, for example, that a female may expect to live 14.40 years on the average when she has attained age 70, according to the 1937 Standard Annuity Table. This is a particularly important point when considering the cost of pension plans, especially if the tendency is to set a younger retirement age for female lives than for males. Not only do the females live longer if they have the same retirement age as for men, but costs will be increased considerably more if their retirement is to take place at a younger age.

Mortality experience continues to improve. A more recent annuity table was based on experience for the years 1939 through 1947 as projected to 1949 and was used as the basis for what has been called the Annuity Table for 1949. By this table the average number of years that a male aged 65 might be expected to live is 15.0 years. However, the more significant mortality improvement has been at the younger ages under 45, where the rates of mortality by the 1949 table and later tables have been less than half those by the 1937 table.

In 1951 a table called the Ga 1951 Mortality Table was published, and this table was based on certain group annuity mortality experience as well as a projection of mortality improvement to 1951. This table, or other projections of it based on future mortality improvement, has been used by insurance companies as the basis for their group annuity rates, and one consulting firm of actuaries has developed a table based on this Ga 1951 table but with the 10 percent loading removed and then projected for future mortality improvement to 1965. This has been designated by said firm as the 1965 Projected Annuity Mortality Table and brings out a level of pension costs some 10 percent higher than does the old 1937 Standard Annuity Mortality Table.

Interest

A second element that enters into determining pension costs is that of interest, and has already been mentioned. A dollar invested at 2 percent compound interest will double itself in 35 years. Therefore, assuming a 2 percent rate, if a person comes into a plan at age 30 and is retired at age 65, any amount that may be considered to be set aside for him at age 30 will be doubled by the time he has attained age 65. Roughly, therefore, amounts that are put into the fund for him uniformly over the 35-year period may be considered to increase by some 50 percent on account of interest. By way of comparison, 3 percent compound interest will more than double a dollar invested at this rate in less than 25 years, and at 4 percent the dollar doubles in less than 18 years; so it may be seen from this that the factor of interest over a long period of time can be a most important one.

Applying the Interest Factor

Now let us consider the cost of an annuity at age 65 for a male life on the basis of the 1965 Projected Annuity Mortality Table. If 4 percent interest is used, $10.36 could provide a life annuity of $1.00 a year. On the basis of 3 percent interest, the cost would be $11.17, and on the basis of 2 percent interest the cost would be $12.09. These figures include only two factors: first, that of mortality, and second, that of interest. It is interesting to note how the cost of the life annuity increases as the rate of interest decreases. Whereas the life expectation is the same in each instance, the amount of interest that can be earned is somewhat less if the rate of interest decreases, and so it is necessary to have more on hand to earn interest for the purpose of paying out the lifetime benefits. As a matter of fact, the cost on the 3 percent basis is some 8 percent less than the cost on the 2 percent basis. This differential is, of course, increased if the period of time over which the fund is to remain invested is increased.

In the above illustration the period of time for which the fund is invested is relatively short. That is, it is assumed that the fund is set up for each male retiring at age 65, and so the investment period is the period of time representing the life expectancy. If the fund is set up at an earlier age, say at age 50, with benefit payments to commence at age 65, the one-sum cost for a life annuity would be $5.97 on a 3 percent interest basis as compared with $7.49 on a 2 percent interest basis. This represents about a 20 percent differential in cost, due to the fact that the average period of the investment would be the life expectation of a person age 50, which is 26 years, about double the life expectation of a person age 65. Hence, it may be seen from this example that a 1 percent differential in the interest rate may make as much difference as 20 percent in costs.

There is another important point to be considered in determining the level of the interest rate to be used. Let us say that investments will bring us a 3 percent return. However, if we have assets amounting to $300,000 of which only $200,000 is invested at 3 percent, then we are only realizing an effective return of 2 percent on our *total* assets. The point is that the rate of interest to be used as a basis for determining pension costs should take into consideration the time during which certain funds are in transition and not invested (sometimes called "fractional cost of interest").

Capital Appreciation and Depreciation

A fund is subject to certain capital appreciation and depreciation, especially to the extent that it is invested in equities. Up to about 1950 the accepted approach in pension fund investments, as well as in the investments of insurance companies, has been to hold bonds rather than stocks on the theory that the benefits (and guarantees where applicable) were in terms of dollars rather than in terms of purchasing power. However, the inflationary spiral of the last 15 or 20 years has indicated the advantages of equity investments to the extent that certain insurance companies are now entering this field by the use of newly legislated "segregated funds." But to the extent that a fund is invested in equities, there is generally more of a problem in the periodic valuation of assets.

Perhaps one of the main advantages of a profit-sharing plan from the investment angle has been that there are no stipulated guarantees, either real or implied, in terms of dollar benefits; each participant simply has a share in the fund, based upon his accumulated units in relation to all units according to the benefit formula of the plan. Consequently, a profit-sharing fund could be invested more in equities without jeopardizing any real or implied guarantees of dollar benefits.

This leads to a consideration of equities as possible investments for pension plans and the possible translation of the benefit formula into shares rather than in terms of dollars. One sizable fund which is in existence is administered by the College Retirement Equities Fund Affiliated with Teachers Insurance and Annuity Association. Under this fund the equities of the teachers who participate are built up on a "money purchase" basis by the fixed percentage of payroll contributions that they make and the contributions that are made on their behalf (not over 50 percent of the contributions are to go to the equities fund).

There are two steps that might be considered in this connection. One step would be to have full participation in the fund until retirement at which time the pension would be determined on the basis of the equity that had been built up at that time. In other words, the equity at the time of retirement would be equated to a certain number of dollars of pension, and the pension would then be payable for lifetime on that basis. A second step, one followed by the C.R.E.F. fund mentioned above, would be to continue participation in the appreciation and depreciation of equities after retirement, so that the amount of pension would vary from time to time, the amount depending on the periodic market value of the equities held in the fund.

The main reason for expressing the pension in terms of equity shares is to hedge against inflation. Certain studies that have been made indicate that, in general, equities have moved up with inflation and down with deflation. On the other hand, this is a relatively new field and is still subject to much experimentation.

Withdrawal

It has been suggested by some sources that the cost effect of taking into consideration withdrawal rates is considerably more than that of taking into account both the factors of mortality and interest. It is certainly true that if an organization has a fairly consistent rate of withdrawal, some recognition can properly be given to this factor in determining the cost of a pension plan if early vesting is not involved. A procedure which is widely used in insured plans is to utilize eligibility requirements excluding employees from participation during the years of high withdrawal.

For example, an eligibility requirement of this sort might be the attainment of age 30 and/or the completion of 3 years of service. The point is that those persons under age 30 and/or those who have not yet completed 3 years of service with an organization would probably account for most of the normal withdrawal. Many of the plans which have been established follow a device of this sort to take account of a large part of the withdrawal. Then the relatively lower terminations among those people who enter the plan after having satisfied the eligibility requirements are recognized by credits for contributions already paid on their account to apply against future contributions required for those who remain.

However, the amount of credit that can be made available, as well as the extent to which withdrawal rates can be used in producing lower cost, depends upon what termination benefit (vesting) is made available according to the provisions of the pension plan. If the termination benefit, in effect, turns over to the terminating employee the full pension value that has been built up for him, then no such credits would be available. On the other hand, if nothing is turned over to the terminating employee, the full effect of his leaving the organization is to reduce costs.

The more direct way of taking into account this factor of withdrawal, which is used extensively in trust fund plans and in some insured plans, is to include in the cost computation a discount for prudently expected withdrawals other than by death or retirement.

The advantage of this more direct approach is that all of the employes are generally included in the cost computations, whereas under the other method certain of the present employees who are excluded one year by reason of not meeting certain eligibility requirements may very well become eligible in the years to come and thereby bring about a much higher level of costs (especially if retroactive pension credit is granted) than was initially anticipated.

The factor of withdrawal is related to the age and service of employees, as noted above. The younger employees with relatively few years of service tend to be subject to the higher rates of withdrawal, but at the same time these are the employees who are the furthest from retirement and for whom the reserves built up and the level of costs are the least. Consequently, there could well be a fairly high rate of annual withdrawal for the whole group of employees, such as 50 percent, or even higher, but when related to the costs of pensions, it would not necessarily mean that the level of costs would be reduced by 50 percent or more. This is because the proportion of older and longer-serviced employees are the ones who primarily determine the going level of pension costs. To mention some extreme possibilities, there are organizations with a fairly high proportion of younger and shorter-service employees who are subject to a high rate of withdrawal, and these organizations might very well find that the level of costs for pensions could be properly reduced by as much as 20 percent or possibly even 30 percent by allowing for this high rate of withdrawal. On the other hand, an organization with a fairly low proportion of younger and shorter serviced employees with a fairly typical rate of withdrawal may find that the level of costs would only be reduced by some 5 percent if a low rate of withdrawal is used in the determination of cost estimates.

This is a matter which is subject to considerable judgment, particularly at the installation of a pension plan, for it is obvious that the very fact of having a pension plan may well serve to change the turnover experience, especially if the pension plan does the job it is supposed to do. One of the reasons generally given for putting in a pension plan is that it will tend to reduce turnover. Another difficulty involved is that, from the economic, political, and labor aspects, past experience may be very little indication of what may be expected in the future. We have been through periods of depression, periods of war, and periods of prosperity, each period necessarily showing a different type of termination experience for each organization. The actuary cannot be considered to be a prophet; he is subject to human limitations just like everyone else; and there is nothing mystical or prophetic attached to a particular set of withdrawal rates that he may come up with, any more than there is attached to the rate of interest or the mortality table which he may choose to use. Generally, the actuary is inclined to use a set of withdrawal rates based on the company experience, if available, or based on an empirical set of rates that may be understating rather than overstating the rate of withdrawal, so that the expression of initial costs may tend to be on the high side. In any event, actual experience will control, for future contributions will be so determined automatically, if a proper actuarial cost method is being consistently followed.

Salary Scales

It is also important to appraise properly the amount of earnings upon which the pension benefit is to be based. This may call for the determination of a salary scale which reflects by sex and age a reasonable increase in earnings until retirement. Of itself, a salary scale is one of the factors for increased cost estimates, if it can be assumed that a person's earnings upon which his benefit is to be based will be greater than his present earnings.

To use an oversimplified example, let us assume that a person's benefit is to be based upon later earnings, say, 25 percent over and above his present earnings. That means that the pension benefit, if directly proportional to earnings, and the cost of this benefit would thereby be increased some 25 percent over what it would be if costs were based merely upon his present earnings.

For many hourly-rate wage groups the level of earnings does not seem to increase appreciably by age, per se, and so if a salary scale is used in determining the level of pensions and costs for a wage group there may be other considerations. One such consideration could be the general inflationary trend in wages, which, although most noted in the last 15-year period, has been more or less evident as long as statistics have been maintained. Another consideration, related in one sense to the first but unrelated in another sense, is the increase in living standards which has been apparent. In mentioning these considerations, it should also be noted that there are factors to be considered which some people feel offset these considerations. Essentially these factors may be boiled down to the idea that any future inflation should in effect pay for itself, and this may also be helped to the extent that there is increased production, which is in the direction of increasing the standard of living. There are certainly other considerations and other factors in addition to those which have been mentioned here. But these are all a part of the problem that has to be faced in deciding whether or not to use a salary scale for a wage group that does not appear to have any very great differential in rates of earnings by age.

On the other hand, for a salaried group where the differential in earnings by age is marked, there is little question about the rationale for using some kind of salary scale if pension benefits are to be based on some future average earnings. For example, the introduction of a moderate salary scale, which would assume that earnings doubled over a 30-year period, might result in the level of actuarial costs being increased by some 10 percent to 20 percent where pension benefits are related directly to some "final" average earnings.

Administrative Expenses

The method of administering a pension plan will have a certain bearing on the cost, and it has not been conclusively proved that either the trust fund or the insurance company funding medium is the least expensive way of handling pension plans. Under the noninsured plan, with a trust fund set-up, there are trustees' fees which tend to grow as the fund grows; there are actuaries' fees, legal fees, and certain other clerical and administrative expenses for keeping the records and handling the many details of operation necessary to make the plan function. Under the insured plan, these expenses are covered by a "loading factor," which also includes the agents' commissions and state premium taxes in certain instances. The margin which insurance companies frequently have included for administrative expenses and other contingencies traditionally has been 8 percent of the gross premiums, charged up until a few years ago when the 8 percent has been reduced, but frequently a constant amount has been added to cover certain of these administrative costs. The loading charge is subject, however, to experience credits, if the loading is deemed higher than necessary.

Both of these methods—trust funds and insurance plans—have their special advocates; an evaluation of the arguments for and against is outside the scope of our more immediate consideration of the cost factors. But anyone weighing the costs of a pension plan would be well served to call in a specialist familiar with both types of plans and to secure estimates of cost from both sides.

Retirement Age

Most industrial pension plans have been initiated or changed over to normal retirement at age 65, probably because since 1935 the Social Security has provided for normal retirement at age 65 (though early retirement is now permitted at age 62 for a reduced benefit and disability retirement at ages under 65 without any reduction in benefit). Also, indications of the level of costs set forth herein have been on the assumption of retirement at age 65. The actual experience to date under many pension plans has been that the average normal retirement has been taking place somewhat after age 65. Some of the reasons for this have been the demand for labor (particularly during the War years when the average age of people retiring under Social Security was about age 69), the continued relative good times with little or no pressure being brought to bear for retiring employees, and the initiation of many new plans which led to the retirement of employees already beyond the normal retirement age who could not have retired on pension any earlier because there was no plan.

On the other hand, when the plan provides for normal retirement at a specific age such as 65, there is certainly a potential liability involved for providing pension benefits from that age. Consequently, this liability is recognized when the expression of costs is in terms of retirement at that age. Furthermore, as more and more benefits become available to older people (through added liberalization of Social Security, veterans benefits, tax credits, etc.), it is quite possible that there may be a more widespread acceptance of retirement at an earlier time. Also, the pressures of fewer jobs for older people will likely be felt more in poor times, and this, taken in conjunction with the pressure of increased production, may very well lead to the automatic retirement of many people when they get to age 65. In many plans that have been adopted since 1950, there is already a noticeable trend towards retirement nearer the normal retirement age.

But let us take the position, for the moment, that normal retirements will not all take place at age 65 as assumed, and we want to know the effect on costs if retirements (including early retirements) take place, on the average, at age 66 or at age 67. On this basis one might count on the long-range costs being reduced by possibly 7 percent from age 65 costs if retirements take place at age 66, on the average, or by 15 percent if retirements take place at age 67.

Other Plan Provisions Affecting Costs

Obviously, the larger the benefits, and the sooner they commence, the more the plan is going to cost. The plan with a benefit formula providing, on the average, a 40 percent-of-pay benefit should be twice as expensive as one providing, on the average, a 20-percent benefit for a particular group of employees. The younger a person is who retires, the longer he will receive benefits. His life expectation at age 60 is about 18 years (by the 1965 Projected Annuity Mortality Table), as compared with about 14½ years at age 65. This does not illustrate the full impact of increased costs, for when interest and other factors are considered a unit of lifetime benefit commencing at age 60 costs about 50 percent more than one commencing at age 65.

Employee Contributions

Let us consider the effect of employee contributions under a pension plan. In the absence of any benefits other than pensions from the plan, the employer costs would be reduced by the exact amount of employee contributions. However, if an employee contributes to the plan, generally, at least, these contributions less any benefits paid should be returned to him in the event of his termination from the plan. It is not uncommon to grant also an additional amount equivalent to interest which has accrued on his contributions. For this reason, each dollar of employee contribution reduces the employer cost by something less than a dollar, perhaps by 70¢, for the younger employee, or by an amount closer to the dollar for the older employee. For example, on this basis, if the annual cost of a pension plan is $400,000 without employee contributions and without any kind of termination benefits, the employer portion of cost, if employees contribute $100,000, might be reduced by about $85,000, leaving a net employer cost of some $315,000. The total employer and employee cost of the pension plan would then, of course, be $415,000 made up of $315,000 employer contributions and $100,000 of employee contributions, the additional $15,000 being required to pay for the termination benefits made necessary by changing to the contributory basis.

Vesting

The vesting provisions of a pension plan define the equity from past employer contributions which the employee receives as a termination benefit in the event of his termination prior to retirement. The larger the vesting, the less there would be credited back (reversions) for offsetting future costs. This is related to the factor of withdrawal in determining costs, and the vesting provision of a plan can help to determine whether or not and to what extent it is appropriate to discount costs because of withdrawal (see above). The longer the employee is with the company, the more likely is he to stay until retirement, so that withdrawal rates are least when the past accumulation of employer contributions is highest. For example, the pension costs may be about 15 percent higher if no rate of withdrawal is assumed, as compared with assuming a moderate rate of withdrawal for a fairly typical group. This 15-percent differential represents the discount taken for withdrawals that are assumed to take place before retirement. If we assume that any withdrawals after age 40 who have 15 or more years of service retain a vested interest, in the sense that their pension accrued up to their date of termination will become payable to them when they reach age 65, then this might reduce the 15-percent discount that may be taken for withdrawals to 10 percent (i.e., increase the cost of the pension plan by some 5 percent). Or if we assume a more liberal vesting provision whereby any withdrawal after 10 or more years of service will be eligible for a vested deferred pension at age 65, then the 15-percent discount may be reduced to 5 percent with some 10-percent increase in the potential cost of the pension plan.

Disability Benefits

A disability provision is not underwritten directly in many insured plans being currently issued. Since the last depression, not many insurance companies have been interested in underwriting a disability provision. However, it can be handled through the deposit administration group annuity as a particular type of early retirement. On the other hand, under the noninsured plan, the disability provision is frequently handled in a more direct manner. A word of caution concerning disability benefits—insurance companies found that their disabilities increased about tenfold during the depression of the 1930's. Although there may be better possible control of this sort of thing in a noninsured plan, the same tendency is possible during a depression for employees losing their jobs to "use" the disability provision of a plan that has an accumulation of reserves. The administrative control is a primary factor affecting disability costs.

In the cost examples given, there was included a fairly common type of disability benefit. Under Formula 1 the disability benefit was the full accrued pension in the event of disability after 15 or more years of service. By way of illustration, that portion of the cost in respect of the disability benefit payable prior to age 65 represented about 6 percent of the total cost.

Conclusion

There is apparently a wide range in the initial level of cost estimates, depending on the actuarial assumptions used as well as the actuarial cost method to be followed. The important point, however, is how much is in the fund, and it follows that the larger the fund, relatively, the greater the assurance that the pension benefits may be met, and the lower the future "cost." Thinking in terms of the cost examples set forth in Table A and the actuarial assumptions used (which involved basically the 1965 Projected Annuity Mortality Table, 3 percent interest, a moderate rate of withdrawal, a modest disability rate, and retirement at age 65), let us estimate roughly what the costs might have been if other sets of actuarial assumptions had been used.

For example, the use of the 1937 Standard Annuity Mortality Table instead of the 1965 Projected Annuity Mortality Table would have led to an expression of costs about 10 percent lower.

The use of $2\frac{3}{4}$ percent interest instead of 3 percent would have increased the expression of costs by about 5 percent, and the use of $3\frac{1}{4}$ percent interest instead of 3 percent would have lowered the expression of costs by about 5 percent.

If no withdrawal rate had been used, the expression of costs would have been about 15 percent higher.

If retirement has been assumed to be at age 66, instead of age 65, the expression of costs would have been reduced by about 7 percent, and if retirement had been assumed to be at age 67, the expression of costs would have been reduced by about 15 percent.

The determination of which factors to use for the purpose of estimating costs is largely an actuarial problem, although the actuary may ask the company for information that would assist him in deciding which factors would be appropriate. Some actuaries feel that the factors that are selected should have certain margins of conservatism for possible future contingencies. Certain insurance company actuaries as well as certain consulting actuaries would fall into this category, and one reason is that the level of long range costs may probably be corrected more easily in the future by a reduction in contribution levels as experience dictates rather than vice versa. There are other reasons that might also be involved in a high rather than a low expression of costs—such as the maximum basis for tax deduction and the fact that the Internal Revenue Service does not permit any direct allocation of funds based on contributions made for contingencies in a trust fund plan (although this, quite inconsistently, is not true for an insured plan).

Other actuaries would prefer to estimate as closely as possible what the long-range cost is going to be, and these actuaries would probably come up with a level of costs that is lower than the first group of actuaries since no margin would be included for possible future contingencies.

In any event, whatever the basis utilized by the actuary, the actual experience of the group and of the fund will control future costs. The actuary can make such calculations as he deems are necessary and sufficient for the purpose of estimating the level of costs, and his valuation results may be thought of as "educated guesses" based on the information made available to him; for the assumptions and methods he uses do not fashion the ultimate costs of the plan, only time does this. Naturally, the employer is very much interested in learning how much an employee benefit program involving pensions is likely to cost. It is primarily for this reason that the actuary is brought into the picture to estimate liabilities and costs. Although the liabilities for pension benefits are not of the sort that are recognized directly on the company's balance sheet (other than by a footnote), the long-range future costs are certainly very real and may get out of hand unless proper recognition is made through some advance provision for funding. This is the area where the actuary can be of considerable assistance.

Chapter 5

DEFERRED PROFIT-SHARING PLANS

By Arthur S. Fefferman

Background

Profit-sharing plans have had a long history. As early as 1794, Albert Gallatin, Secretary of the Treasury under Jefferson and Madison, instituted a profit-sharing plan for the benefit of his employees with the announcement that "the Democratic principle upon which this nation was founded should not be restricted to the political processes but should be applied to the industrial operation"[1] as well. According to the Council of Profit-Sharing Industries, profit-sharing "has been practiced all over the world for as long as the system of free enterprise has been in operation."[2]

Profit-sharing promotes teamwork for labor and management. Since the employee is given a share of the profits, the aim is to encourage him to put forth his best efforts. Profit-sharing plans are also used as an alternative to pension plans to provide retirement income for employees.

While there are basic reasons for the adoption of profit-sharing plans quite aside from the tax laws, in recent years tax considerations have loomed large in the adoption of such plans. This is because the tax laws are designed to encourage the growth and development of profit-sharing plans which do not discriminate as to coverage or benefits in favor of highly paid employees, executives and stockholder-employees as compared with the rank and file of employees.

Where a profit-sharing plan meets the tests prescribed by the Internal Revenue Code for qualification there is an impressive list of tax advantages:

---

[1] Profit-Sharing Manual, published by Council of Profit-Sharing Industries, 1948.
[2] *Ibid.*, p. 5.

(1) Any trust established to administer the plan and manage the funds is specifically exempt from taxation on its income.

(2) Contributions made by employers to the profit-sharing plan are not taxed currently to the participating employees. Instead, the employees generally do not pay any tax until they actually receive payments from the plan.

(3) Employers are allowed tax deductions, within certain limits, for their contributions to the profit-sharing plan even though employees are not taxed currently on such contributions.

(4) Certain lump sum distributions made by the plans to employees are taxed as long term capital gains.

The growth in the number of profit-sharing plans qualified for favorable tax treatment has been spectacular in recent years. Unfortunately, exact records are not available as to the substantial number of profit-sharing plans adopted before 1955. However, between September 30, 1955 and June 30, 1963—a period of less than eight years—over 29,000 profit-sharing plans received favorable rulings from the Internal Revenue Service. In the calendar year 1962 alone, favorable rulings were granted by the Service to 5,016 profit-sharing plans covering 154,000 employees. And in the first six months of 1963 such rulings were issued to 2,757 profit-sharing plans covering 386,000 employees.[3]

There is every indication that the number of profit-sharing plans will continue to accelerate for some time to come. In 1962 a new factor was added with the adoption of the Keogh bill (P.L. 87-792) allowing self-employed people to be covered under qualified pension and profit-sharing plans. Although to date few self-employed persons appear to have adopted such plans, it is quite possible that future years may see many profit-sharing plans adopted by them under the new legislation.

What is a Profit-Sharing Plan?

The Council of Profit-Sharing Industries of America defines a profit-sharing plan as:

> "Any procedure under which an employer pays to all employees in addition to good rates of regular pay, special current or deferred sums based not only upon individual or group performances but on the prosperity of the business as a whole."[4]

---
[3] Internal Revenue Service Press Releases, *Determination Letters Issued On Employee Benefit Plans.*
[4] Council of Profit-Sharing Industries, *op. cit.*, p. 3.

The historic definition of profit-sharing adopted at the International Cooperative Congress in Paris in 1899 is as follows:

> "Profit-sharing is an agreement freely entered into by which the employees receive a share, fixed in advance, of the profits."[5]

These definitions of profit-sharing are broad enough to cover both current and deferred plans. Current profit-sharing is represented primarily by bonuses based on a percentage of profits or by wage dividend plans. At the outset, it should be noted that present law does not grant any special or favorable tax treatment with regard to such plans, but taxes the profits distributed under them as ordinary income to the employee receiving them.

Deferred profit-sharing plans—more specifically plans which delay the distributions to employees for at least two years after the date of the employer's contribution—may qualify for the special tax advantages provided in sections 401 through 405 of the Internal Revenue Code. The discussion of profit-sharing plans contained in this chapter will be restricted to such deferred plans. It should be noted that sections 401 through 405, which set out the statutory tests which profit-sharing plans must meet to qualify for favored tax treatment, are derived from sections 165(a) and 23(p) of the 1939 Code. These sections were first enacted as part of the Revenue Act of 1942. The revisions made in this area in the 1954 Code were not extensive and most of the present statutory language can be traced back to 1942.

The Commissioner of Internal Revenue, in his Regulations interpreting section 401(a) of the 1954 Code, defines a profit-sharing plan as follows:

> "A profit-sharing plan is a plan established and maintained by an employer to provide for the participation in his profits by his employees or their beneficiaries. The plan must provide a definite predetermined formula for allocating the contributions made to the plan among the participants and for distributing the funds accumulated under the plan after a fixed number of years, the attainment of a stated age, or upon the prior occurrence of some event such as layoff, illness, disability, retirement, death, or severance of employment."[6]

---

[5] *Ibid.*, p. 3.

[6] §. 1.401-1(b)(1)(ii). References to sections of the Internal Revenue Code (IRC) are to the Internal Revenue Code of 1954 unless otherwise stated. References to sections of the Income Tax Regulations are to the regulations issued under the 1954 Code unless otherwise stated.

Profit-Sharing Compared With Pension Plans

Any employer intending to establish a deferred compensation plan will do well to consider the relative merits of pension and profit-sharing plans in determining which type of plan better suits his and his employees' needs. The Internal Revenue Code grants favored tax treatment to both types of plans. While the tax treatment of both plans fits into the same framework, there are significant differences in the treatment as well as inherent differences in the types of plans.

(1) *Employer Contribution*: From the employer's viewpoint, perhaps the greatest advantage of a profit-sharing plan is that he has no fixed obligation to make contributions except out of profits. This means that his contributions are automatically larger in years of high profits when it is most convenient for him to make such contributions. Smaller contributions are made in years of low profits, and in loss years no contributions are required. In contrast, under a pension plan, an employer undertakes a fixed commitment to make contributions according to a predetermined formula regardless of his profits in that year.

(2) *Employee Incentives*: Since the amount of the employer's contribution and, hence, the amount of the employees' benefits depend on the size of the employer's profits, many believe that profit-sharing plans provide employees with stronger work incentives than pension plans. On the other hand, some employers feel that profit-sharing plans might encourage employees to question the judgment of executives with respect to decisions affecting profits or tend to encourage undue curiosity in connection with the computations of profits.

(3) *Employee Considerations*: Many profit-sharing plans are used as an alternative to pension plans to provide retirement benefits for participating employees. Since the amount of the benefits depends upon the future profits of the employer and the earnings on the funds, the ultimate amount available for retirement cannot be determined beforehand. This means that under profit-sharing plans, there is no satisfactory way to guarantee that the sum payable to an employee from a profit-sharing trust will be sufficient for the employee's retirement needs. In fact, the Internal Revenue Service regulations specifically indicate that if the employer contributions under a deferred compensation plan

can be determined actuarially on the basis of definitely determinable benefits, the plan will be treated as a pension plan for tax purposes.[7] Some of the uncertainty regarding the extent and duration of the employee's benefits, however, can be reduced by having the profit-sharing trust purchase annuities for the employee on retirement date.

(4) *Flexibility*: A profit-sharing plan may, under certain conditions, possess greater flexibility than a pension plan in providing benefits to employees. Under a profit-sharing plan, forfeitures resulting from termination of employment can be allocated to the accounts of the remaining employees so as to increase their eventual benefits. Under a pension plan, forfeitures generally cannot be used to increase the stated benefits but instead are used to decrease the employer's future contributions. On the other hand, pension plans may be more adaptable than profit-sharing plans in providing adequate benefits for those employees who are approaching retirement at the time the plan is adopted. A pension plan can make provision for the retirement needs of such employees by giving credit for past service in computing the amount of the pension. A profit-sharing plan cannot do this. As a result, it generally requires many years of participation in a profit-sharing plan for the sum credited to the account of an employee to reach the proportions necessary to provide a reasonable retirement income.

An Example of Successful Profit-Sharing

Large rewards are offered by profit-sharing plans which have been managed successfully.

Take, for example, the case of an employee who earns $5,000 a year and participates in a profit-sharing plan from the ages of 30 to 65. Suppose further that the employer contributes for his benefit 15 percent of compensation (the maximum tax deduction[8]) or $750 per year and the earnings rate is 4 percent. Under such conditions, the accumulation at the end of 35 years when the employee retires will be $57,448 ($26,250 of employer contributions plus $31,198 of interest). The sum accumulated for the em-

---

[7] §. 1.401-1(b)(i). Moreover, money purchase plans, where the contributions are fixed and are not geared to profits, are also treated as pension plans. Under such plans, the benefits received by participants depend on the amounts accumulated for them prior to retirement and there is no stated predetermined benefit.

[8] §. 404(a)(3)(A).

ployee at retirement will be even larger than this amount if forfeitures derived from employees who quit or are discharged before retirement are reallocated among the accounts of the employees who remain. Capital gains on the investments made by the profit-sharing plan could also increase the benefits.

If the average salary of the employee is $3,000 instead of $5,000, and all other factors (annual contributions equal 15 percent of pay, 35 years in plan, 4 percent interest) are the same, the sum accumulated in 35 years will equal $34,469. If another employee in the same plan earns $50,000 a year, the sum accumulated in 35 years for his benefit will equal $574,485.

These figures illustrate the substantial results which can be accomplished from investing in a tax-free medium where compound interest tables apply.

A sum of about $14,500 will buy a male employee at 65 a single premium annuity contract providing $100 a month for life. Accordingly, the $57,448 accumulated in the profit-sharing plan for the $5,000 per year employee in the above example could purchase a retirement income of about $397 a month or $4,764 a year, a 95 percent pension without considering Social Security benefits. Commensurate annuities could similarly be purchased for higher-paid employees out of the larger dollar amounts accumulated for them in the profit-sharing plan.

It is obvious, therefore, that a successfully managed profit-sharing plan and trust can provide benefits that are not only reasonable but most generous after the plan has been in existence for a long period of time.

Qualification Rules

Profit-sharing plans must meet the same general rules as pension plans in order to qualify under the Internal Revenue Code.

Any trust established to carry out a qualified plan must be created or organized in the U.S. and must be maintained at all times as a domestic trust. To qualify, the plan must be formulated for the exclusive benefit of the employees and their beneficiaries. The plan must be funded. The employer must make an actual contribution to the plan and part with ownership of the contributed funds. Pay-as-you-go arrangements do not qualify.

To qualify, profit-sharing plans like pension plans must not discriminate as to coverage or as to contributions in favor of shareholders, officers, supervisory personnel and highly compensated employees. These rules are spelled out in Section 401 of the Internal Revenue Code. Considerably stricter rules apply if the plan covers a self-employed individual. The rules applicable to the general run of profit-sharing plans will be described first. Then, the special rules applying to plans covering self-employed individuals will be described.

Non-Discriminatory Coverage

Qualified plans which do not include self-employed individuals may meet the coverage requirements in either of two ways. First, the plan may satisfy the so-called percentage test by covering either 70% or more of all the employees, or 80% or more of all the employees who are eligible to benefit if 70% or more of all the employees are eligible to benefit under the plan. For this purpose, there may be excluded individuals who have been employed for a period not exceeding five years, part-time employees who work for not more than 20 hours in any one week and employees whose customary employment is for not more than five months in any calendar year.[9]

Most profit-sharing plans, however, do not meet the coverage requirement under the above, rather complicated, arithmetical test; instead they generally qualify under a provision giving the Commissioner of Internal Revenue the authority to approve a coverage classification if he finds it not discriminatory.[10] The Internal Revenue Code further specifies that a coverage classification shall not be considered discriminatory "... merely because it is limited to salaried or clerical employees."[11] In other words, the Internal Revenue Service will approve plans which limit coverage to salaried or clerical employees only if the results, when all circumstances are taken into consideration, are nondiscriminatory. On this basis, the Service has approved many profit-sharing plans which cover only salaried or clerical employees and which exclude employees paid on an hourly basis, or a daily basis or on a piece

---

[9] §. 401(a)(3)(A).
[10] §. 401(a)(3)(B).
[11] §. 401(a)(5). In interpreting this provision, the Internal Revenue Service has placed great stress on the words "merely because," holding that the provision does not sanction all plans which are limited to salaried or clerical employees but rather merely indicates that a plan is not automatically deemed to be discriminatory if it limits coverage to such employees.

rate basis. Similarly, where the results are deemed to be nondiscriminatory, the Commissioner has approved profit-sharing plans where coverage is restricted to the employees of one plant without including the employees of another plant under the same ownership.

Nondiscriminatory Contributions

In addition to providing coverage on a nondiscriminatory basis, a profit-sharing plan must provide contributions or benefits that do not discriminate in favor of shareholders, officers, supervisory personnel and highly compensated personnel. In general, qualified plans may, and generally do, provide larger dollar contributions or benefits for higher paid employees than for those who are more modestly compensated, although the employer, as a practical matter, will not contribute more than he can deduct for tax purposes (generally 15 percent of employee compensation). There is no dollar limitation on the amount of contributions that may be provided for any employee. Under a qualified profit-sharing plan, however, the contributions cannot generally constitute a larger percentage of compensation for higher paid employees than for lower paid employees.

The Contribution Formula

It is fairly common for profit-sharing plans to establish a definite formula specifying the portion of profits to be contributed by the employer to the trustee each year. The specific formula used for this purpose varies considerably from plan to plan. One plan, for example, provides that the employer corporation shall contribute five percent of net income before taxes after deducting 10 percent of the stockholders' investment. Under another, the employer contributes 25 percent of net income before taxes after deducting six percent of total assets used in the business. Still another plan calls for annual employer contributions amounting to seven percent of the dividends paid annually to common stockholders.[12]

However, it is important to note that the law does not require a qualified profit-sharing plan to have a definite formula for determining the amount of the contributions to be made by the

---

[12] See the *1963 Study by the Bankers Trust Company of Savings and Thrift Plans, Profit-Sharing Plans and Stock Purchase Plans.*

employer out of profits each year. The Commissioner's regulations under the 1939 Revenue Code sought to impose such a requirement and specified that:

> "A formula for determining the profits to be shared is definite, if, for example, it provides for a contribution equal to (a) a specified percentage of the annual profits (b) a specified percentage of the annual profits in excess of the sum of dividend commitments, plus a fixed amount with an over-all limitation, or (c) a specified percentage of the annual profits not to exceed a specified percentage of the salaries of the participants or their contributions, if any, to the fund."[13]

However, because of the continued refusal of the Courts to sustain this requirement, the regulations under the 1954 Code abandoned the definite contribution formula requirement.[14]

The present income tax regulations, however, specifically indicate that, whether or not a plan contains a definite formula for determining the portion of profits to be contributed by the employer, the plan will not qualify if the contributions are made at such times or in such amounts that, in practice, they discriminate in favor of employees who are officers, shareholders, supervisors or highly compensated employees.[15]

The Allocation Formula

Although the law does not require a qualified profit-sharing plan to have a predetermined formula as to the share of total profits to be contributed by the employer, such a plan must have a definite formula for allocating the employer's contributions among the accounts of the participating employees.

The Regulations of the Commissioner of Internal Revenue provide, in part, that,

> "A formula for distributing the accumulated fund among the participants is definite if, for example, it provides for a distribution in proportion to the basic compensation of each participant."[16]

---

[13] Regulations 118, §. 39.165-1(a)(2). The definite formula for contributions was first required under I. T. 3661, 1944 C. B. 315. The requirement was carried over into Regulations 111, Section 29.165-1(a) by T. D. 5422, 1944 C. B. 318.
[14] §. 1.401-1(b)(1)(ii).
[15] §. 1.401-1(b)(1)(ii).
[16] §. 1.401-1(b)(1)(ii).

Employer contributions may be allocated among the eligible participants of a profit-sharing plan, in part, by reference to years of service to the employer.[17] Thus, an allocation formula generally is acceptable if the annual employer contributions are allocated in accordance with a point system under which each employee receives one point for each full year of service and one point for each $100 of compensation earned during the year. However, if the distribution formula is so drafted as to place greater emphasis on years of service, it may be found that in operation the plan discriminates in favor of officers, shareholders, supervisory personnel and highly compensated personnel because most employees in that group will normally have long years of service in relation to other employees.

Under contributory profit-sharing plans the employer's contributions on behalf of each participant may be geared to the amount of the employee's contribution. It is important, however, that the contribution required of employees before they are allowed to participate in the plan not be so large that only the highly paid employees can afford to participate.

Integration with the Social Security System

Profit-sharing plans which provide benefits only upon retirement or separation from service may take Social Security benefits into consideration for purposes of determining whether the contribution or benefits provided by the plan meet the nondiscrimination test. In effect, such profit-sharing plans are allowed to take credit for a portion of the Social Security benefits provided to employees. The credit given for Social Security under this so-called "integration procedure" is equal to a $9\frac{3}{8}$ percent contribution rate on the first $4800 of pay per annum, the amount of compensation subject to the Social Security system. As a result, if coverage under a profit-sharing plan providing retirement benefits is limited to employees earning more than $4800 a year, then up to $9\frac{3}{8}$ percent of that part of a covered employee's pay which exceeds $4800 a year can be allocated to his account in one year out of employer contributions and forfeitures. This is an example of the so-called "excess plans."

"Offset plans" are also in use. These extend coverage to em-

---

[17] §. 1.401-4(a)(2)(iii).

ployees earning under $4800 a year. However, to take account of the 9⅜ percent allowance for Social Security, allocations for the first $4800 of compensation are at a lower rate than for that part of compensation in excess of $4800. Consequently, when the contributions under the plan and the allowance for Social Security are combined, they together constitute the same percentage of pay throughout the income pay scale. For example, 15 percent of pay may be allocated for that part of compensation in excess of $4800 a year and 5⅝ percent of pay for the first $4800 of compensation. A profit-sharing plan cannot make use of the above described integration allowance for Social Security if the employer also maintains a pension or annuity plan covering the same employees, which is also integrated with Social Security benefits. This is to prevent a firm from taking two integration credits for Social Security benefits by establishing two different types of deferred compensation plans.

Vesting Requirements

The Income Tax Regulations provide that under a qualified profit-sharing plan the sums accumulated for an eligible employee may be paid out by the trustee to the employee after:

> ". . . a fixed number of years, the attainment of a specified age, or upon the prior occurrence of some event such as layoff, illness, disability, retirement, death, or severance of employment."[18]

For the vast majority of plans which do not cover a self-employed person, there is no requirement in the law or the Regulations that the sums contributed by the employer for the benefit of an employee must be fully vested in the employee at all times. In other words, employees covered by such plans do not necessarily have to possess a nonforfeitable right to the employer's pension contributions at all times. The plan, however, must set forth the vesting provisions and enumerate the events on which the trustee is authorized to disburse.

Various kinds of vesting provisions are in use. Some plans grant covered employees complete and immediate vested rights to employer contributions at the time the latter are made. It is more common, however, to provide graduated vesting upon completion

[18] §. 1.401-1(b)(1)(ii).

of a stated period of service or participation in the plan, and/or reaching a specified age. Some plans provide no vesting until the participant reaches retirement age. However, if the firm has an experience of rapid employee turnover, the Internal Revenue Service may not give the plan a favorable advance ruling as to qualification unless it grants covered employees fully vested rights after a reasonable waiting period.[19]

(1) *Retirement*: Benefits must be vested at least by the time the employee reaches the age of normal retirement. The age frequently selected for normal retirement is 65. The sums accumulated for an employee at normal retirement date may, under the terms of a profit-sharing plan, be distributed in a lump sum, over a specified period of years, over the life expectancy of the employee, or may be utilized to buy the employee an annuity contract from a life insurance company.

(2) *Death*: In the event of the death of an employee, many plans provide that the entire sum previously accumulated for his benefits will be paid to the beneficiary selected by the employee. The profit-sharing plan can be drafted to permit the trustee to purchase an annuity contract for the beneficiary of the deceased participant.

A portion of the funds held in a profit-sharing trust can be utilized to purchase life insurance contracts, individual or group, for the benefit of the eligible participants of the plan. In this manner, death benefits are provided through the medium of insurance rather than directly from the funds of the trust.

(3) *Termination of Employment Prior to Retirement*: Profit-sharing plans vary considerably in regard to the rights given to employees who quit or who are discharged prior to normal retirement date. Some plans prescribe no vesting whatever in such event; others provide full vesting. Some plans give vested rights to employees discharged without cause but not to those who voluntarily quit. Others provide no vesting if discharge is due to serious misconduct such as dishonesty or the commission of a felony. Frequently, employees who are discharged or who quit prior to normal retirement date receive vested rights on a graduated scale depending upon the number of years of service (or participation in the plan) with the employer.

---

[19] Rev. Rul. 61-157, 1961-2 C. B. 67, Part 5(c).

Sums not distributed to terminated employees are forfeited and reallocated among the accounts of those who remain, provided, of course, that the manner of reallocation of forfeitures does not discriminate in favor of officers, shareholders, or highly paid employees. In this respect, the qualification rules applying to profit-sharing plans differ from those applying to pension plans. Under the latter, forfeitures cannot be used to increase benefits for the remaining employees, but, instead, must be used to decrease the amount of the employer's contributions in future years.

In order to discourage severance of employment prior to normal retirement date, many plans provide that the sum to which an employee is entitled either will not be paid by the trustee until one year following severance of employment or will be used by the trustee to purchase for such terminated employee a deferred annuity contract providing income at normal retirement date.

Tax Deductions for Employer Contributions

Employers' contributions to qualified profit-sharing plans are deductible for federal income tax purposes under section 404 (subject to certain limits), regardless of whether or not the participants in the plan have a forfeitable or vested right to such contributions at the time they are made. In contrast, if the plan does not qualify, the employer can deduct his contributions only if the employees have fixed rights to such contributions; in that event, the employees are taxed currently on the contributions.

Limits on Tax Deductions

Section 404(a)(3)(A) of the Internal Revenue Code spells out the limits applicable to deductions for employer contributions to qualified profit-sharing plans. In considering these limits, it should be remembered that an employer contribution to a profit-sharing plan, like other compensation for employees, is deductible only if it constitutes a reasonable allowance for services rendered.[20] While the language of the statute is quite complicated, a simple explanation of the limitations is as follows:

(1) The employer is allowed a primary deduction from gross income for contributions made to a qualified profit-sharing trust of

---

[20] §. 1.404(a)-1(b).

up to 15 percent of the aggregate compensation otherwise paid or accrued to the covered employees.

(2) Where the employer contributes in any year less than 15 percent of the payroll of eligible participants, he is allowed to carry over the unused deduction to increase his deduction limit in a subsequent year. If, for example, the employer's deductible contribution in any one year amounts to say, 10 percent of the payroll of participating employees, he is permitted to carry over 5 percent as an unused deduction to raise his deduction limit for contributions in the next year to 20 percent (15 percent primary deduction plus 5 percent carry-over). The amount of the deduction in any one year, including carry-overs, may not, however, exceed 30 percent of the annual payroll of eligible participants.

(3) In any year in which the employer's contributions exceed the amount that he is allowed to deduct under the limitations described above, the excess amount can be carried over and deducted in a subsequent year, provided that the total deduction in that subsequent year (including the amount for contributions made in previous years and not previously deducted) does not exceed 15 percent of the aggregate compensation otherwise paid or accrued to participating employees.

(4) In the event a single employer maintains both a profit-sharing trust and a pension plan (either trusteed or with annuity contracts), the maximum deduction under all plans is 25 percent of the compensation otherwise paid or accrued.[21] If no employee is a beneficiary under more than one trust or plan, however, this over-all limitation does not apply.

The interaction of these deduction limitations is illustrated by the following example: An employer adopts a profit-sharing plan on January 1, 1961. The contribution formula requires the employer to contribute to the trustee annually 20 percent of the net income before taxes. The employer's net income before taxes was $500,000 in 1961; $1,000,000 in 1962; and $200,000 in 1963. Finally, the total compensation paid by the employer to all employees covered by the profit-sharing trust was $800,000 in each of the years 1961, 1962 and 1963.

During the first year of the plan, the employer's contribution would equal 20 percent of $500,000, or $100,000. The total con-

---

[21] § 404(a)(7).

tribution would be deductible because the limit on deductions for such year is $120,000 (15 percent of the $800,000 payroll). Since the employer's contribution was $20,000 less than the maximum sum deductible, a credit carryover arises in the amount of $20,000.

In 1962 the employer contributed 20 percent of $1,000,000 or $200,000. The amount deductible would be $140,000 (15 percent of $800,000 or $120,000, plus a carryover of $20,000). Thus, in 1962 the employer contributed to the profit-sharing trust $60,0000 in excess of the sum for which a deduction could be obtained. This results in a contribution carryover.

In 1963 the contribution of the employer was $40,000 (20 percent of $200,000). Fifteen percent of payroll of the eligible participants in the year 1963 is $120,000 (15 percent of $800,000). Therefore, in 1963 the employer can deduct a current contribution of $40,000 plus the $60,000 contributed in 1962 for which no deduction was previously obtained. This results in a total deduction of $100,000 in 1963, plus a $20,000 credit carryover applicable to future years.

If the employer in the above illustration prefers not to contribute any amount to the profit-sharing trust in any taxable year unless it is deductible in that year, this result could be accomplished by providing the following profit-sharing contribution formula:

> "The employer agrees to contribute to the trustee of the profit-sharing trust annually an amount equal to (a) 20 percent of the net income for each year before state and federal income taxes and before the deduction of the employer's contribution for such year, or (b) the amount deductible under section 404(a)(3)(A) of the Internal Revenue Code for such year, including credit carryovers, whichever amount is the lesser."

In this case, the employer in the above illustration would have been required to contribute to the profit-sharing trust (1) $100,000 in 1961; (2) $140,000 in 1962 and (3) $40,000 in 1963, all contributions being fully deductible. Since the total contributions for the three years amounting to $280,000 would not have averaged 15 percent of payroll (i.e., $360,000), the employer would have an unused credit carryover deduction of $80,000. If, in 1964, net income equals $2,000,000 and 15 percent of payroll still equalled $120,000, the employer would contribute and obtain a deduction that year for $200,000 (15 percent of payroll plus a credit carryover of $80,000) and at that point both contributions and deductions would average 15 percent of the compensation of the eligible participants of the plan.

Affiliated Groups

The 1954 Code made an important change with respect to the deductibility of contributions made by members of an affiliated group of corporations connected through stock ownership with a common parent corporation.[22] Under prior law, where affiliated corporations had established a common profit-sharing plan, the deductible contribution of each member of the group had to be separately computed and determined entirely by reference to its own accumulated and current earnings. Where, for example, one member of the group had no current or accumulated earnings and was unable, therefore, to make any contribution to the trust, no other member of the affiliated group was permitted to make a contribution on behalf of the "loss" member and no shifting of contributions or deductions among the group was permitted.

Under the 1954 Code, a contribution may now be made on behalf of the "loss" corporation for the benefit of its employees by the other members of the group. If the group files a consolidated return, the contribution and the deduction may be divided among the various members of the group at their discretion. But if the group files separate returns, each member's share of the contribution (and deduction) is limited to that proportion of the total contribution made on behalf of the "loss" member that the contributing corporation's current and accumulated profits (after deducting the contribution made on its own behalf) bears to the total current and accumulated profits of the corporation similarly adjusted. There is an excellent illustration of the operation of this formula in the Regulations, Sec. 1.404(a)-10.

Employee Contributions

As noted above, under many profit-sharing plans employees as well as employers make contributions. Under such plans employees may not be allowed to participate unless their contribu-

---

[22] For this purpose the definition of an affiliated group is that set forth in section 1504(a) of the Internal Revenue Code of 1954, i.e., "one or more chains of includible corporations connected through stock ownership with a common parent corporation," and the prescribed stock ownership test is at least 80% of the voting power of all classes of stock and at least 80 percent of each class of non-voting stock.

tions reach certain specified percentages of their compensation. Moreover, the amount of the employer's contributions may be geared to the amount contributed by employees.

Under present law, employees receive no tax deduction for their own contributions to profit-sharing plans. Instead, they make such contributions out of compensation that has been subject to individual income tax. Although contributory plans have certain merits, this tax factor tends to discourage the adoption of such plans. In contrast, the tax law makes it advantageous to the employee to have his employer contribute to the profit-sharing plan. This is because the amounts contributed by the employer are not taxed to the covered employees until they actually receive the benefits under the plan.

In establishing a contributory profit-sharing plan it is important not to set the employees' contributions at so high a level that only the higher-paid employees can afford to participate. In this event, the plan may run afoul of the nondiscrimination rules since, as a practical matter, the lower-paid employees will be excluded from participation. As a general rule, where the plan requires employee contributions as a condition for participation or where the plan gears the amount of employer contributions to the amounts contributed by the employees, the Internal Revenue Service generally holds that employee contributions of up to 6 percent of wages are not burdensome. Larger employee contributions may also be sanctioned under individual plans if the result is not in fact discriminatory against the lower-paid employees. The test is whether the requirements for employee contributions operate to deprive the lower paid employees of benefits at least as high in proportion to compensation as are provided for the higher paid employees.[23]

Under some profit-sharing plans, employees are permitted to make voluntary contributions which do not affect in any way the amount of the employer contributions made on their behalf. Such voluntary contributions obviously cannot cause employer contributions to be allocated on a discriminatory basis. However, because the investment of funds in the plan confers a tax advantage through the tax-free accumulation of earnings, limits are placed on the amounts of these voluntary employee contributions.

---

[23] Rev. Rul. 61-121, 1961-2 C. B. 67, Part 4(g).

198   PENSIONS AND PROFIT SHARING

The Internal Revenue Service has indicated that such voluntary employee contributions are permissible up to 10 percent of compensation.[24] This is in addition to any employee contributions which are made to fulfill requirements for participation in the plan.

Incidental Life Insurance, Hospitalization, and Medical Insurance

Qualified profit-sharing plans may provide covered employees with life insurance, group hospitalization insurance, and prepaid medical care insurance.

The use of the trust funds to pay the cost of such insurance for an employee or his beneficiaries constitutes a distribution for tax purposes. There is no limit on the amount of insurance that may be purchased by the profit-sharing trust from funds which have been accumulated for the period specified by the plan and are available for distribution.

However, if the profit-sharing plan pays the insurance premiums out of funds that have not been accumulated for the period prescribed before distribution, then the amount of the premium payments cannot be more than "incidental." This is to maintain the fundamental nature of the plan as a profit-sharing arrangement. If, under such circumstances, the payment of insurance premiums for covered employees is more than "incidental," the plan is not considered to be a profit-sharing plan and does not satisfy the qualification rules.[25]

Employees who receive such incidental life insurance under a profit-sharing plan are required to pay income tax currently on

---

[24] *Ibid.*, Part 4(h).

[25] In Rev. Rul. 61-164, 1961-2, C. B. 58, the Internal Revenue Service has indicated the guide lines that will be followed in determining how much may be paid by a qualified profit-sharing plan for insurance premiums for employees and their beneficiaries. Premiums paid for such insurance will be regarded as "incidental" under the following conditions:

(1) If only ordinary life insurance contracts are purchased, the aggregate premiums in the case of each participant must be less than one-half of the total contributions allocated to his account.

(2) If only accident and/or health insurance contracts (including hospitalization, major medical or similar types of insurance) are purchased, the payments for premiums may not exceed 25 percent of the funds allocated to the employee's account.

(3) If both ordinary life and accident and/or health insurance contracts are purchased, the amount spent for the accident and/or health insurance premiums plus one-half of the amount spent for the ordinary life insurance premiums, may not, together, exceed 25 percent of the funds allocated to the employee's account.

the value of the protection. The latter is determined on the basis of a table published by the Internal Revenue Service showing the annual cost of $1,000 of group term life insurance at various ages.[26]

Administration

Generally, three or more individuals who are officers or other employees of the employer or representatives of the union are appointed as members of a "Profit-Sharing Committee." This committee is charged with the responsibility of ascertaining the facts and making the decisions which are necessary in the day-to-day operation of the profit-sharing plan. Sometimes the members of this committee are also named as trustees and as custodian of the profit-sharing fund. In other cases, a bank or trust company is designated as trustee of the profit-sharing fund. The Profit-Sharing Committee, if desired, may have the right to instruct the trustee concerning the type of investments which should be made from time to time or may have a veto power over the investments proposed by the trustee. The corporate trustee, however, should have the responsibility of recommending and initiating the investment program. If the trustee is not experienced in the investment field, the advice of competent investment counselors or of competent security brokers should be obtained.

While it is important that the investments made by the profit-sharing trust be conservative to the extent necessary to protect principal, the potential increase in the value of the investment portfolio attributable to dividends and interest compounding annually in a tax-free trust should not be overlooked.

It must be kept in mind that one dollar invested each year for 35 years will increase to about $62 at 3 percent interest compounded annually. The same one dollar invested at the beginning of each year for 35 years will have increased to $77 at the end of 35 years if the trustee is able to earn a return of 4 percent compounded annually, and to $95 if the return is 5 percent. Many observers believe that such differentials justify the taking of some risk, provided that the risk is taken with the advice and consent of competent investment counsel. Considerable flexibility in investment policy results from the fact that the trustee of a profit-

---

[26] Rev. Rul. 55-747, 1955-2 C. B. 228.

sharing fund knows the date on which employees will retire and has no obligation to pay a fixed amount to any such employee—merely his proportionate share of the value of the fund. Because of this, there is little, if any, problem of forced liquidation of securities. Moreover, there is no need to have a large part of the trust fund invested in short-term bonds or other highly liquid investments.

On the subject of investments, the Commissioner's Regulations provide:

> "No specific limitations are provided in section 401(a) with respect to investments which may be made by the trustees of a trust qualifying under section 401(a). Generally, the contributions (of the employer) may be used by the trustees to purchase any investments permitted by the trust agreement to the extent allowed by local law."[27]

It should be noted that a profit-sharing trust is limited to relatively passive investments and may not engage in the active conduct of a trade or business without being taxed on that portion of its income which is derived from a trade or business. Moreover, if the primary purpose of the trust is the carrying on of a trade or business, it would lose its exemption completely and the tax treatment of employer contributions and employee beneficiaries would be the same as under non-qualified plans. The basic rules in this area are identical with those covering pension trusts which are discussed in greater detail on pp. 78-80 of this book.

The funds of a profit-sharing trust may be invested in stock or securities of the employer provided that full disclosure with respect to investments in securities of the employer is made to the Commissioner of Internal Revenue.[28] While advance approval is not required, such approval will be granted by the Commissioner if the investments are made for the exclusive benefit of employees included in the plan and are not made to benefit the employer. An employer may not sell its stock to a profit-sharing trust at an unfair price. However, if the stock of an employer is listed on the New York or American Stock Exchange, or is otherwise actively traded at prices determined at arm's length transactions, and if the stock of the employer pays a fair dividend and is a reasonable

---

[27] Regs. §. 1.401-1(b)(5)(i).
[28] §. 1.401-1(b)(5)(ii).

investment for a trust fund, the Commissioner has no reason for withholding his consent.

The requirement of fair dealing between the employer and the profit-sharing trust he creates was buttressed in the 1954 Code by certain specific rules previously applicable only to dealings between charitable, educational and other eleemosynary organizations and their creators or principal donors. Section 503(c) of the Code lists six types of "prohibited transactions" by the trusts and their creators or corporations affiliated with the creator. If a profit-sharing trust engaged in a prohibited transaction after March 1, 1954, it may lose its exempt status for the taxable years following the year in which it is notified by the Commissioner of the violation. However, if the Commissioner determines that the transaction was entered into for the purpose of diverting the corpus or income, and such transactions involved a substantial part of the trust corpus or income, the exemption may be lost as of the date of the transaction. An exemption so lost may be restored if the Commissioner is satisfied that the organization will not "knowingly again engage in a prohibited transaction." A complete list of the prohibited transactions may be found on pp. 75-77.

Termination or Amendment

In the Commissioner's Regulations it is provided that:

> "The term 'plan' implies a permanent as distinguished from a temporary program."[29]

The same regulations elaborate on this requirement as follows:

> "Thus, although the employer may reserve the right to change or terminate the plan, and to discontinue contributions thereunder, the abandonment of the plan for any reason other than business necessity within a few years after it has taken effect will be evidence that the plan from its inception was not a bona fide program for the exclusive benefit of employees in general."[30]

Thus, while a profit-sharing plan must be intended as a permanent program, the employer may specifically reserve the right to amend or to terminate the plan and to discontinue contributions to the trust. Upon the termination of a profit-sharing plan, the

---
[29] §. 1.401-1(b)(2).
[30] *Ibid.*

sums previously credited to the accounts of the eligible participants of the plan must be fully vested in the employees and must be paid to such employees. The method of payment, however, may be any one of several methods specified in the plan, as determined by the trustees or the Profit-Sharing Committee, including a lump sum cash payment, installment payments over a period of years, or the purchase of an immediate or deferred annuity contract. Or, upon termination of a profit-sharing plan, the trustees of the profit-sharing trust may distribute to the employees, in kind, the investments previously held in trust. The plan must provide that there shall be no reversion of trust funds to the employer.

As pointed out elsewhere in this book, if a pension plan is terminated within 10 years from the date of its adoption, Mimeograph 5717 imposes a limit on the contributions of the employer which can be used to provide benefits for certain highly compensated employees. (See p. 58.) No such limitation is applicable in the case of a profit-sharing plan. However, it must be remembered that a profit-sharing plan may not be terminated within a few years from the date of its adoption except in case of business necessity, or the Internal Revenue Service will argue that the plan was not a bona fide program from its inception. For obvious reasons, it is more difficult to prove a business necessity justifying termination in the case of a profit-sharing plan than a pension plan, since under a profit-sharing plan the employer makes no contributions in years when there are no profits and makes only small contributions in years when profits are small.

Tax Treatment of Distributions

Distributions made by profit-sharing plans to employees and their estates and beneficiaries are generally taxed in the same way as distributions made by pension plans (see pp. 66-73). Employer contributions to the profit-sharing plan as well as earnings accumulated on the funds in the tax-free trust are not taxed until they are paid out as benefits. Employees covered by profit-sharing plans therefore postpone payment of tax on such employer contributions and such earnings until they actually receive them in the form of benefits. This generally reduces their taxes since it tends to shift taxable income from their working years to their retirement years when their income is relatively low and falls in lower tax brackets. The fact that the tax payment is postponed until benefits are received grants employees interest savings insofar as it allows them to use for a longer period of time the amounts eventually paid out as taxes. Long-term capital gains treatment is also accorded to lump-sum distributions paid as a result of the covered individual's separation from service or death.

Some profit-sharing trusts, which invest in the securities of the employer-corporation, distribute such securities as benefits to employees in lieu of cash benefits. In some cases, these securities have appreciated considerably in value between the time of acquisition by the trust and the time of distribution. The Internal Revenue Code prescribes special rules for such unrealized appreciation. Where the distribution of the employer securities is in a lump-sum (i.e., a total distribution) and qualifies for capital gains treatment, the entire amount of the unrealized appreciation is not taxed to the recipient at the time of distribution. On the other hand, where the distribution does not qualify for capital gains treatment, the exclusion at the time of distribution applies only to the part of the unrealized appreciation attributable to employer securities purchased with the employee's own contribution.[31] After this exclusion, the remaining value of the employer-stock distribution is taxed to the recipient with due allowance for the tax-free return of his own contributions to the profit-sharing plan. Of course, the exclusion for unrealized appreciation at the time of distribution described above, is not included in the basis of the securities in the recipient's hands. Therefore, such unrealized appreciation may be taxed in the event that the recipient later sells the securities.

It is interesting that the Treasury, in expanding on the President's 1963 Tax Message, recommended eliminating the exclusion of unrealized appreciation on employer securities distributed under qualified employee plans.[32] This recommendation, however, was not adopted by the Congress.

Profit-Sharing Plans Covering Self-Employed Individuals

The Self-Employed Individuals Tax Retirement Act of 1962 (P. L. 87-792—known as the Keogh Act) allows self-employed

---

[31] §. §. 402(a)(1) and 402(a)(2); §. 1.402(a)-1(a)(6),(7), and (8); §. 1.402(a)-1(b)(1), (2), and (3).

[32] See *President's 1963 Tax Message along with Principal Statement, Technical Explanation, and Supporting Exhibits and Documents, submitted by Secretary of the Treasury Douglas Dillon,* February 6, 1963. U. S. Government Printing Office, pp. 143 and 144.

individuals to be covered by qualified profit-sharing plans as well as by qualified pension plans. The special provisions applicable to such qualified plans are described in detail on pp. 80-85. It should be noted that contributions for self-employed people under such plans are generally limited to 10 percent of earned income or $2,500, whichever is less and that only one-half of these contributions can be deducted. Qualified plans covering self-employed people must also meet stricter rules than those applicable to other plans. If a self-employed person is covered, the plan must generally cover all his full-time employees and give them immediate vested rights to employer contributions made on their behalf. Moreover, in contrast to the situation where no self-employed person is covered, a profit-sharing plan covering such an individual is required to have a definite formula for determining the share of total profits to be contributed on behalf of employees.[33]

The special rules applying to corporate plans covering self-employed people do not apply to plans covering stockholder-employees. The coming years will undoubtedly see many legislative attempts to liberalize the rules applying to plans covering self-employed people.

---

[33] §. 401(d)(2)(B) of the Internal Revenue Code.

CHAPTER 6

BARGAINING ON PENSIONS

By DONALD F. FARWELL

Introduction

Pension planning, complex in itself, becomes more so when it is made a subject of collective bargaining between management and union. No longer can management make unilateral decisions in what it conceives to be the best interests of the business and of employees; pension matters become subject to the pressures and vagaries of the bargaining table.

This implies a number of things—that any actions management wishes to take will have to be discussed with the union, although not necessarily agreed upon; that pension matters, like other issues in bargaining, will become fair game for horse-trading; that management may be faced with demands based upon a "pattern" framed without regard to its own special needs and problems, and that the alternative to granting these demands may be a strike; that it may have to entertain radically differing union proposals for different groups of employees in an area where it usually strives for uniformity of treatment; that any commitments it may make on pensions will be more readily enforceable in the courts; and a multitude of others.

This chapter ignores the traditional arguments for and against pension plans on the ground that these have become largely academic. The negotiated pension plan is a fixture in the collective bargaining picture at practically all larger companies and most smaller ones as well. Discussions as to whether to establish a pension plan now center almost exclusively upon cost considerations; and these are no different from the considerations applicable to all pension plans, as discussed elsewhere in this volume.

The first section of this chapter briefly traces the growth of pension bargaining, from the relatively simple plans of the 1940's to the extremely detailed ones of the 1960's. Special attention is paid to the basic steel plans as typifying this growth.

In the second section, some of the prevailing patterns of negotiated pension plans are outlined—patterns that exert a powerful influence upon the character of any new plans coming into existence.

The third section examines in some detail the major issues confronting negotiators in pension bargaining, and suggests some of those that may bulk large in the future. Following this is a section outlining some of the legal considerations applicable to negotiated pension plans.

The Rise of Pension Bargaining

Pensions for industrial employees have a relatively long history, dating mainly from unilateral programs instituted by management in the 1920's. But pension plans as instruments negotiated with unions on a large scale may be dated, for practical purposes, from the end of World War II.

Several factors combined to create a favorable climate for pension negotiations. One was the proliferation of unilateral plans during the war, as management sought to make employment more attractive at a time when pay increases were blocked by wage controls; this led to union interest and intervention in the field.

A second factor was an action taken by the government at a time when it was operating the coal mines. Secretary of the Interior Krug negotiated an agreement with John L. Lewis, president of the United Mine Workers, for a tonnage royalty on coal to support a pension plan. The hundred-dollar-a-month pension thereby achieved became a target for other unions.

Still another factor was a ruling by the National Labor Relations Board settling the question of pension bargainability. The Board, supported by the courts, ruled in the Inland Steel case[1] that pensions were a proper subject for collective bargaining. Under that ruling, management commits an unfair labor practice under the Taft Act if it refuses to discuss pensions with a union on request. This means not only that management is required to negotiate (though not to agree) on the establishment of a pension plan where none exists, but also that existing unilateral retire-

---

[1] *Inland Steel Co.*, 21 LRRM 1310 (1948); enforced 22 LRRM 2506 (C.A. 7, 1948).

ment plans or policies may not be altered without first consulting the union representing the employees affected. The Board subsequently made an exception to this rule, applicable where the union has expressly waived its right to bargain, but from this time pensions became an issue in practically all major collective bargaining situations.

Recommendations in Basic Steel

The union breakthrough on pensions in manufacturing was achieved with a big assist from the government. A Presidential fact-finding panel, set up when negotiations between basic steel companies and the Steelworkers became deadlocked in 1949, recommended the establishment of noncontributory pension plans. While the panel's recommendations were not immediately accepted, the steel companies capitulated after a strike and agreed to pension provisions in many respects more favorable from the union standpoint than those recommended by the panel. At the same time, pension plans were being negotiated elsewhere (in automobiles and rubber), and the spread to major companies in other manufacturing industries came rapidly.

Expansion of Basic Steel Plans

A Bureau of National Affairs, Inc., study made in 1948 found pension provisions in only 5 percent of collective bargaining contracts. After the establishment of negotiated pensions in steel, there was a sharp and steady rise in this frequency, so that by 1954, according to a similar BNA study, pension plans were incorporated in more than two fifths of contracts. By 1960 the proportion had climbed to two thirds.

Just as negotiated pension plans were gaining in number, so they were being transformed from relatively simple documents to highly complex ones. The process is well illustrated by the evolution of the steel plans.

The first negotiated steel program, Bethlehem's, was built upon an existing unilateral plan. As revised in negotiations, the plan provided a minimum monthly benefit of $100, including primary Social Security, for employees retiring after 25 years' service at the age of 65. (Employees could stay on the job after 65 with management approval.) Proportionately reduced benefits were offered to employees retiring at 65 with 15 to 25 years' service. Employees with at least 15 years' service, regardless of age, who retired because of total and permanent disability were guaranteed minimum pensions of $50 per month.

Higher-than-minimum pensions were possible under a formula based on both service and earnings. This provided a benefit equal to 1 percent of average monthly earnings during the 10-year period preceding retirement multiplied by years of continuous service. Primary Social Security was included in the benefit, so increases in the federal payment operated merely to reduce the amount payable from the pension fund.

The minimum-benefit formula was controlling in all cases where monthly earnings averaged $400 or less. Since the monthly average at that time was under $300, it can be seen that the great majority of employees received the minimum pension.

By 1954 considerable pressure had built up for liberalization of the steel plans—in part because the benefits they provided had been surpassed in other industries, especially autos, and in part because of two successive increases in Social Security, with a third impending. Accordingly, with U.S. Steel leading the way, steel companies agreed to raise the minimum pension benefit upon retirement at age 65, but after 30 rather than 25 years' service, to $140 per month. The deduction for Social Security was set at a maximum of $85, then the maximum benefit, thus assuring that future increases in Social Security would serve to increase minimum pensions. In fact, the federal maximum was raised to $108.50 almost immediately, thereby setting the combined monthly benefit at $163.50.

For each year of service less than 30 the benefit was reduced by $2 per month; thus the minimum pension after 15 years of service became $100 per month. At the same time disability benefits were increased from $50 to $75 per month. Pensions exceeding the various minimums remained possible under the service-and-earnings formula.

Extensive changes were made in the 1956 negotiations, although these did not become effective until late in 1957. The minimum-pension formula was fully divorced from Social Security, and a distinction was made between service before the effective date of the changes and service after that date. The monthly benefit for each year of service prior to November 1, 1957, was set at $2.40; for each year of service thereafter, $2.50. Since the maximum

Social Security benefit at that time was $108.50, the total benefit under the minimum-pension formula became a variable ranging from $180.50 to $183.50 for an employee with 30 years' service. The disability provision was liberalized, also, to provide for application of the minimum-pension formula; in the case of individuals not eligible for disability benefits under the Social Security Act (the payment of such benefits commenced in 1957), the minimum was set at $90 per month.

At the same time, far-reaching changes were made in the eligibility requirements for pensions, bringing several categories of employees into the picture for the first time. First, optional early retirement, with an actuarially reduced pension beginning immediately or an unreduced pension beginning at age 65, was permitted by an employee with at least 15 years' service who had attained the age of 60. More important, deferred (vested) pensions were made available to employees not recalled within two years of layoff and to those terminated in a plant or departmental shutdown, provided they had at least 15 years' service and had attained the age of 40.

Finally, a joint and survivorship option was written into the plans. This permitted an employee to choose to receive a reduced pension, in which case payments to a designated beneficiary were to continue after his death.

Further significant amendments were made in 1960. The minimum normal pension was increased to $2.60 for each year of service beginning on or after January 1, 1960, and $2.50 for each year of service prior to that date. The ceiling on credited service was raised from 30 to 35 years. Together with Social Security, which by then had reached a maximum of $127 a month (its present level), this brought the monthly pension after 35 years' service to a range of $214.50 to $218. The minimum disability pension for those not eligible for Social Security also was increased, from $90 to $100 a month. And the deduction for Social Security under the 1-percent formula was reduced from $85 to $80 a month.

A substantial and wholly new benefit added in 1960 was a lump-sum payment equal to 13 weeks' vacation pay, reduced by any pay for vacation already taken in the year of retirement. This was provided for all retirees except those entitled to disability or deferred vested pensions. Regular pension benefits then became payable upon the completion of three months' retirement.

At the same time, further relaxations were made in eligibility requirements. Full pensions were provided for employees terminated at or after age 55 with at least 20 years' service, by reason of a permanent shutdown or layoff or sickness resulting in a service break, provided such an employee was at least 53 and had 18 or more years' service when he ceased work. Full pensions were provided also for employees retiring at age 60 with 15 or more years' service under mutually satisfactory conditions.

Negotiations in 1962 left the benefit structure basically unchanged but eased the provisions applicable to employees who cease work because of a permanent shutdown, layoff, or disability and are unlikely to be recalled. Whereas these employees, to qualify for pensions, formerly had to be at least 55 and have 20 years' service, they now qualify if their age and service total 80 or, in the case of those who are 55 or over, if their age and service total 75.

More recently, the Steelworkers have achieved pension gains in negotiations with American and Continental Can companies which it is believed represent their objectives in future bargaining with the basic steel companies. The benefit upon normal retirement under these plans is set at $3.25 per month per year of service; added to the maximum federal benefit, this produces a total pension after 35 years' service of $240.75 a month. The can makers' plans also set the minimum disability pension at $120 a month.

Prevailing Pension Patterns

Pattern bargaining—that is, the widespread application of settlements reached by one or more leading companies—has been less marked in the case of pensions than in the case of wage increases and certain other fringe benefits. The reason for this may be that the initial pension negotiations at many companies were concerned with converting established unilateral plans into contractual arrangements, with or without substantial change. In these situations the final negotiated product often was shaped more by the nature of the unilateral plan than by what other companies and unions were doing.

Nevertheless, in some industries and some areas pension patterns have emerged which must be reckoned with in any bargaining on the subject within their respective areas. Generally speaking, this has been true in those industries where one union is dominant, as in automobiles and farm equipment and in basic steel. Here are some of these patterns.

Basic Steel

The benefit structure and eligibility of the plans in the basic steel industry are described in considerable detail in the preceding section of this chapter. Other important aspects are treated here.

There is no provision for compulsory retirement, an employee being eligible for the normal pension but not required to retire when he reaches 65.

Administration of the plans is assigned to boards appointed by management. However, there are joint pension committees which are to be kept informed concerning the operation of the plans. Moreover, special appeals procedures are provided for handling employee complaints regarding benefits. The terminal point of these procedures is arbitration.

Funding provisions are not uniform. All the plans utilize trust funds, but U.S. Steel, for example, is free to determine the manner and means of funding and paying the benefits. Bethlehem and some other companies, on the other hand, must make contributions sufficient to pay all pensions granted through the years.

Autos & Farm Equipment

The pension pattern negotiated by the United Auto Workers in the auto and, to a considerable degree, farm equipment industries is illustrated by the General Motors plan. Normal retirement is at age 65 after 10 or more years' service. A full year of credit is allowed for each year in which an employee has at least 1,700 compensated hours. Pro rata credit is given if the employee has fewer than 1,700 hours.

The monthly benefit upon normal retirement is $2.80 for each year of credited service until age 68, exclusive of Social Security. Thus, if an employee qualifies for the maximum Social Security benefit, his total pension after 35 years' service is $225 per month.

Early retirement at age 60 after 10 or more years' service is permitted at the employee's option, or the company may retire him under mutually satisfactory conditions. The benefit, if retirement is at the employee's option, is a reduced pension beginning immediately or a full pension beginning at age 65. If retirement is by the company under mutually satisfactory conditions, the benefit is double the normal pension until age 65, at which time it reverts to the normal amount. The total and permanent disability benefit, payable after 10 years' service, also is double the normal pension until the employee qualifies for Social Security; then, or in any case at age 65, the normal amount is payable.

Deferred (vested) benefits are available to employees whose seniority is broken between the ages of 40 and 60 after 10 years' service. The benefit amount is $2.80 per month per year of service at age 65, or the employee may elect to take a reduced pension at age 60.

In lieu of normal benefits an employee may take a smaller pension and have half that amount continued for his spouse after his death. The reduced pension, if the employee and spouse are the same age, is equal to 90 percent of the normal benefit—a less-than-actuarial reduction.

Employees are permitted to continue working beyond the normal retirement age, but work beyond the "automatic" retirement age (68) is subject to management approval.

Administration of the plan generally is the responsibility of the company, but there is a joint board, composed of equal numbers of management and union representatives, with an impartial chairman to break deadlocks, to handle benefit-eligibility determinations.

The plan is trusteed, although management has the right to finance the plan through an insurance company if it wishes. Payments by the company each year must be sufficient to cover service credits for that year and to fund past-service credits over a period of 30 years.

Rubber

The pension pattern achieved by the Rubber Workers in their industry is markedly similar to the one that prevailed in the auto industry until late in 1961. Typical of the pattern is the plan of Goodyear Tire & Rubber Co., under which normal retirement takes place at age 65 after 10 or more years' continuous service. Unlike the auto plans, continuous service is the same as seniority, there being no minimum number of compensated hours for a year's credit.

The normal retirement benefit is $2.40 per month for each year of service prior to January 1, 1959, and $2.50 per month for each year of service thereafter, exclusive of Social Security. So the total pension after 35 years' future service, assuming maximum Social Security, is $214.50 per month.

The eligibility requirements for early retirement are different from those in autos—age 55 and 20 or more years' service. Requirements for disability retirement and vesting are the same, and the computation of benefits is similar in all cases. Several survivorship options are available to the retiring employee, each providing the actuarial equivalent of the normal pension benefit.

Administration of the plan is by a company-appointed board. Disputes over benefit determinations may be processed through the regular grievance channels under the applicable collective bargaining agreement. Financing is through a trust fund, the company making contributions in such amounts as may be determined by the board of directors.

Multi-Employer Plans

In certain industries, generally those in which bargaining typically is conducted on a multi-employer basis, employers and unions have negotiated pension plans covering anywhere from a few to a great many companies. These plans vary from one another about as much as single-employer plans, but some general comments can be made about them.

Their most striking common feature is that, even in the absence of express vesting provisions, they make pensions "portable" to a certain extent. That is, so long as an employee remains within a plan's area of coverage, he continues to accumulate pension credits even though he may change his employment. The portability of pensions may be increased in either of two ways. The more common one is the inclusion of vesting provisions similar to those found frequently in single-employer plans; these appear in nearly a quarter of multi-employer plans. The second method, found in fewer than a tenth of multi-employer plans, is the establishment of reciprocity agreements with other such plans. Under these agreements service under one plan may be credited toward benefits under another plan. Reciprocity agreements are characteristic of plans negotiated by the Ladies' Garment Workers.

Benefit formulas in multi-employer plans do not show the great diversity exhibited by single-employer plans—perhaps because the vast majority are of relatively recent origin and were initiated through collective bargaining. More than three fifths, according to a Bureau of Labor Statistics study,[2] base benefits on length of service alone; this is true of about a third of single-employer plans. One quarter provide a uniform benefit for all who meet the minimum eligibility requirements, as against a small fraction of single-employer plans. And a small number express benefits as a percentage of the employer contributions made for each participant—an approach rarely found in single-employer plans.

An arrangement found in some plans, especially those negotiated by the Teamsters, permits the accommodation of employers making contributions at different rates, as negotiated locally. Typical of these plans is the Teamsters' Central States, Southwest and Southeast area program. The retirement benefit for individuals whose employer is contributing at a rate of $6 per week per employee is $200 per month for the first five years of retirement, $90 thereafter. Smaller benefits, not in direct proportion to the contributions, are specified for individuals whose employer is contributing at a lesser rate.

Multi-employer plans are almost all financed wholly by the employers. Of 736 such plans examined by BLS in the study referred to above, only 30 were jointly financed and four were financed entirely by the employees.

A serious problem encountered in multi-employer retirement plans is that of "floating liability." This stems from the fact that employment in many of the industries in which multi-employer plans are found is intermittent, seasonal, or casual; employees, after establishing some equity in a plan, may drift out of the area of coverage, leaving open the question of their return. Accordingly, multi-employer plans place greater emphasis on service-crediting provisions than do single-employer plans. Full-time, year-round employment usually is not required for a year's service credit, but an individual must have had fairly regular employment with one or more contributing employers throughout the minimum service period to qualify for benefits. In addition, workers who do not work for a participating employer during a

---

[2] *Multi-employer Pension Plans Under Collective Bargaining*, BLS Bulletin No. 1326, June 1962.

specified period of time (commonly one or two years) ordinarily are dropped from the plan unless they already have fulfilled the requirements for a pension. If subsequently reemployed, they are regarded as new participants.

Administrative provisions of multi-employer plans contrast sharply with those of single-employer plans. Whereas management generally is charged with sole responsibility for control of the pension fund under single-employer plans, and often for administration of the benefit structure as well, joint administrative boards are the almost invariable rule for multi-employer plans. These boards usually determine both the method of financing to be used in providing benefits and the investment policies of the pension fund.

Multi-employer plans are found most commonly in food, apparel, construction, transportation, mining, and wholesale and retail trade. The union with the largest number of such plans, and also the largest number of covered members, is the Teamsters. Other major unions that place heavy emphasis on multi-employer plans include the Carpenters, Clothing Workers, Electrical Workers (IBEW), Hod Carriers, Ladies' Garment Workers, Meat Cutters, Mine Workers, and Plumbers.

Union Plans

Mention should be made also of pension plans established by some unions to provide benefits for their members wherever employed, provided the required contributions are made by the members or on their behalf. These plans, broadly speaking, are multi-employer plans, but they have certain characteristics which justify separate classification. First, their coverage, at least potentially, is contiguous with that of the union's jurisdiction; the usual multi-employer plan is limited to the employees of one or more employer bargaining associations. Second, their structure is determined unilaterally by the union, participating employers being required to accept the plan as written. And third, they may permit individual employers to make contributions to the pension fund in differing amounts, benefits for employees being geared to the employer's contributions.

Employers participating in such union plans typically are small; indeed, the problem of providing pensions for employees of the small company has been the principal reason for the establishment of union plans. For example, the Machinists reported in October 1963 that the IAM Labor-Management Pension Fund, established in 1960, covered about 10,000 members employed by 250 companies in 32 states. The average number covered at each company was thus only 40.

Paper Mill Workers Plan—A newly established plan of the Pulp, Sulphite & Paper Mill Workers may serve to illustrate the flexible nature of union pension programs. By mid-1963 the plan was just getting off the ground, the union reporting that only a handful of relatively small companies in New York and Massachusetts had elected to participate.

Coverage is open to any employer having a collective bargaining agreement with a local of the Paper Mill Workers. Eligible employee groups are limited, as a general rule, to classifications within the contractual jurisdiction of the union. However, certain nonunion groups, such as clerical employees, may be enrolled if the company agrees to make contributions on their behalf.

The normal pension benefit, payable at age 65 after 25 years of service, may be anywhere from $50 to $250 per month, exclusive of Social Security, depending on the rate at which the company contributes. A proportionately reduced pension is available at age 65 to employees with at least 15 but less than 25 years of service. An early-retirement pension or a deferred vested pension is available to employees who have reached age 55 and have at least 15 years of service. Pensions are payable to totally and permanently disabled employees who are at least 50 and have 15 or more years of service. Benefits continue for life and for three years certain.

Company contributions depend on the benefit level desired and the average age of the local-union membership when the company first joins the plan. To buy a normal pension of $50 per month, the company contributes four cents per man-hour if the average age is less than 32.8 years; 4.5 cents if the average age is from 32.9 to 34.7; and so on up to 12 cents if the average age is from 46.6 to 46.8. Additional pension amounts may be purchased in increments of $10 per month at one fifth the basic contribution rate.

To be eligible for a normal pension, an employee must have at least 25 years' employment in job classifications for which the employer is contributing to the fund, and must have at least two quarters of future service credit. "Future service" is service subsequent to the date on which the employer starts making contributions to the pension fund. Past-service credit is allowed at the rate of one year for each year in which the employee worked 1,200 hours or more. Covered employees may carry pension credits with them as they move from one company to another within the union's jurisdiction.

Administration of the plan, including the pension fund, is by an equal number of employer and union trustees. The trustees are empowered to adjust the nature, amount, and duration of benefits on the basis of availability of funds. Any deadlock of the trustees on benefits or other questions is arbitrable.

Current Issues in Pension Bargaining

Normal Retirement Benefits

As long as wage rates continue their upward march, benefit levels under negotiated pension plans will continue to be a major issue in bargaining. Thus, until 1962, benefits payable under the basic steel plans were increased on each occasion when the plans, by their terms, permitted such action; in 1962 benefit levels remained substantially unchanged, and there were likewise no changes when the two-year contracts signed in 1962 were reopened the following year.

In the early 1950's a number of unions established a pension goal of $200 per month, including the primary Social Security benefit. More liberal benefit formulas and increases in federal payments combined to bring realization of this goal within five years, and pensions in excess of $200 are now quite common. In autos and farm equipment, most major plans provide a benefit upon normal retirement of $2.80 per month per year of credited service, with no limit on the buildup of service credits. Thus an employee retiring at 65 with 35 years' credited service receives a monthly pension of $225, assuming he qualifies for the maximum primary Social Security benefit of $127. A benefit of at least $2.50 per month per year of service has been achieved in major noncontributory plans in many industries, including basic steel, chemicals, electrical and nonelectrical machinery, fabricated metals, nonferrous metals, rubber, stone, clay, and glass, and transportation. The benefit after 35 years' service under a $2.50

plan, again assuming the employee qualifies for maximum Social Security, is $214.50 per month.

Generally speaking, bargaining pressure may be expected from unions wherever pension benefits now fall below $2.50 per month per year of service, excluding Social Security. And in those situations where benefits now are at or above $2.50, the $3.25 benefit provided by the American and Continental can plans can be taken as a union objective.

Relationship of Benefits to Earnings and Service—Benefits under negotiated pension plans may vary with both earnings and service or with service alone, or may be uniform for all qualified employees. A study of 300 negotiated plans (each covering at least 1,000 employees) made by the Bureau of Labor Statistics in 1959[3] found that 46 percent had formulas in which the benefit was determined both by earnings and by credited service; the great majority of these, however, also contained minimum-benefit formulas geared to service only. Close to 40 percent of the plans had formulas basing benefits on service alone. And 10 percent provided a uniform benefit for all qualified employees. (The remaining few plans were combinations or variations of these types.)

Throughout the 1950's there was a trend away from earnings-and-service formulas and toward service-only formulas. There is evidence, however, that unions, believing adequate benefits have been achieved for lower-paid employees, may look upon service-only formulas with less favor in the future. For example, in 1960 the plan of Westinghouse Electric Corporation and the Electrical Workers (IUE) was amended to provide benefits, starting in 1962, ranging from $2.50 to $3.50 per month per year of service, depending upon the employee's earnings; in 1963 the plan was further amended to increase the top and bottom of the range to $2.55 and $3.80, respectively, as of January 1964. The maximum benefit is payable to an employee making $4.25 an hour or more, or its equivalent in weekly or monthly pay. Prior to amendment the plan had provided a benefit of $2.40 per month per year.

Adjustments Based on Living Costs—A union objective that has cropped up in many negotiations, but so far has appeared in few plans, is a provision relating benefits to living costs. The strongest advocate of such an arrangement, perhaps, is the United Auto

---

[3] *Pension Plans Under Collective Bargaining*, BLS Bulletin No. 1284, February 1961.

Workers, which invariably raises the issue in bargaining with the auto companies.

UAW has negotiated a plan with National Lock Company under which benefits are adjusted semi-annually to reflect changes in the BLS Consumer Price Index; downward as well as upward adjustments are permitted. Another example of this approach is a plan negotiated by an independent union of truck drivers in Chicago with three employer associations. The basic benefit is $75 a month, but each July 1 it is subject to adjustment on the basis of the Consumer Price Index for the preceding May. The amount of the adjustment is $5 per month for each three-point change in the index, upward or downward though not below the $75 floor. Pension trustees, however, have the right to amend or terminate the cost-of-living allowance at any time.

Lump-Sum Benefit upon Retirement—An innovation in pension bargaining pioneered by the Steelworkers in 1960 is the special lump-sum benefit payable upon normal or early retirement, described earlier in this chapter. Plans in which this benefit appears include those in basic steel, aluminum, and can manufacturing. It is a rather substantial benefit—in the vicinity of $800, over and above normal pension and vacation payments, for the average retiree.

Other unions may be expected to incorporate a demand for this lump-sum payment in their pension bargaining programs. Two that already have done so are the International Union of Electrical Workers and the United Electrical Workers.

Early Retirement

Early retirement provisions have been a part of many negotiated pension plans since their inception. But whereas the traditional early retirement clause provides for actuarial reduction of the normal benefit, unions are now seeking to negotiate provisions of a very different sort as part of their efforts to combat unemployment, particularly that caused by technological change and plant closures. The aims are to liberalize the conditions under which employees may qualify for pensions prior to the normal retirement age, and to provide them with larger-than-normal pensions until such time as they become entitled to Social Security benefits.

Under the American Motors—UAW pension plan, for example, an employee who is permanently laid off by reason of the discontinuance of a plant or operation is entitled to double the normal pension until he reaches age 65, provided he is at least age 60 and has 10 years' credited service when laid off. At 65 the normal pension becomes payable. Other major auto plans, and also the American Motors plan, specify this benefit when an employee who is age 60 and has 10 years' service is retired at management's option or under "mutually satisfactory conditions."

Similarly, Armour & Company's pension agreements with the Packinghouse Workers and the Meat Cutters provide for the payment of one and one-half times the normal pension to an employee who is at least 55, has 20 or more years' service, and is terminated by reason of a plant or department shutdown or technological change. This special benefit continues to age 62 (at which point the employee may begin collecting reduced Social Security benefits); then the normal benefit becomes payable.

By agreement between Pacific Maritime Association and the independent Longshoremen & Warehousemen, augmented pensions are provided to induce older employees to leave the industry. An employee may retire at age 62, if he has at least 22 years' service, and receive $220 per month in addition to the regular $115 pension until he reaches age 65. The extra sum is paid from an automation fund rather than from the pension fund. If not enough employees retire voluntarily under this provision, mandatory retirement may be resorted to by management.

In the same vein, although not necessarily prompted by unemployment or technological change, is a revision made in 1962 in the Teamsters' Central States, Southwest & Southeast area pension plan. Retirement under this plan formerly was permitted at age 60 after 20 years of service. Benefits vary with contributions paid by participating employers, but in all cases they are much higher during the first five years of retirement—that is, until pensioners can qualify for Social Security benefits—than during the ensuing years. In October 1962 the trustees, with the approval of the Internal Revenue Service, reduced the retirement age to 57. Underlying this change was the fact that retirement at age 62 now is permitted—though with reduced benefits—under the Social Security Act. The plan currently provides a benefit of $200 per month until age 62, in the case of an individual whose employer is contributing $6 per employee per week; thereafter the benefit drops to $90.

A striking example of the high priority being given by many

unions to the matter of earlier retirement was provided in 1963 by the National Maritime Union. To encourage retirement by seamen and thus improve employment opportunities for younger persons, the union resolved to achieve pensions of $150 per month, exclusive of Social Security, payable at any age after 20 years of service. (At the time a pension of $125 per month was payable at age 65 after 25 years of service.) This goal was reached in negotiations with the American Merchant Marine Institute in two stages. First, union members voted to divert 2¼-percent deferred wage increases scheduled to become effective in 1963 and 1964 to the pension fund, and the trustees of the pension fund approved a union proposal to apply additional money, originally earmarked for other benefits, to pensions. This made it possible to drop the minimum age requirement, and to cut the service requirement to 20 years, in 1964. Then the companies agreed, as part of a four-year contract extension, to increase their pension contributions beginning in mid-1965; the pension amount will then be raised to $150 per month.

A highly significant development in this area occurred late in 1963 when Westinghouse Electric Corporation agreed in negotiations with the major electrical unions to pay unreduced pensions to employees with 30 or more years of service who retire at age 62; previously the full pension amount had not been payable prior to age 65. Another change in the pension plan permitted employees to retire between 60 and 65 after 10 or more years of service with substantially higher benefits than previously. Whereas the normal pension formerly was reduced by 7.2 percent for each year short of the 65-year mark, it now is reduced by only 4 percent. The payment of the full pension at age 62 was justly described by the company as a "pioneering provision," at least so far as major manufacturing companies are concerned.

Plans negotiated by the Steelworkers with major steel, aluminum, and can companies make special provision for older employees who are terminated as a result of permanent shutdown, layoff, or disability. To qualify for this "broken service" benefit, an employee must have at least 15 years' service. If he is 55 or older, his age and service must total at least 75; if he is under 55, age and service must total at least 80. The benefit under most plans is the normal pension. However, the plans at American and Continental Can provide a benefit of $5 per month per year of service, as against a normal benefit of $3.25, until the employee can qualify for his full Social Security benefit; then the benefit reverts to normal.

The initiative in this area does not always come from the union. An illustration of management initiative is an offer made in late 1962 by Humble Oil & Refining Company to the Esso Seamen's Association, an independent union representing employees on the company's tanker fleet. As part of a plan to reduce the size of its ship crews by 16 percent to keep the fleet competitive with oil pipelines, the company proposed an early retirement program under which a seaman with 15 years' service could retire with larger-than-normal benefits if he was age 55 or older. The pension for a 62-year-old employee was 96.4 percent of the amount payable at age 65; for a 60-year-old employee, 91 percent; and for a 55-year-old employee, 72 percent. Pensions under the company's regular early-retirement program are 76, 64, and 44 percent, respectively. Deadline for retirement under the special program was set at June 30, 1963.

Disability Benefits

Provisions in negotiated plans relating to benefits for workers who retire because of total and permanent disability vary widely, but an approach pioneered in the automobile industry is gaining in popularity. This provides for a benefit equal to double the normal pension as long as the pensioner is ineligible for Social Security benefits. When he qualifies for any Social Security benefit, disability or regular, or in any case at age 65, the normal pension benefit is payable. The service requirement for disability retirement is 15 years in most cases, but in major plans of the Auto Workers it was reduced to 10 years in the 1961 negotiations. There is no minimum age requirement.

This is the approach seen in many plans in farm equipment and rubber as well as in autos, and it is included in the bargaining program of the Electrical Workers (IUE). A variation negotiated by the Steelworkers at American and Continental Can provides a monthly benefit of $5 per year of service, roughly one and one-half times the normal benefit, subject to a minimum of $120.

Integration with Social Security

Benefits under negotiated pension plans may be so stated as to include Social Security benefits, or they may be wholly divorced from Social Security. In some plans both approaches are seen, the basic benefit formula specifying a pension inclusive of federal payments but the plan guaranteeing to pay a stated minimum benefit without regard to Social Security.

Integration of plan benefits with Social Security may be accomplished in either of two ways. First, all or part of Social Security may be deducted from the amount computed by application of the basic benefit formula. Second, the benefit payable for earnings in excess of the amount considered in computing Social Security may be larger, on a percentage basis, than the benefit payable for earnings up to that amount. The approach found in negotiated plans is usually the first one.

The early negotiated plans for the most part were integrated plans. The auto plans, for example, at first specified a benefit of $100 a month after 25 years' service, inclusive of the full primary Social Security benefit. The steel plans had both a basic and a minimum benefit formula, and both were fully integrated with Social Security.

This arrangement produced much employee and union dissatisfaction because increases in federal payments did not produce higher pensions but merely reduced the amount payable from the private pension fund. So it was not long before steps were taken to divorce pension benefits from Social Security in whole or in part. In the auto plans this was done simply by stating the monthly benefit payable for each year of service (currently $2.80) without regard to Social Security, although for a time the combined benefit was retained in the plans as well. In steel the divorce was partial; a limitation of $85 (subsequently reduced to $80) was placed on the monthly offset under the percentage-of-earnings benefit formula, and a minimum monthly benefit was specified without regard to Social Security. Another variation saw the offset limited to half the Social Security benefit, the basis for this being that employee contributions pay for half the federal benefit.

The trend away from integrated plans has progressed to the point where they are distinctly in the minority, and those which persist are subjected to assaults by union negotiators. Thus, the offset under the Bell Telephone plan was reduced from one half to one third of the primary Social Security benefit as a result of contract negotiations in 1963. A study of 300 negotiated plans made by the Bureau of Labor Statistics in 1959[4] found that three

---

[4] *Pension Plans Under Collective Bargaining*, BLS Bulletin No. 1284, February 1961.

fifths of them had no integration provision whatsoever; and more than half the integrated plans contained a minimum guarantee, unrelated to Social Security, that determined the benefit payable to most covered employees. Similarly, a study of more than 200 negotiated plans made by The Bureau of National Affairs, Inc., in 1961 found that nearly 90 percent contained a benefit formula not geared to Social Security, at least so far as minimum pensions were concerned.

Integration with Social Security has thus been largely removed as an issue in bargaining over the benefit payable upon normal retirement. It continues to figure importantly, however, in bargaining over benefits payable to disabled pensioners or to those who retire for other reasons before they reach 65. Union aims, generally speaking, may be summed up as these: (1) where disability benefits are integrated with Social Security, to eliminate the tie-in or limit the offset, as in the case of normal retirement benefits; and (2) to provide for larger-than-normal benefits until the recipient can qualify for unreduced Social Security benefits.

Benefits for Persons Already Retired

A problem facing pension negotiators when benefits are increased is whether persons already retired shall have their allowances adjusted and, if so, to what extent. Management traditionally has taken the position that the union has no authority to bargain for such persons but, nevertheless, often has made increases in pensions already granted. This may be done in a variety of ways, contractually or extracontractually. The new benefit formula may be applied without modification to some or all previously retired persons; a special formula providing smaller benefits may be applied to them; or their pensions may be increased by a specified dollar amount.

In their pension negotiations with major auto companies in 1958, the Auto Workers, after gaining increased benefits for those already on the retirement rolls, agreed to waive its right to bargain for pensioners. The waiver states that UAW will not ask management to discuss changes in the benefits payable to persons previously retired. It further states that management is not obligated to discuss or to make such changes. A union official stated at the time that the waiver had to be given because it was not the practice in other major industries to make such adjustments. Help for pensioners in the future, he added, would have to take the form of efforts to raise Social Security benefits.

Two questions posed by the waiver were, first, whether the union in fact ever possessed the bargaining rights it agreed to waive; and, second, whether the waiver would be binding upon those who might negotiate for the union in the future. However that may be, benefits under the pension plans were re-negotiated in 1961, and the allowances for persons already retired were left unchanged. It should be noted, however, that if the union should succeed in achieving automatic adjustment of pensions on the basis of changes in living costs, the matter would become largely academic.

Survivor Benefits

Joint and survivor options, under which a pensioner may elect to have payments made to a designated beneficiary after his death, long have been a feature of both unilateral and negotiated retirement plans. The usual option provides for actuarial reduction of benefits payable during the pensioner's lifetime, so that payments to the pensioner and his survivor will be the same, in the average case, as the pensioner would have received in the absence of the option.

Unions, however, are now demanding survivor options differing in two important respects from the traditional ones. First, they are seeking less-than-actuarial reductions in benefits payable to the retired person, and the ultimate goal is said to be no reduction at all. Second, they want employees to be permitted to choose the manner in which payments will be made at the time of retirement. Under the usual option the election must be made well in advance of retirement, or evidence of good health must be shown.

The pension amendments negotiated by the United Auto Workers and the auto companies in 1961 exemplify this new "subsidized" survivor option. At the time of retirement an employee may elect to accept a reduced pension and have 50 percent of the reduced amount paid after his death to his spouse. The reduction depends upon the spouse's age; if it is the same as the employee's, the reduced pension is 90 percent of the normal benefit. The reduced pension under the usual survivor option, in contrast, would be about 83 percent of the normal benefit.

The term "widow's pension" has come to mean something more

extensive in the union lexicon than even the liberalized survivor options now being sought. The survivors of an employee who dies prior to retirement, unions are beginning to argue, should have the benefit of pension contributions made on the employee's behalf. It can be expected that in future pension negotiations they will propose that some provision be made—beyond the mere return of such contributions as the employee may have made—for the widow (or widower) of an employee who dies after a lengthy period of coverage under a pension plan. The thinking was expressed as follows in the 1963 bargaining program of the Electrical Workers (IUE): "Survivors of workers with 15 or more years of service should have survivorship benefits, effective at age 55 or 60."

According to a reference guide prepared by AFL-CIO for its member unions,[5] the general lack of protection for widows "remains a major gap in coverage." "It is important to make some start in this direction," the guide states, "even if initial programs fall considerably short of ideal."

Vesting

Vesting of pension credits in employees prior to retirement age was a rarity in noncontributory pension plans until about 1955. Since then vesting provisions have spread rapidly and may now be found in a majority of negotiated noncontributory as well as in nearly all contributory plans. The union argument for vesting is that pension contributions are the same as wages; accordingly, pension credits earned by an employee should not be lost when he is terminated prior to the time he can qualify for a pension. Considerable bargaining pressure for vesting is to be expected in those situations where it does not already exist.

The great majority of negotiated vesting provisions contain both a minimum age and a minimum service requirement. In autos and farm equipment, an employee terminated at or after age 40 with 10 or more years' service remains entitled to a pension beginning at age 65; the benefit amount is a normal pension based on the employee's credited service at the time of his termination. This is perhaps the most common type of provision. Steelworkers plans provide for deferred full vesting at age 40 after 15 years'

---

[5] *Pension Plans Under Collective Bargaining . . . a reference guide for Trade Unions,* AFL-CIO Publication No. 32, January 1964.

service, but only in the case of employees who are laid off and not recalled within two years or who are terminated because of a plant or department shutdown.

One of the most liberal vesting provisions in a major negotiated pension plan was agreed to by General Electric Company in its 1963 negotiations with the major electrical unions. Vesting now takes place under the GE plan after 10 years of service and the attainment of age 35, or after 15 years of service regardless of age.

Bargaining pressure for vested pension rights, apart from those situations in which vesting is totally lacking, will be aimed at eliminating or easing restrictive conditions. Thus the auto pension plans formerly required exclusion of service prior to age 30 in computing vested benefits; this limitation was removed in the 1961 negotiations. The union's next target, judging from its stated bargaining aims, will be elimination of the age-40 requirement. And the Steelworkers propose full vesting of credits when termination occurs for any reason, not merely in the case of extended layoff or plant closure.

A form of cash vesting is seen in a large number of plans—223 as of September 1962, by the union's count—negotiated by the Electrical Workers (IUE). Employees terminated after three or more years' service, if not eligible for a deferred pension, receive a cash payment equal to $100 per year for each year of future service, plus interest. IUE seeks to negotiate provisions of this type in all of its pension plans; where such provisions exist, "consideration" is to be given to improving the formula and applying it to past service.

Contributory vs. Noncontributory Plans

Unions are strongly in favor of pension plans that are financed wholly by the employer, and the great majority of negotiated plans are noncontributory. Of 100 plans studied by the Bureau of Labor Statistics in 1961,[6] each covering 1,000 or more workers, 81 were found to be noncontributory and only 15 contributory. In the other four situations, noncontributory plans existed side by side with optional contributory plans.

Similarly, a study of more than 200 negotiated plans of all sizes

---

[6] *Digest of One Hundred Selected Pension Plans Under Collective Bargaining, Spring 1961*, BLS Bulletin No. 1307, January 1962.

made by The Bureau of National Affairs, Inc., in 1961 found five sixths of them to be noncontributory.

A major union argument for management financing of pensions is that employee pension contributions are taxable, but company contributions are not. Moreover, generally speaking, the administrative costs of contributory plans are higher. And whereas unions usually are content to have management control the operation of the pension fund, at least in the case of single-employer plans, this may not be the case with a fund that is jointly financed.

It is of course true that larger benefits can be provided if the money paid into the fund by the employer is supplemented by employee contributions. But the employee contributions may then become an issue in future negotiations, the union seeking to eliminate them while preserving the higher benefits they made possible. In any case, few new negotiated plans are being set up on a contributory basis, and most of those in existence are under steady pressure from unions.

Compulsory vs. Voluntary Retirement

Unions traditionally have been opposed to compulsory retirement, and this opposition is reflected in the retirement provisions of negotiated pension plans. Thus, of 300 plans, each covering 1,000 or more employees, studied by the Bureau of Labor Statistics in 1958,[7] about three out of five made provision for involuntary retirement at a specified age. But in only about a third of the plans was retirement involuntary at age 65. In all other cases of involuntary retirement, the employee was permitted to continue working, generally until age 68 or 70.

Involuntary retirement provisions in negotiated plans are of two types, compulsory or automatic. The distinction between the two is that work beyond the compulsory retirement age is discretionary with management or, infrequently, a union-management board; whereas work beyond the automatic age is not envisioned by the parties and not permitted. Compulsory retirement provisions account for about two thirds of the involuntary provisions in negotiated plans.

In a soft labor market the union attitude toward compulsory

---

[7] *Pension Plans Under Collective Bargaining*, BLS Bulletin No. 1259, July 1959.

retirement may undergo a change. When unemployment is high, involuntary retirement may be viewed as an attractive way of removing older persons from the labor force, thus opening up employment opportunities for younger, unemployed workers. There is much evidence of such a change in attitude in today's pension negotiations, but so far it has not resulted in any significant increase in the frequency of provisions for involuntary retirement. Unions, on the whole, still argue that the decision whether to retire should rest with the worker so long as he is able to perform his job in a satisfactory manner.

Instead, unions are seeking to convert involuntary terminations prior to the normal retirement age into retirement situations. That is, they are demanding immediate pensions for older employees who are terminated because of plant shutdowns or extended layoffs—and, as described above, under *Early Retirement*, employers are increasingly receptive to these demands. The possibility remains, however, that unions in the future will become less insistent upon voluntary retirement if, as most observers predict, unemployment remains at a relatively high level.

Investment of Pension Funds

The money in the trust funds set up under negotiated pension plans runs into billions of dollars and represents a very substantial fraction of the capital available for investment in this country. In the case of single-employer plans, the investment policies of these funds as a rule are determined unilaterally by management or by fund trustees selected by management. In recent years, however, unions—particularly the Auto Workers—have begun demanding that the funds be invested, at least in part, in projects that will benefit the employees on whose behalf the money is being accumulated. So far it cannot be said that such demands are being widely reflected in the terms of negotiated plans, but it seems probable that they will increasingly be a factor in future negotiations.

The agreement negotiated by UAW with American Motors Corporation in 1961 touches on the question of pension-fund investment, though without committing the company in any way. A joint group, the American Motors–UAW Conference, is charged with discussing various matters of mutual concern away from the bargaining table. Among these is "the possibility of placing in sound investments some portion of the Pension Fund for the purpose of providing more adequate housing and community facilities in plant communities."

AFL-CIO Pension Goals

A profile of the "ideal" pension plan, from the union point of view, is offered in a reference guide on pensions prepared by AFL-CIO for its member unions.[8] The guide lists 10 ultimate goals that unions, in the opinion of the federation, should strive for, though it concedes that "these goals will not be achieved, except under exceptional circumstances, for a long time to come." The 10 goals are stated as follows:

> 1. The benefit formula should be adequate to provide a basic retirement annuity including Social Security of two-thirds to three-quarters of monthly full time wages for the employees in the lower salary brackets. This proportion may be reduced for the better paid workers. The higher the proportion of this total that is met with Social Security, the less will be the total cost. Benefits should be employer financed.
> 2. The pension benefit formula should be based on earnings prior to retirement rather than upon service alone.
> 3. Pensions for retired workers should provide a cost-of-living adjustment.
> 4. Employees should have a vested right to their pension after 10 years of service, or less, without any age limitation.
> 5. Provision should be made for disability benefits. The benefits should be equal to the retirement benefit that would be payable if the worker were able to continue working to the normal retirement age. The private pension plan should supplement rather than duplicate Social Security, workmen's compensation, Veterans' Administration pensions and other statutory disability benefits.
> 6. There should be a flexible retirement policy. This policy is facilitated by not having any limit on creditable service.
> 7. Pension programs should include survivor benefits.
> 8. Insofar as possible, pension credits should be pooled.
> 9. Labor should have an equal voice in the administration of the pension program.
> 10. The investments of pension funds should include some proportion in soundly conceived projects to benefit workers before they retire as well as after they retire.

---

[8] *Pension Plans Under Collective Bargaining . . . a reference guide for Trade Unions*, AFL-CIO Publication No. 132, January 1964.

Legal Considerations

In addition to the general obligation imposed by the Taft Act upon management to bargain in good faith on the subject of pensions and employee retirement, there are a number of other legal considerations that apply to pension bargaining. These have to do with the requirements of Section 302 of the Taft Act, the enforceability of pension agreements under Section 301 of that law, and the impact of a negotiated pension plan upon the right of compulsory retirement.

Requirements of Section 302

Section 302 of the Taft Act places certain limitations upon employer contributions to a union fund, including a pension fund. These are as follows:

> 1. The money contributed to such a fund must be used solely for certain health and welfare benefits for employees and their families—medical or hospital care, pensions on retirement or death of employees, compensation for injuries or illness resulting from occupational activity, unemployment benefits, life insurance, disability and sickness insurance, and accident insurance.
> 2. The detailed basis on which benefits are to be paid must be spelled out in a written agreement.
> 3. The fund must be administered equally by management and the union, with provision for recourse to a neutral third party in case of disagreement. In the event the parties cannot agree on an impartial third party to resolve a deadlock, either party may ask a U.S. district court to appoint such a neutral. The requirement of joint administration does not apply, however, to funds established prior to January 1, 1946.
> 4. There must be an annual audit, the results of which must be available for inspection by interested parties at the principal office of the trust fund.
> 5. Contributions for pension payments must be kept separately and used only for that purpose.

It should be noted that Section 302 pertains to payments by employers to employee representatives (unions), and the restrictions apply to funds established by unions. Thus they do not apply to most negotiated pension plans, and, more specifically, there is no requirement that the typical negotiated plan be jointly administered.

Holding that it had authority to enjoin conduct in conflict

with Section 302, one federal court concluded that it could compel compliance with these standards: (1) complete records should be kept of all proceedings by trustees; (2) a complete accounting system should be installed; (3) payments to trustees should be made only in accordance with the written trust agreement; (4) trust funds should not be used for union purposes; (5) no expenditures should be made unless necessary to the operation of the fund; (6) no person connected with the company or the union should be permitted to participate in the management of the fund or receive compensation from it; and (7) the trust fund should have completely separate quarters and independent accounts.[9] On the other hand, another federal court decided its authority was limited to enjoining employer payments made in violation of the law.[10]

Employers may sue under Section 302 to test the legality of the administration of welfare funds to which they contribute, one U.S. court of appeals has held. Pointing out that employers may be subject to criminal penalties under the law, the court reasoned that they have a sufficient interest in the legality of a fund to bring an action to restrain violations.[11]

According to one federal district court, a pension fund that gives benefits only to union members doesn't violate Section 302. Welfare funds to be legal need not cover all the employees of an employer, the court said.[12] The National Labor Relations Board, however, has ruled that restricting welfare-fund coverage to union members constitutes discrimination against nonmembers and unlawful assistance to the union under the unfair-labor-practice provisions of the Taft Act.[13]

Enforcement of Pension Agreements

Section 301 of the Taft Act opens the federal courts to suits for violation of contracts between employers and unions without the satisfaction of the usual requirements as to the amount in controversy and the citizenship of the parties. Pension agreements thus are enforceable in federal court, provided the parties are subject to the Taft Act.

---
[9] *American Bakeries Co. v. Barrick*, 41 LRRM 2653 (USDC NOhio, 1958).
[10] *Moses v. Ammond*, 42 LRRM 2200 (USDC SNY, 1958).
[11] *Employing Plasterers' Assn. v. Plasterers*, 46 LRRM 2198 (CA 7, 1960).
[12] *Upholsterers v. Leathercraft Co.*, 23 LRRM 2315 (USDC EPa, 1949).
[13] *Jandel Furs*, 30 LRRM 1463 (1952).

The U.S. Supreme Court has upheld the right of the trustees of a joint pension and welfare fund to sue for recovery of unpaid employer contributions.[14] Similarly, a federal court of appeals ruled that a union could sue under Section 301 to compel a company to resume payment of contributions for a collectively bargained pension plan.[15] Another U.S. appeals court, however, ruled that a union may not sue in federal court for damages caused by a claimed breach of an agreement to make payments to a health and welfare fund. Section 301, in this court's view, does not authorize the federal courts to entertain suits of this nature.[16]

As to the benefit rights of individual employees, the U.S. Supreme Court at one time took the position that Section 301 was not intended to permit actions seeking to enforce the contract rights of individual employees.[17] This prompted the lower federal courts to dismiss suits brought by unions under Section 301 for pensions allegedly due. In December 1962, however, the Supreme Court abandoned this position, ruling that rights of individual employees could be enforced in either federal or state court in suits brought under Section 301.[18] Presumably this would include the right to pension benefits under a negotiated plan.

Moreover, a union may sue under Section 301 to enforce an agreement to arbitrate unresolved grievance disputes, including a dispute relating to employee pension rights.[19] And an award made by the arbitrator is enforceable in the federal courts without further review on the merits.[20]

In actions not brought under Section 301, an individual employee may sue in state court to enforce his pension rights under a collective bargaining contract, and he may sue in federal court if he shows diversity of citizenship and a claim amounting to more than $3,000. The courts usually view pension rights as vested rights which are earned during the life of the contract and are enforceable even after the contract has expired and the employment relationship has ended. The theory is that the employer's pension obligation is incurred in exchange for services rendered

---

[14] *Lewis* v. *Benedict Coal Corp.*, 45 LRRM 2719 (US Sup Ct, 1960).
[15] *Stove Mounters* v. *Welbilt Corp.*, 47 LRRM 2001 (CA 6, 1960).
[16] *Garment Workers* v. *Jay-Ann Co.*, 37 LRRM 2323 (CA 5, 1956).
[17] *Assn. of Westinghouse Salaried Employees* v. *Westinghouse Corp.*, 35 LRRM 2643 (US Sup Ct, 1955).
[18] *Smith* v. *Evening News Assn.*, 51 LRRM 2646 (US Sup Ct, 1962).
[19] *Textile Workers* v. *Lincoln Mills*, 40 LRRM 2113 (US Sup Ct, 1957).
[20] *Steelworkers* v. *Enterprise Wheel & Car Corp.*, 46 LRRM 2423 (US Sup Ct, 1960).

during the life of the contract and the benefits, therefore, are in the nature of deferred compensation.

The problem of enforcing employer commitments to make contributions to a multi-employer pension or welfare fund is one that has plagued a number of unions, particularly the United Mine Workers. The issue in many of these cases appears to have been the factual one of whether an individual employer agreed to the association-wide contract providing for the contributions, not the legal one of whether a commitment to make contributions is enforceable. Some of these disputes reportedly have been compromised out of court, the employer agreeing to make a portion of the contribution assertedly owed to the fund.

Compulsory Retirement

Many negotiated pension plans expressly state that the company may require employees to retire at a particular age. In such cases there is no basis for challenging management's right to resort to involuntary retirement on the ground that it is in conflict with the terms of the applicable collective bargaining agreement. Where, however, management's practice is to permit employees to continue working beyond the compulsory retirement age if they are still in good health and able to perform their jobs, a decision to retire an employee may be subject to challenge in arbitration on the ground that it is arbitrary or discriminatory.

A much different situation is presented where there is a negotiated plan that specifies a normal retirement age but is silent on the question of compulsory retirement. Then the question is whether management violates its collective bargaining agreement if it requires retirement at a particular age. The unilateral adoption of a compulsory retirement policy during the term of a contract has been held by arbitrators to be a breach of contract, usually on the theory that it is in conflict with the seniority and discharge provisions of the agreement.[21] On the other hand, if a unilateral compulsory retirement policy has been in effect for a long period of time without protest from the union, arbitrators generally hold that it is not subject to challenge.[22]

---

[21] *Hunter Engineering Co.*, 37 LA 350 (1961); see also 31 LA 45, 25 LA 77.
[22] *International Minerals & Chemical Corp.*, 31 LA 708 (1958). See also 22 LA 732, 23 LA 214, 27 LA 669, 29 LA 541.

Chapter 7

ADMINISTRATION OF PENSION PLANS

By E. S. Willis

There are essentially only two points from which to view the administration of pension plans. From the first, the plan is seen as one of the most important factors in an employee relations program. The second viewpoint considers the plan as an expensive and long-term management problem not only because of benefits which must be paid, but also because of the extensive administrative procedures and records which must be maintained as the basis for many important decisions such as those involved in financing the program. If either one of these points of view is allowed to dominate the thinking of management, the whole program will suffer.

Basic Questions for the Administrator

It is true that a pension plan is an important and expensive tool to use in improving employee relations. It is also true that only through sound administration can this tool be used effectively. Here is the opportunity for good personal relationships with the employee and the pensioner. Decisions with respect to other aspects of the plan, methods of financing, costs, legal and tax problems, etc., may have a greater ultimate effect on the income of the pensioner, but the attitude of the employee will be influenced more by its administration than by any of these decisions. Each man sees the provisions and procedures as they touch his own life, not as they were conceived to meet the maze of legal and financial problems involved nor as they were planned to meet the needs of some hypothetical average employee. As a matter of fact, from an employee relations angle a good plan has an impact even earlier. If well and smoothly administered, it may be an important factor in good community relations, in better union relations, and in helping to obtain good employees for the company.

Employee Relations

Some of the questions with respect to the importance of the administrative provisions on employee relations which we must ask are:

Is the employee's first impression that the company is sincerely interested in helping him provide for his old age?

If it is a contributory plan, are the procedures for enrolling a new employee such that he knows the bargain in retirement benefits he is getting for the dollar he invests?

If it is a noncontributory plan, does the employee realize what the company is doing for him?

Is he made to feel even as a new employee that the plan will help him not only as a pensioner but also as an employee by providing for the orderly retirement of older workers, thus making his job more secure and opening avenues for promotion?

Are there procedures to inform him periodically of the benefits which have accrued to himself and his family through membership in the plan?

Is the plan used as a means of approach to help in planning his retirement as he grows older?

Is there an easy and natural contact provided at the time of retirement for the purpose of again explaining how much the plan is worth to him?

Are there opportunities for contacts after retirement which will encourage him to continue as a goodwill ambassador of the company?

These questions are typical of those we must answer satisfactorily when we look at the administration of the pension plan from the viewpoint of employee relations.

Good Management

However, we must balance these against the other point of view. The plan must also be administered to serve the interests of management, financial, legal, etc. Here we must seek the answers to an entirely different set of questions:

Are the basic employee records so designed as to have available the essential information with respect to the rights of each employee under the plan?

Are the basic employee records adequate for the periodic valuations of company liability necessary for sound financing, for satisfying the requirements of governmental agencies and for union relations?

Are the records adequate for accurate and reasonably quick cost determinations in the event changes are contemplated?

Is information readily available to supervision to make the necessary contacts with the employee—

a) to get him to join the plan;
b) to inform him from time to time of the benefits accrued to him;
c) to plan his retirement in advance.

Are the procedures and records such as to provide prompt payments of definite amounts easily understood by the pensioners?

Are there procedures for maintaining contacts with pensioners to make sure that they are still alive and receiving their pensions?

Do the procedures insure the teamwork necessary at all stages between the supervisor, the accountant, and the personnel worker?

Finally, is the system installed initially capable of expansion and flexible enough to take care of growth and changes in future years?

These two sets of questions, one from the employee relations point of view, the other from the operations and management point of view, illustrate some of the problems in the administration of a pension plan. Obviously, the answers to many of them will be different depending on many factors which have already been decided before these administrative problems are considered. The answers may be different in contributory plans than in noncontributory; different in self-administered than in insured plans or in those handled by corporate trustees; different depending on many specific provisions of the plan such as those relating to eligibility, vested rights, survivorship options, etc. It would be possible to take up these administrative problems under these several classifications but it seems more natural to take them up as they would arise chronologically and try to examine the several aspects of each. This approach obviously starts with the enrollment of the employee in the plan and ends with the death of his surviving beneficiary.

Enrollment in the Plan

Our concern and the records start with the moment the employee is hired. Whether the plan is contributory or noncontributory, whether the new employee is immediately eligible or is eligible only after a reasonable waiting period of a year or more, the indoctrination program is the first opportunity to explain the provisions of the plan. Here is a chance to make the employee realize at the start of his career that the company is sincerely interested in helping him discharge his responsibilities to himself and his family.

Establishment of the Records

At this point also must start the record which will be discontinued only when the final liability to him or his surviving beneficiary is satisfied.

Careful record keeping, whether by local payroll units or in a central file, involves important basic data such as date of birth, earnings, and complete service record. This basic data must be gathered correctly from every available source, particularly if record keeping has been lax in the past.

If the plan is noncontributory, it is important that arrangements be made to insure inclusion of data for all eligible employees in such records as are maintained for payroll purposes. This may simply be a periodic listing by payroll of all eligible employees showing their age, service, earnings, and sex to be used in annual evaluations and preparation of pensions. In this case, of course, the individual employee's local file must accurately reflect the service he accrues over the years. On the other hand, it may be desirable to maintain a central record for each employee. In the latter case, it is essential that arrangements be made to keep the central records current.

A contributory plan requires that the employee be contacted and enrolled in the plan. The exact time of enrollment may vary somewhat, but in all cases should never be later than the time when the employee becomes eligible. If the employee becomes eligible within, say, one year from the date of employment, it may be more feasible to enroll him when employed, with a follow-up on the date of eligibility to explain again the plan's provisions. A typical enrollment form is shown as Exhibit A. Since contributory plans usually entail at least a refund of contributions to the beneficiary in case of the employee's death, it should be noted that the card includes a section recording the beneficiary designated by the employee.

Exhibit A—Enrollment Card

FN-580-A (10-51)

GENERAL ELECTRIC PENSION PLAN

Pay No. ....

APPLICATION FOR PARTICIPATION

of .... * ....
     First name   Initial   Last name   Social Security No.   Pension Unit No.

I hereby apply for participation in the General Electric Pension Plan and consent to be bound by all the terms of the Plan and the General Electric Pension Trust. I hereby authorize General Electric Company to deduct from my compensation and to pay over on my behalf to the Trustees of the General Electric Pension Trust such contributions as are required of me from time to time under the provisions of the Plan.

I hereby designate, pursuant to the General Electric Pension Plan, as my beneficiary:

.... * my ...., age ....
    First name   Initial   Last name   Relationship

of ....
    No. and street   City   State

if living at the time of my death.

The right to change the beneficiary above designated without the consent of said beneficiary and the right to revoke this authorization by written notice to General Electric Company are reserved.

.... Signed ....
    Witness   First name   Initial   Last name

....
    Date   No. and street   City   State

* Name of participant and name of beneficiary must be typed or printed in ink.

In the event an employee does not wish to join a contributory plan, even after all possible explanation, then a waiver of participation form (Exhibit B) should be signed acknowledging that the provisions of the plan have been explained, that he has received a copy of them, and that he has decided not to join. This card is important years later if an employee complains that he

Exhibit B—Waiver of Participation Card

GENERAL ELECTRIC PENSION PLAN

WAIVER OF PARTICIPATION   Pay No. ....

of .... * ....
  First name Initial Last name   Social Security No. Pension Unit No.

I have been given an opportunity to participate in that portion of the General Electric Pension Plan applicable to my service after the effective date of the Plan.

I hereby acknowledge receipt of the pamphlet which contains the provisions of the General Electric Pension Plan.

I decline to participate.

I understand that I may apply for participation at a later date, if I so desire.

Signed ....
    (First)   (Middle)   (Last)

Date ....

*Type or print in ink.   FN-580-B (5-51)

Exhibit C—Request for Discontinuance of Contributions

REQUEST FOR DISCONTINUANCE OF ENROLLMENT AND CONTRIBUTIONS
GENERAL ELECTRIC PENSION PLAN

PENSION UNIT NO. _____

I, _____ (Type or Print Name), hereby request that my enrollment in the General Electric Pension Plan and my contributions under the Plan be discontinued with the pay period commencing _____. I understand that no benefits or credited service under the Plan will be accumulated during the period that I am not enrolled. I also understand that I may not elect to re-enroll in the Plan before the end of twelve months from the effective date of this discontinuance, my re-enrollment to become effective with the first pay period of the calendar month following the date of my election.

Social Security No. _____

Pay Number _____   Date _____   Signature _____

REQUEST FOR RESUMPTION OF ENROLLMENT AND CONTRIBUTIONS

I hereby request that my enrollment in the General Electric Pension Plan, and my contributions by payroll deduction as required under the Plan, be resumed effective with the first pay period after the end of this calendar month.

Date _____   Signature _____

FOR USE OF PENSION UNIT ONLY

Enrollment resumed effective with pay period commencing _____   Pension Unit Supervisor _____

---

should receive a pension because "he thought he was a member all along and that his foreman never explained the plan to him." Non-participating employees should be contacted periodically, however, to join the plan. Many times an employee initially seeks work for a short period only, but for various reasons later decides to continue with the company on a more or less permanent basis.

Then, in a contributory plan, the new records include the contributions withheld from the earnings and interest, if any, credited thereon. Like the waiver card, it is also important to have a standard record, such as in Exhibit C, for those people who join the plan and later decide not to contribute, at least for some period. Upon retirement, that employee may wonder why his pension is smaller than that of his friends.

Location of Records

Where these records should be kept is an important matter both for good employee relations and for efficient management. In a small company there is probably only one answer, the central payroll will keep the record. In a large company the problem is more complex. Payroll units and employees may be scattered throughout the country. Pension records, financial records, and major administrative matters are usually handled at the headquarters office. There are many occasions when the data for an individual employee should be immediately available to him or his supervisor, notably when he wants to terminate his employment. At the same time information with respect to the total liability of the company for present and past service of employees, with respect to the acceptance of the plan as shown by percentage of participation and much other necessary and valuable information, can usually best be obtained if the basic records are at one central location. Likewise, when an employee terminates his employment under circumstances which give him some continuing rights, whether a vested interest to be paid later, or a pension starting immediately, his record is usually transferred to some central pension office for the final determination of those rights and payment of them. This may involve certification of the amount of the pension to the corporate trustee, insurance company, or self-administered trust which will then pay the employee regularly.

The dilemma of centralized or decentralized records has been solved by leaving the current, day-to-day records of service, earnings, and contributions in the local payroll units with periodic reports (usually annually) to the central pension section where interest credits can be computed, total accrued liability calculated, and the other data needed for management purposes prepared. Exhibit D is a sample used by one company of notice of a new participant which is sent from the payroll sections to the central record section. (It should be noted that the key for reference purposes is the employee's Social Security number.) Exhibit E is a card used to report current year's contributions for each employee to the central record section. Thus, the personal information needed for each individual employee is close at hand and available to him and his supervisor, and the information management needs is also available locally when necessary.

This discussion of the location and nature of the records necessary would not be complete without one word of warning. Plan for the future. The basic records are simple. Your pension consultant can lay them out for you very easily. However, be sure that the system you put in can be expanded without redoing the whole job. Here the advice of a systems expert will be helpful. Do not forget also that expansion may take place geographically as well as numerically. One morning you may find the plan covers plants on both seaboards or that the number of persons covered has been multiplied by 3 or 10 or even 20. A little extra planning and expense in putting in a flexible system in the beginning may well prove to be very worthwhile.

Exhibit D—Notice of New Participant

ADMINISTRATION OF PENSION PLANS 243

Exhibit E—Report of Employee Contributions

Exhibit F—Statement to Employees

Your personal share AS OF DECEMBER 31, 1959

GENERAL ELECTRIC PENSION PLAN

AMOUNT YOU CONTRIBUTED		ANNUAL PENSION CREDITED TO YOU	
DURING 1959	FROM DATE YOU BEGAN CONTRIBUTING TO 12-31-59	FOR SERVICE DURING 1959	FOR SERVICE FROM DATE YOU BEGAN PARTICIPATING TO 12-31-59
$	$	$	$
1	2	3	4

The amount shown in Column 4 should be inserted in the form on Page 3 for estimating your annual General Electric pension at age 65.

GENERAL ELECTRIC INSURANCE PLAN with Comprehensive Medical Expense Benefits

Your Personal Coverage as of January 1, 1960

LIFE INSURANCE	ADDITIONAL BENEFIT FOR ACCIDENTAL DEATH	TOTAL BENEFIT FOR ACCIDENTAL DEATH	ACCIDENTAL DISMEMBERMENT		WEEKLY SICKNESS AND ACCIDENT INSURANCE (UP TO 26 WEEKS)	ENROLLED FOR DEPENDENT COVERAGE
			LOSS OF ONE EYE, HAND OR FOOT	LOSS OF ANY TWO SUCH MEMBERS		
$	$	$	$	$	$	

Comprehensive Coverage For Participants and Their Eligible Dependents
Maximum Benefits per Individual: $7500 in a Calendar Year; $15,000 in a Lifetime.

COVERED MEDICAL EXPENSES	DEDUCTIBLE	CO-INSURANCE	MATERNITY BENEFITS
TYPE A • SEMI-PRIVATE HOSPITAL ROOM AND BOARD (NO LIMIT ON NUMBER OF DAYS). • ALL SPECIAL HOSPITAL SERVICES. • ALL REASONABLE, NECESSARY AND CUSTOMARY SURGICAL FEES. • DIAGNOSTIC X-RAYS. • LOCAL PROFESSIONAL AMBULANCE SERVICE.	$25 PER INDIVIDUAL IN ANY CALENDAR YEAR.	PLAN PAYS 100% OF NEXT $225 PLUS 85% OF REMAINDER OF COVERED "TYPE A" EXPENSES UP TO MAXIMUM SPECIFIED ABOVE.	NORMAL DELIVERY - - -$150 CAESAREAN OR ECTOPIC-$225 MISCARRIAGE - - - UP TO $75 ADDITIONAL BENEFITS IN CASE OF SEVERE COMPLICATIONS.
TYPE B • SERVICES OF PHYSICIANS, INCLUDING SPECIALISTS, OTHER THAN FOR SURGERY. • SPECIAL SERVICES OUTSIDE HOSPITAL—SUCH AS DIAGNOSTIC LABORATORY, X-RAY AND RADIUM TREATMENTS, OXYGEN AND ITS ADMINISTRATION, BLOOD TRANSFUSIONS, INCLUDING BLOOD OR PLASMA, ETC. • REGISTERED GRADUATE NURSES (IN OR OUT OF HOSPITAL). • DRUGS AND MEDICINES (OUT OF HOSPITAL). • RENTAL OF DURABLE EQUIPMENT AND PURCHASE OF ORIGINAL ARTIFICIAL LIMBS OR OTHER PROSTHETIC APPLIANCES.	$50 PER INDIVIDUAL IN ANY CALENDAR YEAR. NOTE: ANY "TYPE A" DEDUCTIBLE INCURRED CAN BE APPLIED AGAINST "TYPE B" DEDUCTIBLE FOR THAT PERSON SO THAT COMBINED DEDUCTIBLE WILL NOT EXCEED $50 IN A CALENDAR YEAR.	PLAN PAYS 75% OF REMAINDER OF COVERED "TYPE B" EXPENSES UP TO MAXIMUM SPECIFIED ABOVE.	See Insurance Plan booklet for additional details about the Plan and more information about Covered Medical Expenses.

Exhibit F—Statement to Employees (continued)

GENERAL ELECTRIC SAVINGS AND SECURITY PROGRAM

EMPLOYEE SAVINGS FOR 1959	INVESTMENT OF EMPLOYEE SAVINGS			INCOME*		YOUR TOTAL CREDITS		
	U. S. BONDS	UNAPPLIED CASH BALANCE	G. E. SHARES	G. E. SHARES	CASH	U. S. BONDS	G. E. SHARES	CASH BALANCE
$	$	$		$				

COMPANY PROPORTIONATE PAYMENTS FOR 1959	INVESTMENT OF COMPANY PAYMENTS			PROMPT ENROLLMENT SHARE
	U. S. BONDS	UNAPPLIED CASH BALANCE	G. E. SHARES	
$	$	$		$

Company Proportionate Payments and the Prompt Enrollment Share are contingently credited.
U. S. Bonds are shown at original maturity value. In some cases, actual maturity value may be somewhat higher. The "Unapplied Cash Balances" were carried forward to 1960 for investment in U. S. Bonds in that year.
The number of G. E. Shares credited to your account is determined by dividing the amount applied to the purchase of stock each month by the "Stock Price" for that month.

*Income represents (1) dividends received on G. E. Shares (reinvested in G. E. stock) and (2) income from the Trustees' investment of unapplied cash. This latter investment income is either (1) reinvested in G. E. Shares if you elected Company payments in G. E. Shares or (2) credited as "Cash" if you elected Company payments in U. S. Bonds.

GENERAL ELECTRIC SAVINGS AND STOCK BONUS PLAN

FRACTIONAL SHARE BALANCE FROM 1954	1955		1956		1957		1958		1959		YOUR TOTAL CREDITS	
	U.S. BONDS	G.E. SHARES	U.S. BONDS	G.E. SHARES	U.S. BONDS	G.E. SHARES	U.S. BONDS	G.E. SHARES	U.S. BONDS	G.E. SHARES	U.S. BONDS	G.E. SHARES	ACCUMULATED INCOME
$	$		$		$		$		$		$		$

G. E. Shares for the years 1955 to 1959 are contingently credited.
U. S. Bonds are shown at original maturity value. In some cases, actual maturity value may be somewhat higher. Payroll deductions not sufficient to purchase an additional Bond as of Dec. 31, 1959, were carried forward to 1960 for investment in U. S. Bonds in that year and are not included in these figures.

The number of G. E. Shares (Stock Bonus) credited to your account each year is determined by dividing 15% of the cost price of the U. S. Bonds shown by the "Stock Price" for that year.

Your Total Credits as of December 31, 1959 exclude any 1954 Bonds, Stock Bonus Shares and accumulated income delivered to you in March, 1960, following the end of the 5 year holding period for 1954 savings.

Contacts with Employees

Contacts with employees and pensioners can be helped by maintaining accurate records. Here we have an important employee relations aspect of sound administrative procedures.

A mistake which is commonly made is to assume that "no news is good news," that, since no questions have arisen during the forty years of an employee's service, there will be no difficulties when he retires. This is far from the truth. There are many surprises awaiting the administrator who is naïve enough to believe this.

The examples are endless: the maiden ladies, whose baptismal records had been reportedly lost in a church fire until the administrator happened to mention this to an elder of the church who could not remember the fire but did find the records indicating the ladies were 6 or 8 years older respectively than the company records showed.

Then there is the prominent employee who remembered distinctly how his supervisor twenty years before had given him leave of absence to help put a distributor on its feet and this assignment had taken him five years. Fortunately, the former supervisor was alive and recalled the incident. He did encourage his somewhat ineffective employee to quit when he had an opportunity to go elsewhere at a higher salary. The supervisor agreed that he may have overdone the encouragement a bit in his desire to have the employee leave, but he had not intended to make it appear the company was giving the man a leave of absence to take the new job.

The employee who gets his union to protest his broken service because he did not receive the notice recalling him to work after a layoff presents another problem. At the time of his recall he happened to have a good job elsewhere but would, of course, "have returned had the notice not been lost in the mail."

Then, there are the marginal cases under which an interpretation of plan language is required, because a plan cannot be written which will fit every possible problem that may arise.

The careful administrator sees in these contacts one thing: better records; real evidence of dates of birth early in the program; a careful recording of the circumstances under which each employee leaves and accurate interpretation well recorded for future use; and the sending of notices of recall to work by registered mail.

Administration of Pension Plans   247

Exhibit G—Sample Benefits Statements

A Personal Report on Your Employee Benefits

This is a report on your complete employee benefits program. It includes information just computed on what the proposed benefit improvements, described recently by letter, will mean to you. These benefit improvements will go into effect at the beginning of the work week in which the Union Committee signs the agreements covering benefits and wages.

Report for:

LIFE INSURANCE
The amount of your group term
life insurance is .... $

SICKNESS BENEFITS
The amount paid to you each week
for up to 26 weeks if you are sick
or injured off the job will be ....

RETIREMENT INCOME
Your estimated monthly income
from the Retirement Income
Plan at age 65 is .... $

Your estimated monthly Social
Security benefits at age 65 are .... $

Total estimated monthly retirement income at age 65 .... $

A spouse's Social Security benefit would be extra.

* *This would be larger if you hadn't withdrawn contributions.*
** *You are not now a Contributory Plan member. Your annuity would be larger if you joined.*
(If either of these conditions applies, star(s) appear after your Retirement Income amount.)

Annual Report to Individuals

Annual statements to individual employees showing the benefits accrued to them under the several company benefit plans have recently been adopted by several companies (Exhibits F and G). In addition to being goodwill builders, they help correct records. An employee who finds his service or other data incorrect is apt to question it immediately.

In addition to these contacts during the working life of an employee, records must be arranged to aid in other contacts with the employees. Notices from either the central pension section or local payroll units may be useful to advise supervisors and employee relations personnel when it is time to start the retirement

Exhibit H—Notice of Termination of Employment (front)

PN-580-G (3-58)

NOTICE OF TERMINATION OF EMPLOYMENT AND REFUND OF CONTRIBUTIONS
General Electric Pension Plan

Company and Employee Trusts Accounting
Room 612, Building #5, Schenectady, New York

Location   Date

The service of_____, Pay No._____
           Last   First   Middle
Social Security No._____, was terminated on_____, 19___. Refund of contributions plus interest was paid during the month of_____, on voucher number_____ in the following amount:

1. Principal at beginning of current year—a) $_____ ☐ Left Service
2. Interest at beginning of current year—a) _____   ☐ Refund because of death
3. Total at beginning of current year—a) _____
4. Contributions during current year—b) _____
5. Interest on item 3 for first six months of current year—c)_____   Payroll Supervisor
6. Total Refund $_____   Pension Unit_____

(a—From trial balance or transfer in.
(b—Include current year contributions transferred from other units.
(c—Use only between June 30 and December 31.

Received payment:
(For cash refunds only)

Employee's Signature

Exhibit H—Refund of Contributions (back)

RECEIPT FOR REFUND OF CONTRIBUTIONS AFTER VESTING
General Electric Pension Plan

To The Secretary, Pension Board
General Electric Company
Schenectady, New York

    I have requested and received refund of the aggregate amount of contributions, ($_____) made by me to the General Electric Pension Trust, plus interest thereon

    I am fully aware that as of_____, 19____, my right to receive a pension from the General Electric Pension Trust vested, and that by obtaining the refund I am hereby forfeiting my right to all benefits provided by the General Electric Pension Plan.

Date_____   _____
                                                       Signature

counseling program for an employee nearing that age, or when the employee should be notified of his rights to elect a survivorship option without a physical examination before retirement. The plan may provide for refunds of contributions when employees leave or die before retirement. Administrative procedures and instructions to exit interviewers must provide automatic checks to make sure that no employee who is eligible for vested rights or for optional retirement leaves without a clear understanding of these rights. He may have the option of accepting the return of his own contributions, but if he elects to do so and to forfeit his other rights, a signed acknowledgment that these had been explained to him should be obtained. (Exhibit H is an example.)

Contacts with Unions

If reasonable care is used in these contacts with the individual employee from the time he is hired until he is retired, little or no difficulty will be experienced in dealing with the unions who represent those employees. This is especially true where the provisions of the plan with respect to such important matters as eligibility, credit for service, calculation of the amount of the pension, etc., are clear and unambiguous and accurate records are maintained.

Contracts with unions provide for various degrees of union participation in the administration of pension plans. In a few, such as the garment trades, the plan itself is administered by the union. At the other extreme are those union contracts which are merely agreements that the company shall put into effect the pension plan described in it or annexed thereto. In some instances —as for example in the contracts in the automobile industry— joint union-management committees pass on pensions, including questions of eligibility, continuity of service, etc. In other cases such decisions are made by management but are subject to the grievance procedure. The absence or presence of collective bargaining agreements has no bearing on the necessity or desirability of careful records of each employee and of all data affecting his rights under the pension plan.

If such records are maintained and the provisions of the plan are clear, little difficulty seems to have been encountered in carrying out the joint administration provided in many recent contracts. Of course, there have been the usual problems connected with setting up the new machinery for the joint administration, which problems were aggravated by the lack of experience of the union representatives and their feeling that the questions to be decided were much more complicated than they really are. Once the machinery has been established and the union representatives gain familiarity with the forms and procedures, there has been little more difficulty than under those plans where management makes the decisions but those decisions are subject to the grievance procedure.

Joint Procedures

Of course, joint administration under either of the procedures developed in the automobile industry is more time-consuming than is administration by management. In the former case every pension application must be reviewed by representatives of the union. In the latter case only those where there is some questionable aspect goes to the grievance procedure. Under one of the joint administrative procedures, a central committee with a full-time impartial staff reviews each retirement case and both union and management representatives must sign even the most routine ones. Under the other procedure, local joint committees review and pass on each case, and only the few on which agreement cannot be reached go to a central committee. Under both procedures, if the central committee cannot agree, the final decision is made by an impartial umpire. It is reported that only a very few cases have gone to the umpire under either procedure. An example of the most difficult type of case is the one where the company doctor says a man is not physically capable of performing the work which the company has available, yet he is not permanently and totally disabled and thus entitled to a disability pension. Such cases, however, are as difficult in a company-administered plan as under a plan which is jointly administered. They are rare and where there is a reasonable service requirement for eligibility for a disability pension, one solution has been to grant the pension.

It can be seen that the ultimate result is no different under joint administration than under company administration with specific decisions subject to the grievance procedure. As a matter of fact, one company reports that its union officials have had an opportunity to watch the jointly administered plans in action. Those officials at each bargaining session make a formal demand for joint administration as instructed by the membership, but are, apparently, perfectly willing to let the matter drop there.

Government Disclosure Reports

Under the Federal Welfare and Pension Plans Disclosure Act, operations of most pension plans must be reported.[1] Certain states such as Wisconsin and Massachusetts also require reports. Under the Federal law, it is necessary to annually report on the plans' financial operations (receipts, disbursements, assets and liabilities, as well as other pertinent transactions which might involve conflicts of interest). The Act requires that a summary report be made available to participating employees. However, it may be desirable to give summary data in advance to employees or publish the data in ads in employee papers or in posters so employees will be fully informed in any event.

Other Annual Reports

Some agreements with unions also provide for annual reports to the union giving over-all data with respect to the operation and financing of the pension plan. Information asked for usually includes such items as the number of employees retired, average pension paid, payments by the company to the insurance company or trustee, and similar information. Many companies include such data in their annual reports to stockholders. Some already give special statements to employee participants also. It is important in planning the records to make sure that such information can easily be obtained in the future if it is not currently needed for these purposes. With the new computer technologies, all the central records can be maintained on tape at headquarters in such a form that the needs for over-all information can be readily met, including the needs for annual valuations and for other management purposes. For example, the data can be summarized for disclosure reports or printed on individual statements for employees. By compiling the appropriate factors, the computer can also fully compute the annual actuarial evaluation, finally printing out only the total liability, if appropriate. In addition, it is possible to arrange for cost data that is basic before and during

---

[1] Federal-State Regulation of Welfare Funds (Revised Edition), 1962, BNA Incorporated, Washington, D.C.

negotiations or at any other time when plan changes are being considered.

Retirement and After

Thus far, this discussion of pension plan administration and record maintenance has dealt with the problems involved from the viewpoint of the active employee. Administrative problems do not end there, however, because the operation for the benefit of the ever-increasing number of pensioners is most important.

Preparation

Records should be arranged so that either the local payroll sections or central pension sections can issue notices to advise supervisors and employee relations personnel that it is time to start retirement counseling for employees nearing retirement. This may begin seven, five, three years, or less in advance of reaching retirement. Also, similar notices must be sent out in case there are advance options, such as election of a survivorship option without medical examination in advance of reaching retirement age (for example, two or three years prior). Careful administration in these matters will save many an unpleasant contact with an employee to whom these matters are important, but who may not have read his copy of the pension plan during the last ten years.

Processing the Pension

Then, just prior to retirement, the forms necessary to process the pension should be started. This, depending on the way the plan is administered, is a responsibility of either the local units or the central pension section. A sample form is included as Exhibit I. It is desirable to initiate the form sufficiently in advance —on a regular log basis—so that there is time for the employee to sign, for an audit of the figures, and inclusion in a pension payroll payable for the month the employee goes on pension.

The increasing size of pension rolls and the long-term nature of pension rolls makes it important that the payroll be mechanized as soon as its size warrants such treatment. Computerization of the pension records will include this.

Contact with Pensioner

Of course, the company whose pension payments are handled by an insurance company or a corporate trustee could cease all contact with the employee at the time of retirement. This rarely happens.

Here, again, we have an employee relations point of view to be considered. The pensioner is a potential ambassador of goodwill for the company not only in the community where he lives, but also among the present employees—his former associates. So regardless of whether pensions are paid by the company, a self-administered trust, a corporate trustee, or an insurance company, provision is usually made for periodic or occasional communications from the company to the pensioner. Arrangements may be made to see that he regularly receives publications sent to employees. In addition, in localities where pensioners are numerous, the company may encourage the organization of clubs and even furnish facilities for meetings and mail the notices. If pensioners are eligible for the continuation of health and life insurance benefits, notices may be necessary from time to time. In many cases pensioners also continue to be eligible for discounts on the purchase of company products. All of these make it advisable to be sure that records are such that notices can be sent easily to all or to any special group.

Payment Problems

There are a few problems from the management point of view which can be avoided with a little forethought. For example, if pensions are paid at the end of the month as wages and salaries usually are, should the final payment be prorated to cover the portion of the month in which the pensioner dies, and, if not, who is entitled to the portion covering the period after his death? Such a problem can be avoided at little cost over the long term by paying the pension in advance at the first of the month with no refund even if the pensioner dies that day. Companies who have made several changes in their pension programs may find themselves with pensioners entitled to receive checks from two or even three or four sources, some for very small amounts. At least one company which found itself in this position formed another

Exhibit I—Application for Pension (front)

AD-255-A (1-52)

APPLICATION FOR PENSION
NORMAL RETIREMENT
General Electric Pension Plan

To THE SECRETARY, PENSION BOARD
GENERAL ELECTRIC COMPANY

.... Location

.... Effective date of pension

I, ..., Social Security No. ....
      Last   First   Middle

hereby make application for retirement on pension under the terms and conditions of the General Electric Pension Plan.

I understand that my total monthly benefit has been computed as follows:

MONTHLY PAST SERVICE ANNUITY (Item G on reverse side)..................... $ ....

MONTHLY FUTURE SERVICE ANNUITY (Item L on reverse side).................. ....

MONTHLY ADDITIONAL PAYMENT, if any, to provide minimum pension under Section XIII as calculated on the reverse side.. ....

    TOTAL MONTHLY BENEFIT... $ ....

I also understand that the calculation of my pension is based in part upon the following data:

Date of birth........................ Age at retirement.............. years............ months

Credited service to date retired............... years............ months

Total contributions which I made toward my pension $ ....

Beneficiary or beneficiaries of any amounts payable under the Plan were designated by me on........................
                                                                                                                               Date

and duly executed designations are attached.

My monthly pension check should be mailed to the following address:

No. and Street	City	Zone	State

                                Signed..
                                           Signature of Participant   Date

Certified Correct:..
                           Pension Unit Supervisor   Unit No.   Date

Approved:..
                           Manager   Date

Calculations certified correct: ....
                                          Company and Employee Trusts Accounting   Date

✦   ✦   ✦   ✦   ✦   ✦   ✦

                            The Pension Board hereby certifies that the above amounts are for the payment of benefits under the General Electric Pension Plan, and hereby directs the Trustees to pay them.

                                                                                For the Pension Board   Date

Exhibit I—Application for Pension (back)

CALCULATION OF PAST SERVICE ANNUITY:

Adjusted service date as of September 1, 1946............ _____
                                              Mo.   Day   Yr.

A. (1.5% women)
   (1.165% men) × _____ × _____ = ... $ _____
                 Past service earnings   Total prospective service
                                    (women to age 60, men to age 65)

B. Less: adjustment under Section IV (3) (b):
   40% of 1st $600 plus 10% of remainder to $3000 (maximum $480)............... _____

C. Remainder.. _____

D. Item C × _____ ÷ _____ = ... _____
            Service to 9/1/46   Total prospective service
                          (women to age 60, men to age 65)

E. Item D increased by 30% effective 1/1/61...................................... _____

F. Annuity per year under survivorship option (Item E × _____ %).................. _____

G. Monthly Past Service Annuity (Item E or F, whichever is applicable, ÷12)............ $ _____

CALCULATION OF FUTURE SERVICE ANNUITY:

H. Aggregate future service annuity at beginning of year............................ $ _____

I. Current year future service annuity (to normal retirement date)................... _____

   (Compensation for current year to normal retirement date $ _____)

   (Contributions for current year to normal retirement date $ _____)

J. Aggregate future service annuity at date of retirement (H plus I)................. _____

K. Annuity per year under survivorship option (Item J × _____ %).................. _____

L. Monthly Future Service Annuity (Item J or K, whichever is applicable, ÷12).......... $ _____

CALCULATION OF ADDITIONAL PAYMENT TO PROVIDE MINIMUM PENSION:

(Only if employee has at least 180 months of full-time credited service under the Pension Plan)

M. Completed months of credited service as a full-time employee:
   (1) Starting 4/1/62............. _____
   (2) Prior to 4/1/62............. _____
   (3) Total..................... _____

N. Minimum annual pension:
   Item M(1) × $2.50....................................$ _____
   Item M(2) × $2.40.................................... _____
      Total..$ _____

O. Annual pension before any reduction for survivorship option (Item E plus J)............ _____

P. Annual additional payment required, if any (Item N minus O)..................... _____

Q. Monthly additional payment required, if any (Item P ÷ 12)......................$ _____

trust for the sole purpose of paying the combined pension amount, the several plans paid the amounts due to the trust each month, and one check for the combined amount was issued to the pensioner.

Problems arise from time to time which may affect only one group of pensioners. Payment of the Social Security pensions and the resulting changes made in plans have increased such problems. A company may have had different pension plans in effect over the last 25 years, and its employees may have retired under the provisions of any one of those plans. The changes in the Social Security Act or even in the company plan may affect one or more groups of pensioners, but not all. It will be helpful if the records are arranged so that explanatory notices can be sent only to the group or groups affected. A notice sent to all pensioners, even though it is perfectly clear who is affected and who is not, will bring a flood of inquiries from those who fail to understand or read the wrong section. A new problem existing in only a few plans so far, but which may increase, is the continuation of payments to a surviving beneficiary or at least to a surviving spouse. This requires adjustment of the pension records and longer-than-ever maintenance of records.

Death of Pensioner

Finally, in the administration of a plan, it is important to establish routinely the fact that the pensioner or his beneficiary is still alive and receiving the monthly check. The story is told of a report by an investigating agency that the pensioner was working for the company. The pension administrator was rightly puzzled because his record indicated the old gentleman was nearly ninety years old. His investigation revealed that it was "Junior," a young man of thirty, who was working in the factory and cashing his father's pension checks as well as his own pay checks. When Junior was approached on the subject, he readily admitted it saying, "Oh, yes; I get the checks regularly. Father left me that annuity in his will." Many of the cases in a large pension roll will not be as amusing or as innocent as that.

There are different ways in which these reviews can be made. Some companies use more than one method.

Twenty-five years ago, it was not too difficult to visit each pensioner at least once a year. They tended to stay near the town where they had worked, and it was a natural and desirable thing to have a visitor from the company call on them, to bring them news of their friends, the changes in the factory, and to inquire about their health and living conditions. The visitors were well received and the case histories in the pension files were accurate and up-to-date.

Today, with pension payrolls running into the tens of thousands for a single company and hundreds of those residing in places as far distant from their work places as St. Petersburg, Florida, the problem is quite different. Annual visitations are expensive, if not impossible. Other methods must be found. There is a natural cross check between group life insurance records and pension records, if life insurance is continued in force on pensioners. Routine comparisons of the endorsements on the most recent check with those for the last few months have proven valuable. In special circumstances, visits by company representatives may still be possible and valuable not only for information but for good employee relations. National or local investigation companies have well-developed services which can be adopted to the needs of most any pension administrator. The administrator will use any of these methods or perhaps a combination of all to keep his information about pensioners current and factual.

The death of the pensioner, or the later death of his beneficiary, if eligible for continuation of benefits, closes the file which may have been opened and active for half a century and more. The pension plan which causes this record to be maintained is a declaration of rights and obligations. Its administration must be careful, just, and humane, and can be such only if the records are accurate and current. The importance of the plan and its just administration can be seen in its true perspective if we realize that on the average the income provided is the chief support of the retired employee for a decade and one-half.

Chapter 8

HOW TO ACHIEVE MAXIMUM RETURN ON PENSION COSTS

By Fred Rudge

Managements rigorously scrutinize the costs of pension programs. Not all managements, however, study with equal care what their company may be able to gain for the expenditures made. The emphasis tends to be on "put" (how do we minimize expense?), rather than on "take" (how can we maximize benefits to the company?).

Maximizing Benefits to the Company

In essence, management has four questions to explore. *First,* what effect might understanding of our pension plan have on:

    a. reducing turnover;
    b. easing recruitment problems;
    c. increasing employee knowledge of the economics of business generally, and of the company specifically; and
    d. building added respect for the manner in which the company views and discharges its responsibilities?

Second, what have we got to sell? How, for example, do our pension benefits compare with our own industry and with the patterns of others in the communities where we operate? What in fact led to the benefits—management initiative? a union contract as it affected the non-exempt? a union contract which led to upgrading the benefits of the exempt?

Third, what is the "climate" at various levels of the organization, as it affects management's effort to communicate about pensions? Is there felt to be (or known to be) a high, middle, or low level of management credibility? Does management communicate regularly, occasionally, or infrequently on matters of economic importance to the company and its people? Will an effort to intercommunicate on pension benefits be looked upon negatively as "management grinding its own ax," or positively, as being information of pertinent interest to the individual and his family?

Fourth, what climate, candidly, is management trying to create in encouraging understanding of pension benefits? One or a combination of the following is possible. The examples do not seek to set a value judgment on what is right; rather, they suggest that appraisal by management of what it really wants to accomplish (before communication attempts are undertaken) is highly desirable. Possible company aims:

> a. To stop pressure for added increases which are not justified, because of competitive, or other pressures;
> b. To win understanding of the company's own people (and other publics such as the plant community, stockholders, government officials) that the management comprehends, faces up to, and solves problems in the mutual interest;
> c. To utilize a subject area of crucial economic importance to the individual, as a legitimate "reason why" for exploration of economic considerations as they affect the company and the individual.

Why Analyze?

Management can answer the four questions above as applicable to its own company's unique circumstances without undue difficulty. In so doing, management will prepare the way for an effective educational program and avoid communication expenditures that won't pay off.

"*Company* benefits" in the pension area are dependent on what people *think*. One-way, downward communication from management about what *management* thinks (and wishfully hopes others will think, too) can be wide of the mark and wasteful. A modest amount of analysis of the very specialized situation of any individual company can assure that communication expenditures are warranted.

Communication Policy and Method

The guidelines that follow depart somewhat from most currently available literature on corporate communications in general, and pension plan education specifically. Management, it is recommended, should critically examine its ability to communicate effectively before it assumes that simple language, aided and abetted by pictures and charts, will automatically affect the attitudes of others. A step-by-step procedure might include:

First: Evaluation of already existing channels of communication. Is reasonably up-to-date, factual information available regarding the readership of the corporation's publications and the degree of management credibility on both noncontroversial and controversial subjects? If not, consideration should be given to a "spot check" which can be handled inexpensively by a letter or even postcard questionnaire mailing to a small cross section of company personnel. If the "spot check," which might be a 5 percent sample where employees total more than 10,000 (and a higher percentage with smaller employee totals), reveals that there seem to be problems of readership or credibility, further data should be sought. Questionnaires can be supplemented by a relatively small number of face-to-face interviews to provide understanding, in depth, of *what* people think and, to a considerable degree, *why* they think as they do.

Such audits of readership and credibility are valuable, not only for planning pension communications, but as they throw light on the problems and opportunities in all areas of corporate information efforts.

Second: Consideration of the "climate" of relationships as it may affect pension communication. Is management justifiably secure in believing that employees at the various levels of the organization are "able to hear" what management wants to communicate about pensions?

In the minds of any employee group at any level, there may be, from *their* point of view, one, several, or many questions which are compelling. Where this is the case, those who are disaffected, concerned, or uncertain tend to have little or no interest in what management communicates on what they consider "peripheral issues."

What they want to hear about is what concerns them. Meantime, messages about any other subject areas (including pensions) will be like water off a duck's back. The reaction will be: "I don't give a damn about what you (top management) are interested in until you react to the problems *I* think are important to me and to our company."

Management may ask, "Do you recommend *not* communicating on pensions until *all* other problems are settled (which they most certainly never will be)?" The answer is, not at all. As Dale Carnegie emphasized in "How to Win Friends and Influence People," the best way to begin to intercommunicate effectively is to do some listening *first*. Moreover, it is every bit as easy to take a reading on what pivotal problems people think they have on their minds, as it is to assess readership of company publications or management credibility. It can be spot checked or analyzed in depth.

Granted, fact-finding of this type is not always popular with top management, and, indeed, line management at all levels. Harassed managers usually have a vast number of compelling demands that "should have been settled yesterday," and they are aware of a host of problems that they feel certain they could solve if only there were time to get to them. Consequently, there is an understandable allergy to the process of finding out from lower levels what the bosses already feel they know all about.

Despite the obstacles, the upward communication first is the best guarantor that subsequent downward communication is properly planned. Experience offers abundant testimony that even if he can communicate with the economic lucidity of a Sylvia Porter, the charm of Art Buchwald, and the perceptivity of Raymond Moley, nobody, but nobody, is going to "hear" if the reader has other, to him, much more important problems on his mind.

Any one of hundreds of problems (as often emotional as logical), ranging from parking lots to conflicting policy, may exist. It is very simple to find out about them; just ask. First ask just a few people. If this preliminary effort suggests that there are trouble spots of possible significance, then sample more widely and in greater depth.

Third: Setting the stage for pension communications. Is management enough aware about employee knowledge (or lack of it) or level of interest (high, medium or low), so that pension communications can be sensitively addressed to those whose thinking management wishes to affect favorably?

With minimum trouble and expense, a minuscule cross section can be asked in effect, "What questions would *you* like answered as these bear on your interests, that of your family, and, incidentally, of the well-being of your company?" To many, such an exercise may seem academic when management *has all the facts and simply wants to communicate what is logical.*

Nonetheless, there is a vast distinction between answering questions that have been asked, and stating facts about which only the communicator is certain he is interested. Moreover, as further amplified below, the process of "asking, then answering" should not only be a part of the initial effort, but a fundamental aspect of the continuing informative endeavor by management. Without such a continuing interchange, it is possible for management to say what it wants to say, but highly unlikely that it will add to the knowledge, or affect the attitudes of, its audience.

Fourth: Continuous "marketing" as opposed to one-shot "sales efforts." Can management honestly say to itself, "We've got a solid proposition, so self-evident that it will be both understood and supported when we first state it simply and graphically (as we in management see it)"?

Consumer product advertisers have had to be reasonably accurate about breadth of coverage, message repetition, and consumer recall, since their economic survival has been directly dependent thereon. Far less rigorous standards are applied to "idea selling," as in the pension area. Success or lack of it in this area impinges apparently less directly on the cash register. Further, the measurement of attitudes and their resultant effect on the company is far less developed than is the more urgent question of buyer response as it affects sales and profits.

In any event, it is apt to be a safe assumption that one or a few communiques in areas of "ideas" about equate to the same amount of effort in product selling. Neither produces *anything.* Possibly, too, it may be that in "idea selling," just as in product selling, more attention has to be paid to putting the audience in a mood to listen than to the phrasing of the "commercials," once a hopefully attentive audience has been created.

Fifth: Facilitating intercommunication so that a majority of employees really understand pensions and their significance to themselves and to the company. An affirmative answer to the question, "Can our management develop some new simple method of adult education?" is a tricky gamble.

The processes through which adults learn have been well explored. Among other valid conclusions is the fact that people's comprehension increases as they become interested and involved to the point where *they* want to know more. Someone else telling them what the someone else wants them to know or to believe more often than not is self-defeating.

Management's best bet for creating employee interest and involvement is stimulating intercommunication of sufficient duration so that the facts can be comprehended and absorbed.

A number of methods are available and can be tailored to the circumstances of the individual plant or office. None of them, however (and unfortunately from the standpoint of "time" and cost-conscious management), is "apparently" as inexpensive as printing a few booklets and messages and letting it go at that.

Some Guidelines to Content and Style

The executive faced with preparing a pension education program will find it helpful to keep in mind that:

1. The word "pension" automatically suggests to many "the money I live on after I retire." The company pension needs to be explained as a supplement to Social Security and to other forms of individual saving. Standing alone, monthly pension payments as compared to wages or salary are more apt to breed disappointment than satisfaction. The company pension needs to be related to a total plan for retirement, with emphasis on the fact that the individual's responsibility for his future is still *his* responsibility.

2. The perspective of those who are in different age brackets will almost certainly differ. Older people, faced with retirement soon, are apt to look at only the amount of monthly benefits without regard to the time it takes to build contributions, or the amount of their own payments to the fund, if any. Younger employees, conversely, may feel resentment about a contributory plan, which they will help support over a long period of years, while those with long service reap seemingly disproportionate benefits.

Such gaps in understanding can be answered only if management explains in detail exactly *how* the company's plan will operate, and *why* it will be equitable to all groups. The insurance carrier or the banking trustee can help the company communicator by providing at least a check list of the salient features of the plan as these features will benefit the employees covered.

3. "Customer analysis" is as valuable in selling an idea as it is in selling a product. If the company is going to gain stature

with its employees, as it should, through its pension plan, the company must then assume the role of "seller" and consider the employee its "customer." Discussed above is the use of research in studying the employee climate in which management will communicate about pensions.

Similarly helpful to management will be some preliminary analysis of what kinds of questions people have on their minds, and what attitudes they have toward the problems of old age generally and pensions specifically. Knowledge of these questions and attitudes helps management to communicate *with* (rather than *at*) its people in terms of *their* frame of reference and *their* language.

A questionnaire (with plenty of room for the recipient to write in his comments) will provide ample leads on how management might respond effectively about a) the ever increasing number of older people; b) the problems of younger people coping with dependents; c) compulsory retirement to give others a chance; d) the advantages (*and disadvantages*) of federal government involvement; and e) above all, the cost of company pension programs and the *sources of support* on which such programs *are dependent*.

4. The benefits of a pension program can and should be personalized. The story should be told both from the standpoint of the individual and his family. When the plan is initiated, and perhaps annually thereafter, each person can receive a pay envelope enclosure (or be told by his supervisor) where he stands.[1]

5. While the language should be simple, the facts should be explicit. Most executives will realize without the point being belabored that the legal language of the insurance company or bank plan should be avoided.

However, it is worth emphasizing that adequate "selling" of the program requires the answers to many, many questions. What led to the plan's adoption? What are the cost factors? What would similar benefits cost if the employee had to pay for them himself? How is life expectancy determined? How do mortality tables work?

---

[1] Management representatives were apparently making no headway in trying to convince a distrustful (and illiterate) local union president that their pension offer should be accepted. The problem was solved when management brought $3,180.00 in cash to a bargaining meeting and said to the local union president, "This is what your share would be worth."

How is the money invested, and how does interest build up equities?

Further, the practical questions uppermost in the mind of the employee are:

1. What do I get out of it?
2. What do I put into it?
3. What does the company put into it?
4. When do I join?
5. When do I start to collect?
6. Will I be able to live on the pension?
7. What happens if I leave the company?
8. What happens if I'm disabled?
9. How will my family benefit if I should die?
10. How do I know my money is safe?
11. What happens if I get laid off?

From the management's point of view, the following realities are somewhat parallel, and their inclusion in an educational program should be carefully considered:

a. What does the company get out of it?
b. What are the competitive economic forces faced at home and abroad, and, as these forces impinge on our company, how do we meet added pension and other costs?
c. What side effects do pension expenditures have on capital expenditures, research and development, and profit?
d. Is the American economy, our industry, and our company in a position where increasing wage-salary costs can be balanced against compensating consumer price increases?

Some Guidelines to Method

While a well-illustrated booklet telling the whole story is essential, in and of itself it is not enough. Several ways to tie in pension education with other normal on-going activities in many companies, or with special "selling" efforts, are suggested.

Indoctrination

Many progressive companies have found that indoctrination efforts (which may range from several hours to several days), or training courses (weeks or months in duration), do pay off. Pension education can be made a part of such programs. Initial presentations can range from easels; black-board illustration or slap boards; to sound-slide films such as that of Dan River Mills (see page 266).

How soon can I join up?

As soon as you've passed 30 years of age and have at least 5 years of continuous service to your credit. Like any other plan of this kind, the Dan River Retirement Plan can't work for people who sign up and then leave the company just as their savings start to grow—so these two simple rules help the Plan, and also make it work best for everybody.

You see, young folks usually do some moving around before they finally settle down. Besides, the 35 years between 30 and 65 give you a good deal of time to build up a retirement income, from your contributions and those of the company! Then, too, it stands to reason that once anybody has been with us 5 years, there's a pretty good chance he'll stay on until he reaches retirement age.

This page from the Dan River Mills pension booklet shows that, with imaginative treatment, the much-abused Question and Answer technique can make very interesting reading. The booklet is in color and is 9" x 12". The booklet is first introduced in a sound-slide film.

How to Achieve Maximum Return on Pension Costs 267

WILLIAM BENDIX and TOM D'ANDREA in

CASH ON THE BARRELHEAD

An employee communication film on an issue of tremendous importance to management and employees alike

Many companies use this film to dramatize their pension program and other benefits. For information on purchase or rental, write BNA Incorporated, 1231 24th Street, N.W., Washington, D.C. 20037.

The important thing, however, is the face-to-face discussion that follows on several or more occasions. There should not be an effort to teach by rote; rather the conference leader should raise questions about the thinking of the conferees and then help talk out the facts and the implications thereof.

Progress Report Meetings

Some companies have felt it better to work hard to get along with their people than to await a degree of deterioration of employee morale in which some outside third party has to settle the disputes. Those companies which have been successful (and there are many) recognize communication not as *the sole* key to their success, but certainly as an essential back-up to a sound philosophy and well-defined, equitable policy. Pension education can be woven and rewoven into "annual report" employee meetings, "tool box meetings," "for your information" meetings, and "let's share ideas" meetings.

Letters to the Homes and Responses Thereto

It has long been recognized that communications to the home can affect management-labor-employee relations. During strikes, for example, managements have successfully raised a back-wash of marital discussions addressed to the question, "Don't you think, dear, it's time you and the other boys stopped hitting the bricks?"

The wife is also interested in her (and the children's) security in non-crisis situations. She will probably read letters providing the FACTS about pension plans, and they will probably do some good providing they don't stress too blatantly how great the management is and how lucky her husband is to be an employee of dear old American Nuts and Bolts, Inc. Most certainly such letters *will* be useful if it is made easy for those on the home front to raise questions, (or to comment) both to their husbands and to the company.

A resultant second (third or fourth) communique which can truthfully state, "Minnie Z—— raised this interesting point," and "Sophie I—— reminded us that we gave no attention to these points," constitutes intercommunication that is effective. A good communicator, of course, can think up all the questions in advance that Minnie Z—— and Sophie I—— might ask, and save time, stationery, and postage by laying out the whole case in lavender on the first go-around.

The thoroughly experienced communicator knows he'll never match the way the gals express themselves. More important, he'll know it's not the initial statement, but the continuing interchange that counts.

Contests

As another possibility, the pump can be primed by varying types of "fill in the last two lines," "write 50 words," "ask the best question (or questions)," or prizes for the best letter on "why our plan is 'good' or why it is 'bad'."

The employee relations department facing the development of such a pump-priming effort may feel itself in rather deep water. However, if the company is even medium size, the probability is that within the company there is requisite knowledge (in the sales department, or the dealer contact department) on how to set up such a contest to get sufficient response, to arrange for prizes that will motivate, and to budget the moderate total costs.

The Challenge To Management

It may be that the economics of pensions could be the fulcrum of much broader economic education efforts by individual companies. For many years company presidents have exhorted fellow presidents on the point that widespread understanding of economics is a necessity. Relatively few companies to date, however, have taken any action. Pension education opens up a golden opportunity for the company to communicate not only the specific economics of this particular cost item but how, in turn, it relates to the business and the economy as a whole.

The main consideration from the individual's point of view, of course, is what a pension will do for him. But there are many other compelling considerations about pensions, each of which, as it is amplified, can provide knowledge of the economics of business.

What, for example, are the sources of the money that companies put into a pension plan? Are these sources guaranteed, as is a savings bank loan by the Federal Deposit Insurance Corporation, or are they dependent over the long haul on the company's ability to compete and to make a profit?

What are some of the factors which should determine the level of pensions? Should the level automatically be reasonably comparable to those of other companies in the industry or geographic area in order to attract and hold desirable employees? Or must market conditions, demand for the product, and product vulnerability to foreign competition also be determinants of the level?

What consequences of investing corporate funds in pensions deserve consideration? What, for example, happens if profits are affected (and why are profits important?)? Or what if capital expenditures have to be reduced (and what "good" does capital investment do for the people of a company?)?

Are pensions something different and distinct, a special obligation of management and a special right of employees, or are pensions, in economic terms, simply a part of a total wage and salary cost? (And what is this total picture as it affects the company and employee job security?)

Are company pensions, generally speaking, a desirable part of the problem of providing for retirement, or should new social security legislation replace what business is now doing (and what are the cost implications if the government does "take over" in the retirement area?)?

Certainly for those in the business community who mean what they say about the desirability of economic education, pension communication offers a way to get started.

Finally, the pension area permits a way to get started simply and naturally. Virtually any executive who wants to intercommunicate can handle the basic what and why and meaning of a pension program to employees, to the company and to the common welfare of both. In the process, the return on the pension investment will be maximized, and knowledge of the enterprise system enhanced.

Illustrative Pension Brochures

On the following pages are reproduced excerpts from material prepared by different companies to inform employees of their pension benefits:

How to Achieve Maximum Return on Pension Costs 271

Folks...
meet Danny Donmoyer

That's Danny over there—all dressed up in his Sunday best. He looked that way when he walked in a few days ago to apply for a job at Circle "L."

We asked Danny a lot of questions about himself before we hired him. But Danny had a lot of questions to ask us, too. And one thing he really went into was our Retirement Plan for salaried employees.

Danny asked us some pretty sharp questions. We found ourselves whipping out our pencil and making calculations. We spent a good hour explaining the why's of this and the wherefore's of that.

Afterward, it occurred to us that the things Danny wanted to know might be just the sort of questions you would ask if you were sitting down with us to talk over the provisions of the Plan. And that gave us the idea of explaining the Plan the way we explained it to Danny— and with Danny asking the questions.

So here goes

The excerpts of this and the following page illustrate effective introduction of a fictional character to personalize pension details. (From the Lebanon Steel Foundry pension booklet for salaried employees.)

I'm interested in the money end of it. How much am I going to get when I retire?

That will depend on how many years you work for us before you retire — and how much money you earn while you are a member of the Plan.

To figure out retirement benefits based on *current service* (i.e., benefits which are built up during membership in the Plan), we use this formula:

THIS IS KNOWN AS OUR "CURRENT SERVICE" FORMULA

¾ OF 1% OF (ANNUAL EARNINGS UP TO $4200) FOR EACH YEAR YOU ARE A MEMBER = X

1½% OF (ANNUAL EARNINGS ABOVE $4200) FOR EACH YEAR YOU ARE A MEMBER = Y

X + Y = ANNUAL RETIREMENT BENEFITS BASED ON CURRENT AND FUTURE SERVICE

You will notice in this formula that the retirement benefits based on earnings above $4200 are twice as much as benefits based on earnings below $4200. This is because Social Security will provide us with Old Age Benefits based on our earnings up to $4200 but will not provide us with any benefits based on our earnings above $4200.

How to Achieve Maximum Return on Pension Costs

Let's take a look at the years ahead...

UNITED STATES TOBACCO COMPANY
RETIREMENT INCOME PLAN

LET'S LOOK AHEAD

SUN	MON	TUES	WED	THURS	FRI	SAT
						5
6						12
13						19
20						26
27						

IT'S HARD TO REALIZE time passes so quickly ... but the years slip by faster than we think.

Most of us, as we look ahead, see a day coming when we would like to have a chance to enjoy some of the good things of life without continuing to work so hard for them.

We try to prepare for such a day as best we can. We want to live our lives in our own way after we get older, without being a burden to our children, or to our relatives, or to our friends.

To help you live more comfortably after you are 65, your Company has developed a Retirement Income Plan for you.

This booklet explains how the Retirement Income Plan works ... how it adds to the provision you are now making for later years, and to the Social Security income you will have then.

The money your Company is putting into the Plan will give you a more comfortable income than you could have otherwise. This booklet will help you "take a look at the years ahead" —years that will be made more pleasant for you because of the United States Tobacco Company Retirement Income Plan.

I urge you to join the Plan as soon as you are eligible, because the sooner you join, the greater your benefits from it will be.

Cordially yours,

J. W. Peterson

PRESIDENT, UNITED STATES TOBACCO COMPANY

WHEN YOU RETIRE ... THERE'LL BE NO LIMIT TO THE TIME YOU CAN TOAST YOUR TOES BY THE FIRE

SUN	MON	TUES	WED	THURS	FRI	SAT
			1	2	3	4
5						11
12						18
19						25
26	27	28	29	30		

HOW THE MONEY IN THE PLAN IS PROTECTED—The money you save and the money the Company adds to it will be deposited with the Central Hanover Bank and Trust Company in New York. This bank is responsible for investing the money safely so it will earn compound interest.

When you retire, the Central Hanover Bank and Trust Company will mail your retirement income check to you at the beginning of each month.

A Pension Committee, appointed by the Board of Directors of the Company, is in complete charge of the Retirement Income Plan. It is the job of this Committee to see that everything works smoothly. If any questions come up, the decision of this Committee will be final.

The Company will pay all the expenses for the operation of the Plan.

Page 10

United States Tobacco Company dramatizes its plan's salient points, using a calendar page for each feature.

274   PENSIONS AND PROFIT SHARING

GOLDEN
ESSO EXTRA

ANOTHER Esso FIR...

...And

NEW RETIREMENT ANNUITY PLAN

ESSO STANDARD OIL COMPAN

THE NEW RETIREMENT ANNUITY PLAN

is designed for today's conditions and for the years to come.

It will:

1 PROVIDE FOR A HIGHER LEVEL OF ANNUITIES AT NO GREATER COST TO YOU.

2 RECOGNIZE HIGHER EARNINGS AT RETIREMENT.

3 ASSURE ADEQUATE ANNUITIES FOR CAREER EMPLOYEES.

4 IMPROVE TEMPORARY EARLY RETIREMENT ALLOWANCES (TERA).

5 RECOGNIZE ANY FUTURE CHANGES IN THE SOCIAL SECURITY TAX BASE.

Each of these 5 new areas is discussed in the following pages.

[2]

Esso Standard Oil Company (now a division of Humble Oil & Refining Company) emphasizes five principal features of its new retirement annuity plan.

INDEX

A

Acquisitions by trusts 43, 44
Actuaries
    in general, advice 13, 173
    assumptions, cost of plans 139, 140, 179
    self-administered trusts 135
Administration of pension plans
    annual report 251, 268
    application for pension 254
    brochures, illustrated 271-274
    changed plans 256
    communications (see Communications)
    contributory plans 248
    disability benefits 30, 250
    early retirement benefits 249
    education and training programs 263 et seq., 269
    enrollments 17, 18, 114, 236-239
    expenses (see Administrative expenses)
    forms, illustrated 239, 240, 242-245, 247, 248, 254, 255
    group annuity contracts 89, 111, 113
    joint union-management administration 215, 249, 250
    management considerations 236, 265
    ordinary life insurance with supplemental trust 135
    profit-sharing plans 199
    records 114, 236-238, 240 et seq., 252
    self-administered trusts 30, 139
    statutory required summary report 251
    waiver of participation 239
Administrative expenses
    contributory plans 38
    cost of plans generally 175
    individual contract pension trust 127, 129, 131

Affiliated companies 196
AFL-CIO pension goals 226, 230
Age requirement (see Retirement age)
Allocation formula, profit-sharing plans 189, 190
Amendment of plans
    in general 13
    disclosure to Revenue Service 54
    group annuity contracts 106
    involuntary 54
    profit-sharing plans 201
    "reserved right" provisions 53
    tax aspects 54
Annuities (see specific plan names)
Annuity tables 167
Arbitration, negotiated plans 211, 233, 234, 250
Automotive industry plans
    current benefits 217
    death benefits, subsidized survivor option 224
    disability benefits 222
    early retirement benefits 219
    equity investments 229
    formula earnings class table 151, 152
    pattern bargaining 211
    social security integration 223
    vesting provisions 226

B

Bargaining (see Negotiated plans)
Benefit formulas
    average earnings basis of payment 23, 24
    "classical" without social security offset 153, 154
    final years' earnings basis of payment 23, 24, 93, 115
    flat benefit formulas, cost table 151, 152, 154, 155
    group insured annuities 90
    group permanent life insurance 118
    multi-employer plans 214

275

INDEX

Brochures, illustrated 271, 274
Business lease income 79

C

Capital appreciation and depreciation (see Equity investments)
Charitable organizations, retirement age 21
Collective bargaining and pensions (see Negotiated plans)
College Retirement Equity Fund 25, 26, 171
Communications
    with employees 113, 114, 118, 236, 237, 246 et seq., 251, 259 et seq., 268
    with pensioner 252, 253
    with unions 249
Compensation basis of payment 22, 23
    average earnings basis 23, 24
    death benefits 32
    final pay basis 23, 24, 93, 115
    negotiated plans 218, 230
Compulsory v. voluntary retirement 21, 228, 234
Contributions by employees (see Contributory plans)
Contributions by employer (see Cost of plans)
Contributory v. noncontributory plans 38
Contributory plans
    additional contributions, voluntary 95
    advantages and disadvantages 37, 38
    benefits 24, 94, 108
    cost of plans 177
    enrollment of employees 17, 18, 114, 236, 238
    excess payments 95
    labor position 38
    money purchase plans (see Money purchase plans)
    profit-sharing 190
    ratio of benefits/contributions 94, 95
    self-employed persons 82
    taxation 65
Cost-of-living adjustments, BLS
    negotiated plans 218, 219, 230
    variable annuities 140, 142

Cost of plans
    (see also Financing methods)
    actuarial assumptions 139, 140, 179
    administrative expenses 175
    calculations, draft plan 19
    contributory plans 177
    disability benefits 178
    employee contributions 177
    factors affecting 20, 165
    interest 146, 156, 157, 169
    minimum contribution requirement 159, 161
    retirement age 175
    salary scales 174
    vesting 34, 177
    withdrawal 178

D

Death benefits
    capital gains treatment 68, 71
    change from life annuity to guaranteed annuity 101, 102
    computation 32
    contingent annuitant 71, 72, 101, 122, 123
    contributory plans 32, 36, 66, 99, 100, 137, 139
    earnings basis of payments 32, 33
    estate tax 73
    flat amount 32, 33
    group annuity contracts 99, 100
    group permanent life insurance 117, 119 et seq.
    guaranteed pension payments 37
    joint and survivorship annuity 71, 73, 101
    life insurance benefits 132, 192
    modified cash refund 100, 101
    negotiated plans 212, 225, 226
    optional benefits 36, 100, 101, 122, 123
    ordinary life insurance with supplemental trust 132
    profit-sharing plans 192, 202, 203
    selection charge 123
    self-administered trusts 137, 139
    service requirement 32
    tax exclusion 42, 72
    widow's benefits, annuity 33, 101, 225, 226

INDEX

Death of pensioner, investigations 256, 257
Deductions (see Tax aspects of plans)
Deferred retirement (see Retirement age)
Disability benefits
  administration 30, 250
  computation 31
  cost of plans in general 178
  group annuity contracts 98
  group deposit administration 115, 178
  importance of 29, 30
  negotiated plans 30, 208, 209, 212, 222, 224, 230
  noninsured plans 178
  self-administered trusts 29, 137, 139
  separate long-term insurance contract 98
  social security supplemental benefits 31, 224
  temporary illness 13, 29
  underwriting of 29
  union plans, Paper Mill Workers 216
Disbursement phase of plans, defined 88
Discharge 192, 209, 210, 220, 221
Disclosures
  amendment of plans 54
  equity investments 44, 68, 251
  profit-sharing plans 200
Discontinuance (see Termination of plans)
Dividends (see Equity investments)

E

Early retirement benefits
  (see also Vesting)
  administration 249
  advantages and disadvantages 34
  company approval 35
  computation 36
  defined 34
  eligibility 35
  group annuity contracts 96, 97
  negotiated plans 209, 211, 213, 219, 221, 222, 228, 229
  profit-sharing plans 192
  reduced annuities 96, 97
  social security adjustments 97
  union plans, Paper Mill Workers 216
Education programs, guidelines 263 et seq.
Equity investments
  College Retirement Equities Fund 25, 26, 171
  disclosures 44, 68, 251
  group deposit administration 117
  group insured annuity contracts 112, 113
  negotiated plans 229, 230
  profit-sharing plans 170, 171, 199, 200, 203
  separate accounts procedures 117, 141, 170
  unsecured bonds 76
  variable annuities 141, 142
European plans 33, 43

F

Federal Welfare and Pension Plans Disclosure Act 251
"Feeder organizations" 77
Final pay plans
  flat-benefits type plans 23, 24, 93, 115
  group annuity contracts 93
Financing pension plans 87
  (see also Cost of plans)
  estimated annual amounts 89
  group insured annuities 89
  methods of financing 87, 88
  real costs 88, 89
  safety margins 89, 112
  tabular analysis of financing methods 144
Flat benefit type plans
  actuarially sound basis 45, 46
  computation of benefits 25
  cost example 151, 152
  final average pay percentage 23, 24, 93, 115
  minimum service requirement 22
  negotiated plans 25
  size of benefits 28, 93
Forfeitures
  discrimination in benefits 51
  group annuity contracts 104
  profit-sharing plans 185, 191, 193
  self-employed persons 82
  termination of plans 57, 58, 106

278 INDEX

Forms illustrated 239, 240, 242-245, 247, 248, 254, 255
Funding methods
    aggregate-cost 150
    entry-age-normal cost 150, 151, 156, 157
        illustrative costs tables 152, 155, 158
    level cost 150
    "pay-as-you-go" arrangements 155, 156
    self-employed persons 82
    terminal-cost (one-sum) 149, 156, 157
        table 158
    unit-cost (see Unit-benefit funding)

G

Group deposit administration contracts
    aggregate-cost funding 150, 151
    costs 116
    defined 114
    discontinuance 115
    employer credits 115, 116
    "immediate participation guarantee" (IPG) 116
Group insured annuity contracts 89
    application for 90
    contingency reserve 112
    deposit administration (see Group deposit adm.)
    discontinuance 105
    earnings class schedules 91, 93
    employee contributions 91, 94, 108
    employer credits 98, 104, 112
    investment earnings 112, 113
    money purchase pension plans (see Money purchase plans)
    premiums and rates 106
    size of group 89
    split funding 87
    state premium taxes 111
Group permanent life insurance 117
    advantages over individual policies 118
    conversions to individual contracts 125
    defined 117
    employer credits 125
    level-cost funding 150
    premiums and rates 125

    profit-sharing, comparison with 184
    profit-sharing, purchases of 198
    "retirement annuity" excess fund 121
    salary class schedule 119
    size of group 117
    termination value 124

H

High paid employees
    nondiscrimination, qualification of plan 47, 49, 56
    profit-sharing plans, deferred 187, 188, 189, 190, 197, 262
    termination of plans, discrimination 56
Hospitalization benefits 198

I

Income tax (see Tax aspects of plans)
Individual contract pension trust
    application 128
    defined 127
    dividend credits 130
    employee credits 129, 130
    "guaranteed issue" 128, 129
    premiums and rates 129
    reinsurance contracts 128
    size of group 127
    termination values 129, 130
Insurance companies
    premium rates 110
    rate reductions 112
    separate accounts procedures 117, 141, 170
    underwriting 29, 140
Interest
    cost reduction 146, 156, 157, 169
    death benefits 99
    fractional cost of interest 170
    money-purchase plans 24, 25
    past service credit, liability 107
    profit-sharing plans 199
    savings, tax deferment 42, 147
    valuation rates 164
    vesting, early retirement benefits 36
Internal Revenue Service approved plans
    application 51 et seq.

INDEX

bona fide requirements 42 et seq., 159, 163
number to date 40
Investments (see Equity investments)

K

Keogh-Smathers Act 40, 80, 182, 203

L

Laid-off employees 192, 209, 210, 220, 221
Life insurance
    death benefits 132, 192
    group permanent life insurance (see Group permanent life insurance)
    individual contract pension trust 129
    individual insurance contracts 150
    ordinary life pension trust (see Ordinary life insurance with supplemental fund)
    profit-sharing plans 192, 198
    tables 167
    taxation 66
Loading factor 175
Low-paid employees
    benefits for 23, 50

M

Medical insurance benefits 198
Mergers
    survival of carryover credit 62
Modified cash refund 100, 101
Money-purchase plans 136
    actuarially sound basis 45, 46
    benefits, computation 24, 25
    College Retirement Equities Fund 25, 26, 171
    defined 92
    group insured annuities 92, 149, 171
    salary class schedule 93
    self-administered trusts 136
Mortality tables 165 et seq.
Multi-employer plans
    employer contributions 214
    enforcement of contracts 234
    "floating liability" 214
    IRS rulings, application 52

"portability" 213
reciprocity agreements 213
tax considerations 65
union pension plans 214, 215

N

National Labor Relations Board
    bargainability of pension plans 206
Negotiated plans 38
    actuarially sound basis 45, 46
    AFL-CIO pension goals 226, 230
    apparel industry, multi-employer plans 213
    arbitration 211, 233, 234, 250
    augmented pensions 219, 220, 222
    automotive industry (see Automotive industry plans)
    "broken service" benefits 221
    can companies 210, 222
    cents-per-hour index 154
    compulsory v. voluntary retirement 21, 228, 234
    contributory v. noncontributory plans 227
    cost-of-living adjustments, BLS, 218, 219, 230
    current issues in pension bargaining 217 et seq.
    employer contributions 228, 229, 231
    enforcement of agreements 232
    "fringe benefits," combinations 64
    government role 206, 207
    group deposit administration 115
    growth to date, history 206, 207
    joint and survivorship benefits 209, 213, 225
    lump-sum benefit 209, 219
    multi-employer plans (see Multi-employer plans)
    pattern bargaining 210 et seq.
    pensioners already retired, bargaining 224
    rubber industry, pattern bargaining 212, 213
    steel industry (see Steel industry plans)
    Taft Act, effect 206, 231 et seq.
    Teamsters' plans 214, 215, 220
    waiver of benefits 224, 225
    widow's pension 225

280   INDEX

Nondiscriminatory qualification classifications, IRS 47 et seq.
   profit-sharing plans 187, 197
   self-employed persons 80
Noninsured plans 175, 178

O

Open market purchases 134
Options
   death benefits 36, 100, 101, 122, 123
   negotiated plans 225, 226
   pension plans generally 36
Ordinary life insurance with supplemental trust conversion to annuity 132, 134
   defined 131, 132
   employer credits 134
   open market purchases 134
   premiums and rates 133
   termination values 133

P

Paper Mill Workers' plan 216
Past service benefits
   credit 94
   entry-age-normal-cost funding 150, 154, 156, 157
   negotiated plans 107
   payments 107
   profit-sharing plans 185
   unfunded costs, tax deduction 55, 60, 61, 107, 163
   union pension plans 217
   variable annuities 142
"Pay-as-you-go" arrangements
   funding methods in general 155, 156
   profit-sharing plans 186
Pension plans generally
   analysis in preparation for 13
   cost of plans (see Cost of plans)
   coverage generally 17, 46 et seq.
   death benefits (see Death benefits)
   disability benefits (see Disability benefits)
   diversion of funds 44
   early retirement benefits (see Early retirement benefits)
   eligibility requirements 17
   existing benefits, treatment 15
   financing (see Financing pension plans)
   funding methods (see Funding methods)
   growth to date 40
   guaranteed payments 37
   multi-employer plans (see Multi-employer plans)
   normal age retirement 21, 96
   optional benefits 36
   post-review, IRS 54
   retirement age (see Retirement age)
   service after retirement age 21, 98
   size of benefits 28
   tax aspects of (see Tax aspects of pension plans)
   union approval of 14
   union plans 215, 216
   vesting benefits (see Vesting)
Pensioners already retired, union as bargaining agent 224
Policy charges
   group insured annuities 90, 110
   group permanent life insurance 118
Profit-sharing plans, deferred
   affiliated companies 196
   allocation formula 189, 190
   annuities, purchase of 185, 192
   contribution formula 188, 189, 195
   defined 182, 183
   distributions, taxation 202, 203
   employee contributions 182, 190, 196, 197, 202
   employer contributions 182, 184, 193 et seq., 202
   hospitalization benefits 198
   "incidental" benefits 198
   investments, disclosure 200
   medical insurance benefits 198
   nondiscriminatory coverage, 187, 197
   pension plans, comparison with 184, 185
   prohibited transactions 200, 201
   qualification rules, IRS 186
   self-employed individuals 182, 203, 204
   voluntary contributions 197, 198

INDEX

Prohibited transactions 75 et seq.
   profit-sharing plans 200, 201
   self-employed plans 85
Public corporations
   in general, benefit plans 25, 33
   retirement age 21
   retirement income credit 71
   variable annuity plan 25

Q

Qualification tests, Revenue Service
   in general 42 et seq.
   profit-sharing plans 186

R

Reciprocity agreements 213
Records 114, 236-238, 240 et seq., 252
Retirement age 175
   compulsory v. voluntary retirement 21, 228, 234
   cost of plans in general 175
   group permanent life insurance 120
   individual contract pension trust 128
   pension plans generally, normal age 21, 96
   public organizations 21
   women employees 21

S

Salaried employees
   enrollment considerations 19
   profit-sharing plans, nondiscrimination tests 187
   salary scales 175
   social security integration 48
Salary scales
   costs computation 174
Self-administered trusts
   actuarial assumptions 139, 140
   defined 135
   employee contributions 136
   employer contributions 136
   premiums and rates 138
   salary increase factors 139
   trust indenture 135
   underwriting 140
   variable annuities (see Variable annuities)

Self-employed persons
   contributions and benefits 80, 81
   coverage 81
   excess contributions 83
   funding 82
   Keogh-Smathers Act 40, 80, 182, 203
   nondiscrimination, qualification 80
   profit-sharing plans 182, 203, 204
Service requirement 22, 25
   death benefits 32
   flat-benefit type plans 22
   multi-employer plans 214
   negotiated plans 218
   vesting in general 35
Social security integration
   in general, plans independent from Social Security benefits 15, 16, 25
   adjustments within plans 27
   contributory and noncontributory plans 38
   defined 26
   development of 38, 49
   disability supplementary benefit 31
   early retirement discount 97
   earnings in excess of social security wages 23, 27, 91, 190
   group insured annuities 90, 91, 97
   negotiated plans 157, 207-209, 211, 220, 223, 224
   nondiscrimination test, IRS 47, 48
   offset 97, 151, 154, 157
   "over $4800" plan 48
   present rate 50
   profit-sharing plans 190, 191
   salaried employees 48
   saving clause 16
   self-employed persons 82
"Split funding" 87
Steel industry plans
   in general 207-210
   "broken service benefit" 221
   current benefits 217
   formula cost, tables 151, 152, 156, 157
   pattern bargaining 211
   social security integration 223
   vesting 226, 227
Stockholders
   nondiscrimination, qualification of plan 47, 49
   profit-sharing plans 186, 187

282 INDEX

termination of plan, discrimination 56
thirty percent rule 51

T

Taft Act, effect 206, 231 et seq.
Tax aspects of pension plans 40
   accrual basis payments 62
   bona fide qualification tests, IRS 42 et seq.
   capital gains treatment 68 et seq.
   employee deductions 42, 65 et seq., 147
   employer deductions 42, 59, 147, 163
   estate tax 42, 73
   estimated maximum contribution 161, 163
   "excess" carryover credit 62, 194, 195
   investments, disclosure (see Disclosures)
   level amount deduction 61, 163
   negotiated plans 41, 45, 64
   ordinary life insurance with supplemental trust 70
   past and future service cost deductions 55, 59, 60, 61, 107, 163
   post-retirement exclusion ratio 67
   profit-sharing plans 181, 182, 184 et seq., 193 et seq., 202, 203
   qualified plans' approval, procedure 51 et seq.
   recovery of investment 67, 68
   reports 60
   self-employed individuals' plan 40, 80, 84
   single-year distribution 68
   suspension 55
   termination (see Termination of plans)
Temporary illness 13, 29
Termination of employment (see Vesting)
Termination of plans
   benefit distribution, capital gains treatment 69
   "business necessity" 56, 57, 58
   defined 58
   disclosure 57
   discontinuance of contributions, exhibit 240
   discrimination in benefits 56, 58, 59
   employee tax liability 57
   forfeitures 57, 58, 106
   group deposit administration 115
   group insured annuities 45, 95, 103, 105
   profit-sharing plans 201
   self administered trust 138
   survivor of carryover credit 62
   temporary termination 55
Training and education programs 263, 265, 266, 269
Trust indenture 135

U

Underwriting
   disability benefits 29
   self administered trust 140
Union pension plans 215 et seq.
Unit-benefit funding
   group insured annuities contracts 90, 108, 109, 149
   group permanent life insurance 119
   self-administered trusts 136
Unrelated business income 78

V

Variable annuity plans
   actuarially sound test 46
   College Retirement Equity Fund 25, 26, 171
   cost-of-living adjustment, BLS 140, 142
   defined 46, 140
   fixed dollar income 141, 142
   separate accounts procedures 117, 141, 170
Vesting
   advantages and disadvantages 34
   company approval 35
   contributory plans 36, 103
   cost of plans in general 34, 177
   discrimination in benefits 51
   eligibility 35
   graduated vesting 191, 192
   group annuity contracts 103, 106
   minimum age requirements 35
   multi-employer plans 213
   negotiated plans 35, 209, 212, 226,

227, 230, 233
partial vesting 36
profit-sharing plans 191, 192, 202
self-administered trusts 138
service requirement 35

W

Wage and salaried employees
    combination plans 25
    separate plans 19
Wage employees
    enrollment consideration 19
    flat benefit plans 25
    salary scales 174
Westinghouse Electric Corp. 218, 221
Withdrawal
    cost of plans in general 178
    discount assumption 172
    exclusions from plans 172
    group insured annuities 99, 103
    group permanent life insurance 124, 125
    older workers 173, 175, 178
    post-retirement withdrawal 171
    self-administered trusts 139
    surrender charges 124
    vesting 172, 178
Women employees
    normal retirement age 21

Y

Young employees
    rate of contributions 95
    withdrawal factors 172